Azúcar!

Azú

Eduardo Marceles

Translated by Dolores M. Koch

car!

The Biography of

Celia Cruz

Reed

PRESS

Published by Reed Press ™
360 Park Avenue South
New York, NY 10010
www.reedpress.com

Library of Congress Cataloging-in-Publication Data

Marceles, Eduardo, 1947–
    [Azúcar! English]
    Azúcar! : the biography of Celia Cruz / Eduardo Marceles ; trans-
lated by Dolores M. Koch.
        p. cm.
    "This translation is based on a revision of the original Spanish
edition"—T.p. verso. Includes discography (p.), bibliographical references (p.).
    ISBN 1-59429-021-0 (hardcover : alk. paper)
    1. Cruz, Celia. 2. Singers—Latin America—Biography. I. Title.
    ML420.C957M3713 2004
    782.42164'092--dc22
                                                            2004013129

Book designed by Neuwirth & Associates
Composition by John Reinhardt Book Design

Printed in the United States

10 9 8 7 6 5 4 3 2 1

For Nubia Medina,
painter of dreams and steadfast companion
in the adventure of life.

And also for my Triple A: Anneli,
Andrea and Alyssa,
restless muses that surround my
work table with their jovial sounds of youth.

Translator's Note

This translation is based on a revision
of the original Spanish edition.

• • •

Musical terms that appear in italics throughout the text
can be found in the Glossary.

When she sings, you hear angels.

—ALEJO CARPENTIER

Contents

Acknowledgments

This biography of Celia Cruz would not have been possible without the generous contributions of a significant number of friends and collaborators who, at each stage of its development, offered their talent and experience to make it come to fruition. In the first place, I wish to give thanks to Leyhla Ahuile, my agent, who saw fit to suggest my name for this project.

To my wife, painter Nubia Medina, for providing the domestic logistics that allowed me to concentrate all my energy on the writing, and also for indicating disagreements and repetitions in the first draft, as well as for her patience during the time I needed for the basic research.

I wish to thank also, my daughters Anneli and Andrea, and my granddaughter Alyssa Montijo who, during this process, had to face on their own a few emergencies without protesting.

In New York, my sincere gratitude to Diana Vargas, colleague in some journalistic adventures, for her valuable suggestions and corrections that improved the original draft considerably. In the same way, to José Luis Llanes, brilliant journalist, for his timely indications and for allowing me to use some fragments of his chronicles about the funeral of the Guarachera de Cuba; and to Adriana Collado and Fernando Velázquez, from the newspaper *Hoy*, for their stimulating observations about the manuscript.

In Miami, thanks to Jaime Cabrera for his hospitality and his advice, for allowing me to see his videos about Celia, and helping me locate interviewees Eloy Cepero and Tita Borggiano, Laserie's widow. Also to Alfredo Arango and Colombia Páez, for their interviews with Celia and for their kindnesses.

In Colombia, I wish to express my appreciation for the hospitality offered me by Gabriel Beltrán in Bogotá, and by my mother, Imperia Daconte de Márceles, in Barranquilla, as well as the cooperation given by César Pagano, Rafael Bassi Labarrera, Mariano Candela, Guarino Caicedo, and Enrique Caviedes, for sharing with me what they knew about the Cuban vocalist; to Lorenzo Sierra for copying essential videos for me from his extensive collection with the best information about Celia and the Fania All Stars; as well as Mirta Villamil for her guidance in Cartagena de Indias.

In Havana, I would not have been able to find out about Celia's years in Cuba without the fundamental assistance of the poet and literary scholar José Luis Díaz-Granados and his kind wife, Gladys. They lit my way to the Santos Suárez neighborhood and the Museo de la Música; my thanks also for the wondrous hospitality offered me by María Antonia and her winsome son, Luis Ángel Monest, who scanned some of the photographs in this book.

And speaking about photos, without the collaboration

of poet and musicologist Sigfredo Ariel, musical historian Helio Orovio, and journalist Alex Fleites, we would not have the photos that are reproduced in this book. Thanks a hundred times, and thanks again for their limitless generosity.

In México, thanks to writer Fernando Vallejo for his suggestions and for effectively making possible my contact with Iván Restrepo, close friend of the Knights, who was kind enough to share with me intimate details of his long-lasting friendship with the couple.

Despite the good will demonstrated by all my friends and collaborators—and despite all my efforts—any error or omission in this book is totally my own responsibility, though I hope that, in a biography that is so long and detailed, these have been reduced to a minimum. I do not wish to omit mentioning the numerous researchers and journalists who, directly or indirectly, referred to by name or left anonymous, have helped me with their reflections and pertinent information in each case. To all of them, my cordial embrace and deep gratitude.

Azúcar!

1

**Farewell to the Great Queen,
New York, Tuesday, July 22, 2003**

Morning began with a security mobilization surrounding the Frank H. Campbell Funeral Home at Madison Avenue and Eighty-first Street in Manhattan. A large number of New Yorkers had come to pay their respects and sad farewells to the one and only *Guarachera* of Cuba. It was cloudy on that Tuesday morning, the twenty-second of July, 2003, and rain was expected as if to underscore the sadness of the New York Hispanic community. At one P.M., the funeral procession headed for Fifth Avenue past a general ovation and a chorus of voices singing her songs. At the head of the procession, seven black carriages transported the dozens of floral arrangements Celia had received, including one made in the shape of a Cuban flag in red, white, and blue carnations with a plastic star. A silk ribbon from a wreath of white roses read: "Thanks for taking our Cuban music all over the world. Celia, we will never forget you."

Following these vehicles, a light tan convertible carried an image of the *Virgen de la Caridad del Cobre* (Our Lady of Charity), patron of Cuba. Next came a white carriage pulled by two showy horses wearing plumed helmets, driven by a black coachman. It carried the Diva's golden bier, also covered by her country's flag. Twenty-two black limousines followed, with Celia's relatives and friends, closing the long funeral procession. Along Fifth Avenue the procession was greeted by shouts and a sea of multicolored flags from every imaginable country. Her admirers lined both sides of the avenue. The Ebony Goddess had stopped traffic in the great metropolis. Four helicopters flew above the funeral cortège as it moved down the famous thoroughfare beside Central Park.

By the time it reached Fifty-ninth Street, so many people had joined in that they were blocking the way for anyone who might have wanted to ignore what was going on around them. Tourists, bystanders, and passersby stopped to ask why there was such a concentration of people. Many expressed sorrow upon hearing the news. Two blocks away from Saint Patrick's Cathedral came the shouts, singing, and loud *vivas* heralding the arrival of the *Guarachera*. Suddenly, a thick shroud of dark clouds obscured the sun. The city seemed to dress itself in rigorous mourning to pay its respects to the singer with the wondrous voice who had brought joy to the hearts of millions all over the world. Then, there was a clap of thunder, as if nature were expressing her sorrow. Large drops of rain fell, blending with the mourners' tears. At two P.M. the cortège arrived at the cathedral, a neo-gothic structure with a capacity of fifteen hundred people. Its two towers were overshadowed by the forest of midtown skyscrapers.

The image of the Virgin, Our Lady of Charity, surrounded by pink and red roses, was the first brought in and then placed to the left of the atrium, beside the Cuban flag. Next came the attending clergy, headed by Reverend Josú Iriondo, Assistant Bishop of New York, who was to deliver the homily. Father Alberto Cutié, who had presided over the Miami vigil, was among the celebrants. Next the coffin of the Queen appeared, followed by her widower, a serene Pedro Knight in an impeccable gray suit who walked arm in arm with Mayor Michael Bloomberg, and then came Celia's relatives and close friends.

Her sister Dolores Ramos was there, and her niece Celia; her manager and right-hand man, Omer Pardillo-Cid; and her colleagues Johnny Pacheco, Willie Colón, La India, Rubén Blades, Ray Barretto, Antonio Banderas and his wife, Melanie Griffith; along with Patti LaBelle, Jon Secada, Victor Manuelle, Chita Rivera, and Marc Anthony, just to mention the ones closest to her. Many others came to bid farewell, such as José Alberto (el Canario); Calixto Leicea, Sonora Matancera's ex-trumpet player who was ninety-four years old; and Puerto Rican musician Nelson González, who took part in the album *Regalo del alma*, Celia Cruz's musical testament. The crowds unable to enter the church could follow the mass by listening to loudspeakers that had been placed outside in anticipation of the overflowing crowd.

"No matter how high she climbed, Celia never distanced herself from her people, because when she climbed high, she took the people with her," said Assistant Bishop Iriondo, whose family has its roots in the Spanish Basque provinces. "Celia Caridad Cruz Alfonso, you live and will continue to live, like good sugar, dissolved in your people's black coffee." Celia was lying in state. Three large ovations thundered inside the cathedral during the mass, which was performed in English and in Spanish. The first occurred when Iriondo introduced Pedro Knight. The second happened at the end of the "Ave Maria," interpreted by Celia's friend, singer Patti LaBelle. The rendition brought Antonio Banderas to tears. And the last ovation was heard when Victor Manuelle sang his farewell, in the best Celia Cruz style, rendering a capella "*La vida es un carnaval*" and ending with a moving solo that surprised everybody with his ability to improvise in the best Caribbean *sonero* tradition.

"Celia's light did not go out, it flared brightly," concluded Bishop Iriondo. And at the close, interrupting the silent and solemn occasion, Omer Pardillo-Cid offered an emotional farewell to the one he considered his adoptive mother: "You left Cuba, but Cuba never left you. Please, Celia, help us make Cuba free."

2

*Simón Cruz, Catalina "Ollita" Alfonso,
and Celia's Early Years*

The birth of the Ebony Goddess was recorded in the civil registry of El Cerro district, a neighborhood in the city of Havana, on January 16, 1939. Entered there was the fact that Celia Cruz had been born to music and joy on October 21, 1925, under the sign of Libra, in a house on Serrano Street, close to Enamorados. She was the only daughter of Simón Cruz, a railroad worker from the town of Los Palacios, and Catalina Alfonso, who was also from Pinar del Río. Catalina was a housewife with the same prodigious voice that Celia had inherited. Before her relationship with Simón, Catalina already had a daughter, Dolores, with Aquilino Ramos. After Celia, she also had two other children, Bárbaro and Gladys, with Alejandro Jiménez. Celia never revealed these details about her siblings.

Contrary to tradition, Celia was not named after her mother or her grandmothers, Luz Cruz and Dolores Alfonso. She was named Celia Caridad Cruz Alfonso (as is customary, she carried both her father's and her mother's surnames). Celia's grandfather, Ramón Cruz, had been a soldier in the Cuban Revolutionary Army and, as a *mambí*, fought in the War of Independence against Spain's colonial regime.

Catalina, born on April 30, 1900, was known as "Ollita" to family and friends. This was a nickname given to her mother by an orphan child she had adopted. According to Celia, the boy had a speech impediment that caused the mispronunciation of her name. But the nickname stuck, and everybody called her Ollita. Even Celia called her Ollita and not Mother.

The Alfonso-Cruz family was Catholic. Early on, Celia was eager to start reading so that she could learn the catechism and celebrate her First Holy Communion. It finally occurred at the church of La Milagrosa, in the Havana neighborhood of Santos Suárez.

Celia grew up in a very poor home. As a stoker for the Cuban railroad, the first in Latin America, Simón Cruz brought home a modest salary, which barely covered basic expenses for his immediate family, let alone the fourteen other relatives living in his home. These relatives included Aunt Nena (Agustina Alfonso) and her four children; Celia's cousin Serafín Díaz, with his two children; and the orphan child Catalina had adopted. Ollita had her hands full as a housewife, and was never able to contribute money to the household budget.

Adding to the financial strain of the Alfonso-Cruz family was Cuba's economic decline as sugar and tobacco exports became a casualty of the Great Depression, which affected so many countries after 1929. The radical drop

in the stock markets brought a severe reduction in manu-
facturing, a rise in unemployment, and an increasing lack
of cash reserves. These circumstances made the country
poorer, since its economy depended heavily on U.S. buyers
for its agricultural products.

In spite of these hardships, Celia had happy memories
of her home and of her youth. She remembered her father,
tired from the day's work, sitting in the communal patio
of the tenement house, or *solar*, enjoying a Havana cigar
and singing songs like *"Capullito de Alelí," "Blancas
Azucenas," "Las Calles de San Juan,"* and *"¿Y tú qué has
hecho?"* Her parents enjoyed music, and Santos Suárez
was a neighborhood with a joyous spirit, home to a good
number of musicians. It had its own *comparsa de carnaval,*
(carnival parade group), as did most Havana neighborhoods, called *Las Jornaleras.* Every year during the carnival season the *comparsas* came out with their dancers in
brightly-colored costumes, thundering drums, and Chinese
cornet, giving rise to carnival joy, and inciting everybody
to join the festivities.

It was very clear that Celia was born to sing. Still in
the cradle, she would awaken humming the lullabies her
mother sang to her at bedtime. She was doing this even
before she was able to speak, astonishing her family members. Celia's mother recognized her child's talent for singing, and was so proud of Celia's artistic disposition that
she took advantage of every opportunity to encourage her
daughter to sing and show off, particularly when they had
visitors. And Celia remembered her grandmother telling
her that she was predestined to a life in music.

Celia's voice always caught the attention of passersby,
who would stop to listen as she sang her siblings and cousins to sleep at bedtime. Ollita once recalled that the chil-

dren would not want to go to sleep: they preferred to listen to Celia's amazing voice. Celia's favorite lullaby was a song by Manuel Prado: *Duerme, duerme mientras yo te arrullaré / con el hechizo de esta canción / que para ti canté /.*

Ollita knew that Celia would be famous after hearing her sing for a tourist. As Ollita remembered, she had taken Celia window shopping to the big stores in Havana. They entered a shoe store. Celia loved the shoes, but the family had no money to buy them. To pass the time, she began singing. An American tourist, enraptured, stopped and listened. Encouraged and even more inspired, Celia sang one of her father's favorite songs, "*¿Y tú qué has hecho?*" by composer Eusebio Delfín, which begins: *En el tronco de un árbol una niña / grabó su nombre, henchida de placer... /.* Celia's tourist admirer told Ollita that, if she would not feel offended, he would buy a pair of shoes for the young singer. This was a gesture for which Celia was very grateful because, as she once commented, at times she had gone to school with torn shoes.

When Celia was five she contracted a rare disease that brought her near death. Family and friends gathered around her bed to pray for her recovery. To everybody's surprise, one day she came out of her severe illness singing an unknown tune. Her mother was frightened, convinced that such behavior could only be a bad omen for a very sick person, and she begged her to stop singing. But Celia recuperated quite well after that, and again became the healthy, happy child she had always been.

In spite of the love and admiration she felt for Ollita, when Celia was six, she went to live with her aunt and godmother, Anacleta Alfonso (known as Ana), who lived in the tenement of La Margarita, in Santos Suárez. It was an old building, shaded by a centenary oak tree. "Aunt

Ana was like a mother to me," Celia confided in an interview. "She had a daughter who died before I was born." As the child lay in her coffin, Ana broke her daughter's little finger in order to recognize her after reincarnation. "My cousin died when my mother was pregnant with me, and when I was born, the little finger on my right hand was twisted. Aunt Ana thought that I was the reincarnation of her daughter. That is why my aunt loved me so much." This incident confirmed Celia's belief in reincarnation.

Aunt Ana loved the innocent fun of dance halls and radio programs that featured orchestras playing popular music. Her favorite vocalists, and instrumentalists were Abelardo Barroso, Fernando Collazo, Pablo Quevedo, Arsenio Rodríguez, Antonio Arcaño, and the ever-popular Paulina Álvarez. During Celia's childhood, the radio was the principal means of entertainment in Cuba, so every week she listened to the soap operas and contests from her favorite broadcasting stations. Celia remained with her Aunt Ana until her aunt moved back to her hometown in Pinar del Río, at which point Celia went back home to her mother.

With her girlfriends, Celia listened to music and went dancing at night to clubs such as Las Águilas, Los Tulipanes, El Antillano, and Los Jóvenes del Vals, where she heard Arcaño y sus Maravillas for the first time. Popular orchestras like Hermanos Contreras played local rhythms, and the singers were Abelardo Barroso, Conrado Cepero, Joseíto Fernández (composer of the famous *"Guantanamera"*), Pablo Quevedo, and Paulina Álvarez, *la Emperatriz del Danzonete* (The Empress of the Danzonete). The *danzonette* was derived from the dance craze then, the *danzón*. Álvarez was Celia's favorite singer, particularly in her rendition of *"Dulce serenidad"* with the Zenón González orchestra.

The friends would also frequent the neighborhood movie theaters. They preferred theaters like the Apolo because it was closer to home, and because it played weekly episodes of *The Lone Ranger*—a favorite of Celia's—as well as films with Shirley Temple or Lily Pons. Sometimes they would go to the Santos Suárez, the Dora, or the Moderno cinema, which showed Mexican films with Tito Guízar. Celia had a clear preference for musicals and comedies over war films.

Celia's older sister, Dolores, once organized a musical group named The Golden Button with neighborhood friends. Under the direction of *marímbula* player Francisco Gavilán, they would perform at neighborhood parties and celebrations at no charge. In return for their performance, they would accept refreshments, candy, and cake. When Dolores later went to live with her godmother, Celia replaced Dolores in the group.

As a youngster, Celia was slender like a Caribbean palm tree. She was described as a sensible girl with a charismatic personality and an innocent impishness who could be both sensitive and mischievous at once.

Her Aunt Ana would encourage Celia to participate in contests sponsored by radio stations that were in search of new talent. In one of these contests, her aunt watched Celia, a shy girl, standing stiff while singing a very danceable *guaracha*. Aunt Ana gave her a piece of advice that Celia never forgot. She told Celia that in order to express herself more fully in front of an audience, she should learn to dance and sing at the same time. Taking her aunt's advice, Celia began to dance in all her performances. Adding dance rhythms to her singing was not the only advice she received from family and friends throughout her life. Celia was always open to suggestions, which she pondered and then either accepted or rejected. It is this same consideration and respect that Celia would always show other people, both personally and professionally.

In spite of the encouragement Celia was receiving from Ollita, her Aunt Ana, and cousin Serafín Díaz, plus praise from neighbors who would come to listen as Celia sang at bedtime to the many children in the always joyful household, Simón Cruz was totally against the direction his daughter's life was taking.

At that time, young girls aspiring to the limelight quite often had to pay their way onerously by consenting to sexual favors with the owners of the clubs or of the radio stations. The machismo that was rampant then prevented people from realizing the tremendous prejudice this prurient behavior engendered.

Celia's career advanced nonetheless, and newspapers and magazines began to take note of this emerging star on the Cuban musical scene. At work, her father began hearing comments about a young singing sensation whose last name just happened to coincide with his. At first, Simón denied any relationship to the young singer, but later, after a newspaper published her photograph, he could not hide the fact that she was indeed his daughter. There was nothing but praise for Celia, and her father, without retracting his admonitions against her career or revealing his emotions, felt proud of his daughter. From that day forward, Simón Cruz knew that Celia's future was inextricably linked to music.

Sadly, her father would not live long enough to enjoy her later successes abroad. In 1960, before Celia left Cuba with her touring orchestra for Mexico, her father's doctors warned of his imminent death. On July 22, 1960, seven days after Celia left Cuba, Mr. Cruz died at the age of 78.

Celia always felt a sense of responsibility and duty toward her family and she managed to leave enough money to cover all of her father's funeral expenses.

Celia was preparing for a performance and did not immediately know of her father's passing. Her family withheld the news from her until a month later when, almost casually, she was informed that her father had died from the disease he had suffered in the final stage of his life.

Ollita was also sick by the time Celia left Cuba. Celia once commented that one of the reasons she left Cuba was to make enough money so that her mother could obtain better medical treatment and the best nutrition available. Fish and seafood were essentially unavailable due to the country's strict food rationing, and could only be found on the costly black market. Ollita, already weakened by cancer, was able to remain in contact with Celia through weekly telephone calls, and even later, during the critical stages of her illness, when it became difficult for her to hold a coherent conversation.

Celia gave variously detailed accounts of how she received the news of her mother's death. Interviewed in Bogota, Colombia, by a Cuban journalist named Guarino Caicedo, she said, "On the evening of April 7, 1962, I was to perform in an important show at the Teatro Puerto Rico in New York, with Lucho Gatica, Armando Manzanero, and Lucecita. I suddenly learned that my mother had died in Cuba. The news floored me. I had to perform, though I was dying inside. I cried a lot. Those were very dramatic moments. But I did go onstage, and no one in the audience noticed anything out of the ordinary. The show had gone on."

In another interview, Celia remembered that upon returning from a manicure, she heard the trumpet player with the Sonora Matancera and her future husband, Pedro

Knight, telling of her mother's passing the night before to someone on the telephone. He explained that Celia had not been told so that she could be relaxed and ready to perform in the show that same evening.

Celia broke down crying. Between numbers during the show that evening, she would burst into sobs. Her fans knew nothing of her sadness. They would find out a few days later. Once the band arrived in Miami, Tita Borggiano, Rolando Laserie's widow and Celia's neighbor and intimate friend, revealed that *she* was the person Pedro Knight was talking to that day on the phone and she rushed to be with Celia that evening. "We got together to cry over the death of her mother."

According to music writer César Pagano, "Celia's example confirms the belief that the descendants of former African slaves in San Juan de Puerto Rico, Santiago de Cuba, New Orleans, Port-au-Prince, Bahía, or Cartagena de Indias, even though suffering due to very depressed, often even subhuman economic conditions, had the capacity to overcome their difficulties and create a persona that demonstrated the indomitable optimism they have in their heart. For instance, Celia was never able to have a child, and neither could she ever return to her country. However, she always presented herself as a happy person, vital and playful."

Celia once said that she left her homeland because Fidel Castro's revolutionary government had taken measures that violated people's freedom of expression, as well as freedom to travel. After her mother's death, Celia applied to be granted permission to return to Cuba to visit her mother's tomb, but was denied entry. "It's really absurd that one had to ask permission to enter one's own country," she sorrowfully commented, remembering that while

Ollita was in the hospital, she had been allowed to talk to her mother on the phone just for a few minutes and only on Sundays.

Today, some of Celia's family members remain in Cuba. Her sister Dolores married Francisco Hernández Torres, and they had four children: Francisco (Pipo), Irene (better known as Lolina), Ángel, and Hugo. Lolina resembled her aunt Celia, and also inherited a vibrant, resonant voice that perhaps could have led her to musical successes also, but an early marriage, children, and economic limitations have kept Lolina in domestic surroundings all her life.

Celia's brother, Bárbaro, devoted himself to Santería and distinguished himself in ritual ceremonies by singing Afro-Cuban rhythms dedicated to the Lucumí pantheon.

Celia's other sister, Gladys, lived in Santos Suárez in the home of a schoolteacher, Lorenza García, who raised and educated Gladys all through her youth. In 1960 when *La Guarachera* left for exile in Mexico, she invited Gladys to come along. Living abroad, Gladys remained close to Celia before settling in the United States, where she married baseball player Orlando Bécquer. They had four children for whom Celia felt special affection.

3

Celia's Early Career

After grammar school, Celia attended the Academy of the Oblate Sisters, a Catholic school for black girls, where she studied typing, shorthand, and English. Her parents wanted Celia to be a schoolteacher, and to please them she then attended the Escuela Normal, a teachers' school. However, once again it was her singing voice that got noticed.

Although Celia would never get to teach, she never forgot her first career ambition. She once confided that had she not ultimately chosen singing, she would have followed her first vocation. "It so happened that while I was at school, I began singing in radio contests and I won cash prizes. It was only with this money that I was able to buy my books, because my family was very poor. By the time I graduated, I had become rather well known. One day a teacher asked me to sing *"República de México"* at the end of the school year celebration at Public School No. 6, which was close to my home. I said to this lady, 'Look, I graduated from teachers' school, and now I have to start looking for a job.' And she told me, 'Don't teach, honey. Sing, and in one day you'll make as much as I do in a month.'"

"In a sense," Celia finally conceded, "I have fulfilled my mother's wish for me that I become a teacher, since, through my music, I can teach generations of people about my culture, and about how much happiness one can find by giving joy to other people. As an artist, I want to make everybody's heart sing and spirits overflow with joy."

Celia began her career singing at school concerts and community gatherings in the tenements of Havana. Her first public appearance as a singer was in 1938, when her cousin Serafín convinced her to enter a radio talent show called *Los Reyes de la Conga* (The Kings of Conga) sponsored by Radio Lavín, an affiliate of the 1010 Broadcasting Network. Her cousins Serafín and Nenita (Luciana García Alfonso, daughter of her Aunt Nena), and her sister Gladys accompanied her for support. Celia won the contest by unanimous vote and was selected as the Queen of Conga by a truly impressive panel of judges consisting of singer Rita Montaner (la Única); Miguel Matamoros, famous composer and leader of the Trío Matamoros; Gonzalo Roig, pioneer of Cuban symphonic music, and composer of the perennial favorite "*Quiéreme mucho*"; and Eliseo Grenet, composer and musicologist, author of the book *Música popular cubana,* published in 1939.

Encouraged by her success, Celia's cousin Serafín also took her to *La hora del té*, a radio program emceed by Edulfo Ruiz on Radio García Serra. Celia shone in her rendition of the Argentine tango "*Nostalgia,*" a song inspired by composers Cadícamo and Cobián, which sounded more like a *bolero* because, inspired by the style of the popular singer Paulina Álvarez, it was played with an underlying *bolero clave*. Celia was nervous, shy, and insecure; after all, it was only the second time the adolescent had been handed a microphone. Notwithstanding, she received a cake as a prize for participating in the contest. Given her family's circumstances, a cake was a luxury, a gift from heaven that all enjoyed. Celia was beginning to realize that her singing could bring joy to her family. Four weeks later the finalist was chosen, and Celia won a silver chain necklace. It was her first real piece of jewelry.

Most of her early prizes were the sponsor's modest products: chocolate bars, cans of condensed milk, boxes of crackers, bars of soap, and with her winnings, she complemented her father's meager earnings. Remembering those times would always make her sad. "We were so poor that often I did not have money for the trolley fare and I had to walk a lot to get to the contests or else sing to the driver for my fare."

In 1940 she participated in *La Corte Suprema del Arte*, an immensely popular radio talent show in Cuba. She received a more tangible reward: fifteen pesos, which was a significant amount at that time. Celia had chosen for the occasion *"Mango mangüé,"* a composition by Gilberto Valdés (which Isolina Carrillo would later arrange for her), and *"Arrepentida,"* by José Carbó, both sung in duet with the young vocalist Vilma Valle. Havana's music world was becoming aware of her wondrous voice.

With her developing talent and the stirrings of an inevitable vocation, she took up a more formal musical education, which included musical theory, voice, and piano at the Conservatorio Nacional de Música de La Habana. Her voice teacher, Marín Mir, who had connections with CMQ Radio, helped her to develop her own style. Even with her newly-trained voice, she didn't lose the timbre of Afro-Cuban chanting. Her piano lessons were interrupted for her refusal to trim her long fingernails, which infuriated her teacher, Óscar Muñoz Boufartique (composer of the popular *"Burundanga"*).

Celia would often sing tangos in contests. The tango was very popular in Cuba at that time, and it could be heard on radio programs all over the country. Celia's natural versatility and ability to improvise in any rhythm, allowed her to deal comfortably with many styles during her career: *son montuno, danzón, mambo, guajira, conga, chachachá, cumbia, porro, merengue, omelenkó, calipso, rumba, balada, bolero,* rap, rock, *guaracha,* and much later, with what came to be called *salsa.* As Celia Cruz gained experience with her first forays into the world of music, the clear ring of her voice delighted those who heard her. She was asked to sing with the many emerging groups on her joyful and polyphonic island.

Composer and pianist Isolina Carrillo was one of the first to recognize Celia's talent for performing Afro-Cuban music. Carrillo, a distinguished musician who had founded the Orquesta Gigante of Radio Cadena Azul (a local radio station), developed a real interest in Celia, and suggested that with Celia's African ancestry it would be better for her to sing Caribbean dance music. Carillo arranged two *guarachas* for her: *"Que vengan los rumberos"* and *"Mango mangüé."*

Isolina Carrillo introduced Celia to Obdulio Morales, a pianist and orchestra conductor, whose group performed on the programs at Radio Cadena Suaritos with singer Merceditas Valdés. With Obdulio, Celia made her first

Isolina Carrillo (born in Havana in 1907) had been recognized in Cuba for her dynamic career as pianist, composer, and orchestra leader. She was also the teacher of several generations of musicians and singers. In 1933 she had played the trumpet in an all-female septet, Las Trovadoras del Cayo, and later she founded the Conjunto Siboney, with Celia Cruz and Olga Guillot (*La Reina del Bolero*). In 1942, Isolina Carrillo organized the first orchestra devoted only to *danzones*, when the *danzón* was becoming passé. Among the vocalists in her orchestra were Alfredo León, Gaspar Pombo, and Hortensia López. Later, Gilda Cánovas also joined them and, occasionally, Isolina invited Celia to sing with them. She is best remembered for her hit torch song "*Dos gardenias*," a *bolero* immortalized by *El Inquieto Anacobero* (Daniel Santos) with the Sonora Matancera, and sung later, very successfully, by Pedro Vargas, Toña La Negra, Vicentico Valdés, Elena Burke, and many others. During the 1990s it attained worldwide popularity once again due to the smash hit film *Buena Vista Social Club* and its soundtrack, performed by Ibrahim Ferrer and Omara Portuondo.

Afro-Cuban recordings, "*Changó*" and "*Babalú-Ayé*" (sung in Lucumí), with *batá* drums and the Coro Yoruba. Then, at the beginning of 1949, she made a 78 rpm record with the group La Gloria Matancera, conducted by Juan Manuel Díaz, of the *guaracha* "*Ocanosordi*," by Gervasio Kessell, which later became very popular with the Sonora Matancera and the voice of Bienvenido Granda.

On the international level at this time, from 1940 to 1945, World War II was being fought. Cuba's commercial dealings with other countries became extremely limited. Its dependence on a single export product, sugar cane and its byproducts, had been radically reduced due to the presence of German submarines on Caribbean patrol. This also affected the flow of tourists who normally flocked to nightclubs and cabarets in Cuba, an important source of income for popular music professionals.

Despite these circumstances, Celia was able to continue building her career by appearing regularly at the CMQ radio station. She and other vocalists were presented on Sunday afternoons, accompanied by the station's orchestra, in the program called *Estrellas Nacientes* (Rising Stars). In addition, she performed regularly at dance parties given by the regional social clubs from Spain, such as El Centro Gallego (Galician Center) and El Centro Asturiano (Asturian Center), and those held in the gardens of the Tropical Brewery. She also sang at the Cuatro Caminos Theater, the Belacoaín, and at festive occasions organized by labor unions. In addition, Celia sang for a short time with an all-female (the eight Castro sisters) orchestra called Anacaona, a group with whom Celia toured Maracaibo (Venezuela).

In 1947, Celia recorded four songs with Ernesto Duarte and his orchestra, which were precursors of the Afro-Caribbean style that would make her famous later: *"El cumbanchero"* by Puerto Rican composer Rafael Hernández, *"Mambé"* and *"La mazucamba"* by composer Orlando de la Rosa, and *"Quédate negra,"* an African lament by pianist Facundo Rivero.

To protect Cuban artists, a law had been created in which movie houses showing foreign films had to offer live shows with Cuban artists during intermission. Celia sang in one of those shows, at the elegant Teatro América, with her friends Olga Guillot and *El Bárbaro del Ritmo*, Beny Moré.

In 1948, Celia met Roderico (Rodney) Neira, choreographer of the popular shows at the Tropicana nightclub.

Bartolomé Maximiliano Moré, born in Camagüey in 1919, was one of twenty children. In 1945 the Trio Matamoros took him on tour to Mexico as a singer. His nickname, Bartolo, was used there as a name for donkeys, so he became Beny, and later, Benny. He stayed in Mexico, finally singing and recording with Pérez Prado. Returning to Cuba in the fifties, he organized a gigantic orchestra and was given the moniker of *El Bárbaro del Ritmo*. He was a much-loved singer and instinctive musician (he could not read music), and composed many numbers by humming them to his pianist. His sure rhythm and very melodic voice was very much sought after, leaving him very little time for sleep. He died young, in 1963, in Cuba. A movie of his life was made but it was soon banned.

Roderico invited Celia to appear at the Teatro Fausto, in his show *Sinfonía en Blanco y Negro* (Symphony in Black and White), with a group of *rumba* dancers, Las Mulatas de Fuego (The Red-Hot Mulatto Women), who later became a sensation in Latin America. Sharing the stage with Xiomara Alfaro, Elena Burke, Vilma Valle, and two chorus girls, Celia sang "*Pulpa de tamarindo*," "*Puntillita*," or "*Meneíto pa'cá*." Celia did not possess one of those exuberant Cuban figures that were characteristic of the group. Still, she brought them great success. The show was held over for more than two years and included a tour of Venezuela and Mexico, where they recorded several numbers.

4

New York, Monday, July 21, 2003

The *day before the high mass* at St. Patrick's Cathedral in New York, Celia's fans marched to the funeral home where her body lay in state. They sang Celia's songs and cried. People came from all parts of the city, the country, and the world, to revere the queen, Celia Cruz, a black Latina woman. They arrived carrying flowers, flags, photos, posters, worn recordings, religious images, little bags of sugar, and their tears—lots of tears. Each in his or her own way had indelible memories of the performer who had inspired them, had given them joy or, through her music, had touched their lives. They came singing *"Guantanamera," "El yerbero moderno," "La negra tiene tumbao," "Bemba colorá,"* or any song that brought them closer to Celia and made them feel better about their loss.

People came to the funeral home in groups and holding

hands, like small families joined in sorrow. The children came, men and women, the young and the old, the frail and the handicapped—all to catch a glimpse of Celia one last time. *"La negra nos tiene tumbao,"* said an anonymous voice, out of the crowd piling up at the door, making a clever play of words with the title of one of her famous songs. "And that is true, she has felled us to the ground," agreed a woman in mourning black, drying her tears with a crumpled hankie. Thousands of citizens filed past Celia Cruz's coffin to bid farewell to the one who so many times had brought happiness into their lives with her unique cry of joy, *"Azúcar!"* "She was from Cuba, but she also belonged to Puerto Rico, Mexico, Colombia, the world!" said New York City Mayor Michael Bloomberg in reference to the Latina superstar with the universal following.

Appointed and elected officials coming to pay their respects included Mel Martínez, U.S. Secretary of Housing and Urban Development; Congressman Charles Rangel; and New York Governor George Pataki, whose office announced that Tuesday, July 22 was to be officially proclaimed Celia Cruz Day in New York State.

A smiling girl about eight years old emerged from the chapel holding a photo of Celia Cruz taken at a concert in the Blue Note Club. "She signed it for me and since then I have always had it in my room," said the girl, as a Hispanic woman next to her suffered an attack of hysteria.

Inside the chapel, the Cuban diva was attired like a queen, carefully made up, wearing a blond wig and a white dress speckled with diamonds, a rosary with a silvery crucifix in her impeccably manicured hands. Her nails were long and polished, and she was bedecked with her favorite jewels, as if ready for her next concert. The inside of her coffin was golden, and to the left, near her face, was an image of her revered *Virgen de la Caridad del Cobre* (Our Lady of Charity), patron of Cuba, to accompany her into eternity. There was also a copy of her last album, *Regalo del alma* (Gift from My Soul), and a handful of Cuban soil that she had collected on a visit to the U.S. naval base in Guantánamo Bay (Gitmo) when she sang there for exiles in 1994.

The funeral parlor's large hall was flanked by two enormous photos of the Queen of Salsa, and filled with thousands of bouquets of every variety of white flowers. Above her coffin, crowning the space like a shield of honor, was a huge Cuban flag. Inside, the songs of the *Guarachera* were heard, mixed with the ceaseless sobs of visitors throwing kisses and rose petals at her as they filed past making the sign of the cross. The list of celebrities paying their final respects to Celia that day seemed endless: Marc Anthony, La India, Johnny Pacheco, José Luis Rodríguez (el Puma), Isidro Infante, Tito Puente Jr., Jon Secada, Cheo Feliciano, Ralph Mercado, José Alberto (el Canario), Sergio George, and many more.

"She was my goddess," said a saddened Johnny Pacheco, the Dominican musician and a *salsa* legend in his own right. "She is having a funeral fit for what she was, a queen," added her Cuban-American manager, Omer Pardillo, whom Celia considered her adopted son. Paquito D'Rivera, the famous saxophone player, added, "There will be no other Celia. No way will there ever be anyone who could replace her."

In this mournful scene, the only one who seemed immutable, among the more than fifty thousand people flocked at the door, was Rebecca Scott, an African-American woman dressed in yellow (the color of the *Caridad del Cobre*). She was sitting on the sidewalk across from the chapel playing a small drum. "I'm going to be playing here until the last person leaves the funeral home," said Scott. She told the story of how she met Celia Cruz years ago at a concert of the Fania All Stars in Madison Square Garden. "I was sitting in the audience with my little drum when she saw me and said: "*Sube pa'cá!*" (Come up here!), and I played onstage with her," she said emotionally. "That is why all these people are here. She was genuine, and extraordinarily unpretentious."

5

Santería and Afro-Cuban Music

The Yoruba religion in Cuba, also known as Lucumí, is better known as *Santería* (cult of the saints). This Yoruba religion has not only survived but developed, and is practiced today also outside Cuba, in Puerto Rico, the Dominican Republic, Haiti, Jamaica, Brazil, and even in cities like Cartagena de Indias in Colombia or Colón in Panama. With the Cuban exodus, it reached Miami, Elizabeth (New Jersey), and New York City.

It is difficult to separate this religion of African origin from the Cuban culture, and therefore, from its music, art, or literature. The African deities (*orishas*) came to the Americas when Spanish colonists brought African slaves to labor in their sugar plantations. Isolated in their rural *barracones,* the slaves held on to the tribal gods that they worshiped before, mostly Yoruba from the region now known as Nigeria. In time, many of the Catholic saints, symbols, and other elements were assimilated to such an extent that they became an integral part of the slaves' beliefs.

Celia had this to say about the Afro-Cuban religion of *Santería*: "This is a religion that is loved very much by the people, even though at present it has lost its prestige because it has become commercialized in a sinful manner. But it is a religion I respect, and besides, I play a *santera* in the soap opera *Valentina.*"

On one occasion she confided, "I am a religious person, not a *santera*. I believe in God and I always put myself in His hands. I am a devotee of Our Lady of Mercy (*La Virgen de las Mercedes*) and I like to dress in white, her color. I am also very devoted to the patron saint of Cuba, Our Lady of Charity (*La Virgen de la Caridad del Cobre*), in whose honor I keep a beautiful altar at home. I sing *Santería* rhythms because I can sing them easily."

While Celia was trying to make her voice known through radio contests, she did not sing African rhythms but all kinds of musical genres, and she kept exploring. Over years of hesitation, advice, and audience reaction to her performances, she grappled with her repertory and what songs were best for her to sing.

Very early she began singing a variety of music: *afros*, *rumbas*, *guarachas*, *sones*, tangos, even flamenco tunes from Spain. Her style was very far from being defined. In time, all of her extraordinary intelligence and sensibility led her to start evaluating and discovering that her fate fundamentally connected her with the *rumba*, the *guaracha*, the *guaguancó*, and *santería* chants. In a word, this was Afro-Cuban music and this was where she shone. "Onorio Muñoz, together with composer Isolina Carrillo, arranged a few numbers by Gilberto Valdés for me," Celia said. "That is how I began to sing *guarachas*, and people began calling me *La Guarachera de Cuba*. Today they call me the Queen of Salsa. They are just names, and they don't displease me."

She was such a complete artist that she also sang *sones* and *boleros* beautifully. From 1947 on, she performed in the most prestigious nightclubs in Havana, such as Montmartre and Sans Souci, where she took part in the production of *Maracas en la noche*. She also performed in cabarets: Tambú, Zombie, Topeka, and in shows in the best movie theaters of those times, such as Encanto, América, and Fausto. She was often accompanied by large bands, from fourteen to eighteen musicians, like the Sans Souci orchestra, led by Maestro Rafael Ortega, who often used arrangements by the well-known Bebo Valdés. Celia was singing African themes, and one day she said, "A man came, introduced himself, and told me, 'Look, you should be singing everything.' *Afros* were really nice and I had the voice to shine in them, but *afros* were like sad laments of black slaves, and at that time, not very commercial."

After singing with a band called La Gloria Matancera, and with the orchestras led by Bebo Valdés and Edelberto Guzmán, Celia recorded an LP with the Sonora Caracas. She followed this with a show at the Tropicana, the famous nightclub and casino, where she took turns with Paulina Álvarez in the show *Pregón negro, danzonete, bembé santero*. The bandleader there, Obdulio Morales, knew deeply about *Santería* and practiced it. Every night Celia sang whatever fit the choreography of the show: Caribbean, Brazilian or French songs (her favorite was "*La Vie en rose*," made famous by Edith Piaf, the Little Sparrow of Paris). Her appearances at the Tropicana nightclub became decisive in her career development. There she met

Rogelio Martínez, bandleader of the Sonora Matancera, a musical group that was beginning to be noticed for its outstanding repertory.

Celia had vivid memories of the Tropicana in the fifties. "I did a lot of shows on *Santería* then." It had an effect on her. Even after settling in the United States, she kept a copy of *El Monte,* by Lydia Cabrera, which is not easy to understand. "Anyone who goes deeply into it becomes a *santero.*" She also had a book on the *orishas* (African deities) and another one on the meaning of *caracoles* (snail shells that are used to predict the future). "I don't sing to the saints very often now," she once said in an interview. "I explore other themes, like '*Químbara*,' '*Toro mata*,' '*Sopa en botella.*'"

Although it was popularly believed, Celia insisted that she was never a *santera,* but she was indeed superstitious. She never took a hotel room with the number thirteen on it or any room on that floor. No one could whistle in her dressing room while she was getting ready or talk about flying or crawling insects. She would dress in white for her first song or her first appearance on a new stage, whether in Paris or in Buenos Aires. She said it was for good luck, and because it was the color of peace and purity. It was also the color of the *Virgen de las* Mercedes (Obatalá). Later in her career, she opted for costumes in spectacularly brilliant colors, very different from the slim dresses with long trains that she wore while still in Cuba.

She was also superstitious about real pearls, after hearing that if a bride wore pearls on her wedding day, she would cry a lot during her marriage. Early in her career, while she was on tour abroad, an impresario gave Celia a brooch in the shape of a flower, with a genuine pearl in the center. Upon her return to Cuba, contracts for singing

Throughout her long career, Celia sang many *Santería* rhythms. They are contained in two CD's under the title *Tributo a los orishas*, with the Sonora Matancera. Among them, *"Guede Zaina,"* (Haitian *congo* by D. en D., 1952), *"Elegguá quiere tambó"* (*afro* by Luis Martínez Griñán, 1955), *"Canto a Yemayá"* (*montuno* by Enrique Herrera, 1955), *"Oyá, diosa y fe"* (*bolero-afro* by Julio Blanco Leonard, 1956), *"Baila Yemayá"* (mambo by Lino Frías, 1960), *"Baho Kende"* (*guaguansón* by Alberto Zayas, 1960), "Mulense" (*guaguancó* by Florentino Cedeño, 1960), *"Maitagua"* (*guaracha* by Jesús and Rogelio Martínez, 1960), *"Saludo a Elegguá"* (*bolero-afro* by July Mendoza, 1961), *"Lalle Lalle"* (*guaguancó* by J. C. Fumero, 1961), *"Yemayá"* (*bembé* chant by Lino Frías, 1962), *"Yembe Laroco"* (*guaracha* by Blanco Suazo, 1962), *"Changó"* (*afro* by Rogelio Martínez, 1965), *"Palo mayimbe"* (*bembé* by Javier Vázquez, 1965), *"Para tu altar "* (*guaracha-pregón* by July Mendoza, 1965), *"Changó ta vení"* (*guanguansón* by Justi Barreto, 1965), *"Óyeme, Aggayú"* (*guaracha-afro* by Alberto Zayas, 1965) and *"Plegaria a Laroye"* (*bolero-afro* by Francisco Varela, 1965).

engagements mysteriously dried up. Some time later, while she was wearing the same brooch, her flight was canceled when the plane developed mechanical problems. She promptly pulled the pearl out of the brooch and returned it to the sea to get rid of its bad luck.

Celia had a terrible fear of flying. Saint Christopher was the first saint she packed in her portable pantheon. As she said to Umberto Valverde for his book *Celia Cruz: Reina Rumba*: "When I am traveling by air, I prefer to listen to classical music because it relaxes me; perhaps for the fear I have of airplanes, I begin to panic. It is a strange panic, and people ask me how is it possible then that I can sleep during flights. And I think it's that my nerves make me sleep. I was not always afraid, not until about 1961: one day we visited some friends and they began to talk about this and to tell stories. Somebody said that a plane went down because a few flying swallows got into the plane's turbines. Since then I began to be afraid of flying, and I couldn't get rid of that fear."

Celia always traveled with her little mass book, which she read in spare moments. She would also carry thirty small pictures and miniature images of her favorite saints, such as Saint Lazarus (Babalú-Ayé, for protection against disease); *la Virgen de Regla* (Yemayá, queen of the waters); Saint Gregorio Hernández, the anointed Venezuelan, to stop pain; *la Virgen de las Mercedes (Obatalá,* for peace and harmony); Saint Jude Tadeus, patron of impossible causes; Saint Martín de Porres, the canonized Peruvian friar; *la Virgen de la Caridad del Cobre* (Oshún, goddess of love and marriage), patron of Cuba; Saint Christopher, protector of travelers; and Saint Barbara *(Changó,* deity of fire, thunder and lightning). As Celina González used to sing, / *Santa Bárbara bendita,* / *para ti surge mi lira.* / *Santa Bárbara bendita,* / *y con emoción se inspira* / *ante tu imagen bonita.* / *¡Que viva Changó!, ¡Que viva Changó, señores!* /. Celia would turn to her saints for small favors: good luck in a concert, or no rain before her show so her admirers would show up.

One of her most famous numbers was *"El yerbero moderno,"* or *"El yerberito,"* as she used to call it: *Casera, traigo mis flores* / *acabaditas de cortar.* / *Las hay de todos los colores,* / *mis flores para tu altar.* / *El girasol como llama, para Ochún,* / *y la rosa nacarada de Obatalá,* / *príncipe de pura sangre para Changó, / las Siete Potencias y Yemayá, / y para Babalú-Ayé, gladiolos blancos. / Para Changó y Yemayá, mis flores traigo, / mis flores para tu altar.* (Lady, I have fresh flowers, just cut. / I have them in all colors,/ my flowers for your altar. / Sunflowers like tongues of fire for Ochún, / and the pearly roses for Obatalá, / the princes of pure blood for Changó, / the Seven African Powers, and Yemayá; / and for Babalú-Ayé, white gladioluses. For Changó and Yemayá I bring to you my flowers, / my flowers for your altar.)

6

New York, Sunday, July 20, 2003

Celia's *New York vigil* was to be held in the Frank H. Campell funeral home and her remains then transferred in a horse-driven carriage to the majestic Saint Patrick's Cathedral on Manhattan's Fifth Avenue, for the last religious service before her remains were laid to rest in Woodlawn Cemetery in the Bronx.

When Celia Cruz's body arrived in New York on Sunday, July 20, hundreds of fans were there to receive her. The cortège arrived at 6:23 in the afternoon, and was received with applause and shouts of "Celia, Celia!" and "Pedro, we love you!" Her arrival was greeted, amid magnificent floral arrangements and bouquets of white flowers, by the international press, her fans, cars passing by waving Cuban flags and blasting her music on their radios.

After the grandiose vigil in Miami on Saturday, more than a million people crowded the streets to say their final farewell to "their Queen," and hundreds flocked to the funeral home entrance to await the arrival of her remains.

"Cuba's soul has died," said Paquito D'Rivera. From the rank and file to the president, no one could overlook the death of the beloved Cuban singer. There were photos of her on magazine covers and the front pages of newspapers, with lengthy articles and interviews, personal testimonies, quotes from friends and colleagues. All the while her songs could be heard at events in her honor and on special radio and television programs.

Exhaustion was evident in the faces of Pedro Knight, and of Omer Pardillo. For two days, they had followed a marathon itinerary which amazed Latinos and Anglos alike.

In all corners of the city, Celia was the topic of conversation. "Celia was always big, but people did not realize it," said Antonio Mora, owner of the Botánica Santa Bárbara in Upper Manhattan, which the Queen of Salsa had visited, looking for religious images. "Besides being an extraordinary singer, she was also important for her position against Castro," said a businessman who had come from Cuba many years before. Watching from his restaurant El Mambí, Cuban owner Rafael Morales would see Celia coming and going to her bank across the street. "The nicest thing about Celia was her lack of self-importance. One day she told me, 'The name of your restaurant is El Mambí, so you *must* be Cuban!' and she started laughing. Both Celia and Pedro were very polite, really," Morales said.

Enrique Tejada, a Dominican musician who works at Rufi's Music at 172 Street and Broadway, sold every Celia recording he had in the store. He wasn't celebrating his good fortune, however, but commented sadly, "It's an irreparable loss, she just went like that, and it's very sad."

"Celia taught us that we must always move forward, no matter what," said Julio Meneses, a *marielito* who had come to the Bronx in 1980. "That is why I am here, because she was an inspiration for me and for many exiles."

Ángela Lebrón, a Puerto Rican, was clutching a bouquet of white roses and sunflowers. "The white ones were her favorites, and also the sunflowers, because they are yellow and that is the color of the *Virgen de la Caridad del Cobre*, the patron of Cuba. Celia was very devoted to her," Lebrón said.

Henry Alonso and his family had come from Washington, D.C. to deliver a poster signed by her fans from the capital of the United States. Among them, there was an eighty-three-year-old woman. "We Cubans were most proud of her, she was our last glory," said the grandmother, leaning on a cane. "That's why I am here," she added in a quivering voice, "to honor her."

7

Celia's First Taste of Success

Before joining the Sonora Matancera, Celia worked with many musical groups, using them as so many stepping stones on the way to her dream of working with the famous orchestra and its impressive roster of singers. Daniel Santos, Bienvenido Granda, and Miguel D'Gonzalo (who also sang with Aldemaro Romero and his orchestra) were considered to be among the best singers of popular Cuban music. Celia also performed with Jesús Pérez and his drums; Papín and his Rumberos, La Gloria Matancera; Alfonso Larraín and Leonard Melody in Venezuela; and later with Ernesto Duarte's band, and of course with the Tropicana orchestra.

For her appearances at radio station Mil Diez (1010), she performed with such accomplished conductors as Adolfo Guzmán, Facundo Rivero, Enrique González Mantici—whose talented *bongosero* was Ramón (Mongo) Santamaría—and Obdulio Morales, the musical arranger who had worked on several Santería numbers that Celia recorded. Also appearing on the same radio station were the Trío Matamoros, Los Jóvenes del Cayo, Arsenio Rodríguez, the Trío Hermanos Rigual, the so-called Radiofónica of Arcaño y sus Maravillas, Olga Guillot, and the ever-popular Benny Moré. This station transmitted tangos, jazz, classical music, programming from Spain and, of course, Cuban music.

During this time, Celia first met Paulina Álvarez. Paulina's style had inspired Celia's rendition of the tango *"Nostalgia"* using the Cuban *clave* to give the number a Caribbean sound.

This was also the time that Celia first learned from Rita Montaner to combine song with dance to create what would later become her signature performance style. By then, Rita Montaner (*La Única*) already had a list of musical hits that stretched back to 1922.

Celia was beginning to develop her own artistic style, combining that vibrantly sonorous voice and its plethora of nuanced cadences with her charismatic, spontaneous personality to create a whirlwind of joy on the stage. Due to her growing popularity, 1010 began to invite her on its tours of the island. A pianist whose job it was to coordinate her music with local bands always accompanied her. On more than one occasion this person was Dámaso Pérez Prado, the future King of Mambo.

What was to become Celia's long relationship with the Sonora Matancera began in a roundabout manner. Celia knew from the beginning that she needed the Sonora Matancera to solidify her artistic career. Rafael Sotolongo, manager and publicist for Crusellas & Co., which sponsored the Sonora Matancera program at Radio Progreso, and Roderico (Rodney) N eira, the Tropicana's choreogra-

Rita Montaner debuted in the first regional Cuban concert organized by Jorge Anckermann in the Payret theater in Havana, where she also performed popular dances. During her long career, she distinguished herself as a singer, but also appeared in theater, film, and *zarzuela*, or musical popular in Spain. She popularized *"El manisero"* (the Peanut Vendor), written for her by Moisés Simons.

pher, introduced Celia to Rogelio Martínez, the Sonora's bandleader. They wanted him to hear her sing and consider the possibility of using her as a substitute for the orchestra's soloist, Myrta Silva, who had left. Martínez received these kinds of requests and recommendations often. So, politely but without making a commitment, he agreed to call her. The manager eagerly gave Rogelio Celia's telephone number. In reality, it was the number of a store on the corner near Celia's home, whose owner would relay messages for her.

Weeks went by and the Sonora Matancera's leader with his many social and professional commitments forgot his promise to call Celia. Then one day, by chance, Celia met the bandleader. She took advantage of the opportunity and asked if he would listen to her sing one song, because she valued his opinion highly. He graciously accepted.

Rogelio Martínez would later confide, "When that black woman opened her mouth, my hair stood on end. After I heard her, I featured her in my program at Radio Progreso in Havana, and I created a new repertory of songs for her. I do not compose," Martínez explained. "What I do is choose the appropriate repertory for each singer, and I have never failed, I think. When Sidney Siegel, producer for Seeco Records, came to see me at the radio program, and I told him that I was going to record with Celia Cruz, he asked, 'How come? Are you out of your mind?' I told him that if he did not want to produce the record, I would look for another studio. And I added, in an urgent tone, 'This is what we'll do: I'm going to make the recording and send you the tape. If you don't like it, you return it to me, and we'll do it ourselves.'"

The *pregón* Martínez gave Celia to record was *"El yerbero moderno,"* which later became a big hit in Latin America and all over the world. Celia's followers see this song as a letter of introduction for the young singer, who, somehow, never received a gold record for it.

"Fifteen days later, I am at home and the phone rings at two or three in the morning," remembers Rogelio Martínez. "We began talking, but I did not understand what it was all about with Sidney, until he told me: 'Rogelio, that girl I told you not to record, well, I'm going to give her an exclusive contract.' 'That is something you have to take up with her,' I said."

At the time, the principal female vocalist with the Sonora Matancera was Myrta Silva, also known as *"Café con Leche."*

August 3, 1950, marked a change for Celia's career. Her opportunity materialized when Rogelio Martínez asked Celia to replace Myrta Silva who had left the country. Myrta returned to Havana only briefly in 1952 in order to record the *son montuno "Qué corto es el amor"* and the *guaracha "Loca,"* with the Sonora, for Seeco Records.

During the next fifteen years, Celia sang with the Sonora Matancera. Her years singing with the band are regarded as Celia's golden period, as she starred in some of the best moments in Afro-Cuban music.

Celia has told the story of her first meeting with the

> Severino Ramos earned the nickname *Refresquito* because
> when he was out for drinks with his friends or other
> members of the orchestra, he had the habit of asking only
> for a *"refresquito"* (a small soda). He was the musical ar-
> ranger for the Sonora and a wizard at harmonizing instru-
> ments and voices to obtain the unique sound for which
> the orchestra was famous.

Sonora Matancera many times. She arrived early, before
eleven in the morning, which was the regular starting time
for rehearsals at Radio Progreso *La Onda de la Alegría*
(The Joyful Wave). As fate would have it, the handsome
trumpet-player Pedro Knight, her future husband, also
arrived early to rehearse. Celia brought two *guarachas*
to sing for the audition, *"No queremos chaperonas"* and
"El tiempo de la colonia." Knight politely offered to help
and he passed the scores on to Severino Ramos (*"Refresquito"*).

In the beginning, Celia's participation in the Sonora
Matancera, *"Decano de los Conjuntos de América"* (the
Dean of Orchestras in the Americas), was not as propitious
as she had expected. Myrta Silva had a large following.
She was a sensual woman who performed with an exciting
dose of eroticism. This, coupled with the fact that she was
white (a real advantage given the underlying racism at the
time) gave Myrta an edge over Celia. Celia was dark black
and a little too skinny. Superficial as it may seem, her physical appearance was a hindrance to the development of
her career as a popular singer. At first, listeners called the
radio station demanding the return of Myrta Silva. "They
used to say my voice was too strident, that I was not right
for the Sonora," Celia recounted much later. "People have

always preferred sassy performers," she said, referring to Myrta Silva's suggestive dance movements.

Cuba's racist heritage persisted in different ways even as Celia started drawing attention in the Cuban musical scene. Cuba was one of the last countries in the Americas to abolish slavery, which it did in 1886. One of Cuba's most notorious incidents occurred in the 1930s when Joe Louis, the World Heavyweight Champion boxer, was denied lodging in the most exclusive hotel in the city, the Hotel Nacional, because he was black.

During the forties, "white" bands like the Orquesta Casino de la Playa, Riverside, Hermanos Castro and bandleaders Julio Cueva or René Touzet played in clubs for white people. Despite the fact that the musicians of the Sonora Matancera were mostly black, they enjoyed great success and performed for thirty years at Radio Progreso before leaving Cuba in 1960.

Sidney Siegel, owner of Seeco Records, would later explain his initial reluctance to hire Celia. Sidney was convinced that a female black singer could not succeed, but he (and everyone else) changed his mind after hearing Celia sing.

In addition to racism, sexism was also a very real negative factor for Celia. With few exceptions there was a preference for male artists that extended beyond music to the fine arts and literature. This machismo mentality started to recede with the breakthrough of women like María Teresa Vera, Justa García, Rita Montaner, Paulina Alvarez, and the handful of other female artists that paved the way for Celia. The first big opportunity for Celia was at the 1010 radio station. Her voice was so rich in timbre and nuance that it seduced anyone who heard it. Her talent overcame all the obstacles.

Calixto Leicea, an ex-trumpet player from the Sonora Matancera who lives in New York, remembers first seeing Celia and knowing she was destined for greatness. "Celia had something special that we all could feel, something different; and when I met her in the forties at Havana's Radio Progreso, I told her so, and I was right," Leicea reminisced, biting a Havana cigar.

One of Leicea's unforgettable moments with *La Guarachera* happened after a gig one night in Cuba. "A man approached us to say, 'Hey, what a pity that Celia is so ugly.' Rogelio Martínez grabbed the man by the neck, and roughed him up for being so rude. How dare he? How is he going to say something like this about the orchestra's darling pet? She was not only talented, she was a beautiful woman, and she had always been beautiful."

José Pardo Llada, a well-known radio commentator, says: "I met Celia Cruz in early 1950, when Havana's Radio Progreso contracted her to perform with the Sonora Matancera. The musicians did not want her because they thought she was too skinny and ugly, but its bandleader, Rogelio Martínez, had faith in her talent and in her voice from the start." Celia's early act was a far cry from the spectacular attire, the wigs in all colors, the exotic costumes, and the fanciful shoes she gradually began wearing in the 1970s. The very slender Celia still combed her straightened hair back into a fashionable bun or a braid or wore it under a turban, following the stereotype of beauty created by movies and fashion magazines, imposing an esthetic pattern that copied the women of Europe and the United States. These women had "delicate" features, blond hair—natural or dyed—and light complexions. Mulatto women were more acceptable than dark-skinned ones.

According to César Pagano, "Dark-skinned women

were only admired as dancers, and once in a while as singers in groups that performed in black clubs or associations, such as the Buena Vista Social Club. Celia Cruz, dark-skinned and thin, with a hooked nose, large mouth, kinky hair, strident voice, and a repertoire of black chants in black *patois*, did not enjoy the best of conditions for the start of her musical career. Her undeniable talent, self-confidence, patience, and professionalism saved her from the expected rejection." Rogelio Martínez's confidence in Celia's inimitable voice and unique style was growing, and he approached José Carbó, a composer from Santiago de Cuba—on the eastern end of the island—to compose a few numbers for the young newcomer. Celia was taking her first steps with the Sonora, and Carbó was responsible for her initial success, "*Cao cao maní picao*," a *guaracha* that made her a star of Cuban popular rhythms in early 1951. Once it was stamped on those brittle 78 vinyl discs, the number became an instant hit that brought her fame throughout Latin America. It was followed by "*Tatalibabá*," "*Ritmo, tambó y flores*," "*La guagua*," and "*El yerbero moderno*," among others.

With Celia Cruz at center stage, the Sonora Matancera orchestra reached the highest radio ratings ever for their live presentations broadcast each evening from seven to eight at Radio Progreso. The joy of her joining the Sonora was darkened by sad news. Her cousin Serafín, the first one to detect her musical talent and to encourage her to compete, died just as Celia was beginning to be recognized. He left behind his widow, Evangelina, with five children. "It is a pain that I always carry inside of me," said Celia some time after his untimely demise.

With its tropical rhythms, the Sonora Matancera propelled itself like an electrical charge onto the international music scene. On the flip side of "*Cao cao maní picao*" was "*Mata siguaraya,*" an *afro* attributed to Lino Frías, a pianist with the orchestra. Carbó felt hurt by the title "*Reina de la Salsa,*" given to Celia in New York. To Carbó, her music was Cuban. "She should only be called *La Guarachera de Cuba.*" In his New Jersey home, Carbó has Celia's first LP, where she wrote by hand, "*Gracias, mano Carbó, por la suerte que me dio tu número*" (Thanks, my friend Carbó, for the good luck your number has given me).

8

New York, Friday, July 18, 2003

With passionate cries of *"Azúcar!,"* many tears, and a shower of red rose petals, all accompanied by the strains of *No hay que llorar / que la vida es un carnaval / y es más bello vivir cantando. /* (You don't have to cry / because life is like a carnival / and it is much better to live singing.), Celia Cruz's adoring fans bid farewell to her remains, which left for Miami on Friday, July 18.

At about two in the afternoon, Luis Falcón, a young fan who considered himself Celia's "son," and her personal assistant, Omer Pardillo, arrived at the funeral home for the drive to the airport. Her widower, Pedro Knight, chose to stay inside the car that would take them to Kennedy Airport. They were headed to Miami, the capital of the Cuban exile community, where *La Guarachera* was expected to receive the homage of thousands of people.

The Frank H. Campell Funeral Home was also host to the memorial services of Rudolf Valentino, the idolized actor, in 1926. The funeral home was then located on Sixty-sixth Street and Broadway.

Pall bearers carried Celia Cruz's bier on their shoulders. The moment expected by all those attending had come. As her remains were exiting the chapel, shouts of *"Azúcar!"* burst forth. It was the expression that the singer had popularized throughout her artistic career in the United States. Celia's remains were to leave on an American Airlines flight at five-thirty in the afternoon, accompanied by relatives and close friends.

When her body was placed in the hearse headed for Kennedy Airport, some of those present lunged toward the limousine in order to touch it, but were prevented by security. Fans who had gathered early in the morning on the sidewalks in front of the funeral home were still standing vigil, and waving white handkerchiefs. The funeral director placed a commemorative book for visitors so they could leave messages of condolence for Celia's relatives. Some people brought bouquets of flowers with ribbon messages, others lit candles, and someone laid a Cuban flag over an impromptu altar on the sidewalk.

A street performer of Colombian descent, who earns his living dancing with a rag doll on the streets of New York City, asked permission from her relatives to render the Queen of Salsa one last homage. A spokesman for the funeral parlor approached and told the perfomer that, although Celia's family was sad, they understood that he interpreted life the way she did, with joy and hope, and gave him their blessing. After the street performer danced with his doll to the rhythms of "*La vida es un carnaval*," he waited until Celia's remains left the chapel, letting his tape machine run on, playing her song, to bid her a joyous farewell.

9

A Historical View of the Sonora Matancera

The Sonora Matancera Orchestra came from humble origins in the city of Matanzas, on January 12, 1924. Founded in 1693, Matanzas had become a commercial and industrial center, with a very active seaport. Valentín Cané, a *timbalero* who had the initiative of gathering a group of musicians from the city neighborhood called Ojo de Agua, founded the Sonora. Cané was also deft at playing the *tres*, a guitar with three pairs of strings tuned in octaves. He formed part of this string group, which he called Tuna Liberal, whose name coincided with the political party of the Governor of the State, Juan Gronlier. The founding members of this group, besides Cané, who also played the *tumbadora*, were Pablo Vázquez on bass, Manuel Sánchez (el Cojito Jimagua) on *timbales*, and Domingo Medina, José Manuel Valera, Juan Bautista Llopis, and Julio Gobin, all on guitar, and Ismael

Goberna on the trumpet. By 1932, the group had adopted the name Septeto Soprano. Later, the band became known as Estudiantina Sonora Matancera.

Throughout its development, some of the founding members of this modest neighborhood *tuna* left and were replaced with more recognized musicians. Owing to his old age, Maestro Cané was one of the first to go, in 1942. The rigors of the profession had proved too much for him, and the well-liked Alfonso Furias (Yiyo) replaced him. Other members who joined at different times were Raimundo Elpidio (Babú), son of founding member Pablo Vázquez; and José Rosario Chávez (also known as "Manteca"), who replaced Jimagua. One of the oldest members who was part of the initial Sonora was Carlos Manuel Díaz (the famous Caíto), on *maracas* and backups, who had joined in 1926.

The original group used to play in the open-air concerts held in the Central Park of Matanzas. They also provided music for dances at private parties, at the sugar mills—especially those at the Hershey Sugar Mill—and at the large farms of Río Potrero.

In Havana, the Sonora played for festivals organized by political parties, and it was invited to play around the country during the dictatorship of Gerardo Machado (1929-1933), a declared admirer of the group. The group was asked to perform in the capital in social clubs such as Los Anaranjados, Los Veinte, Los Treinta, La Casita de los Médicos, and Café La Mora. In addition, they began playing at the Teatro Alhambra in 1927. The group was a fixture at Marte y Belona for eighteen years. They played there until 1950, when they left for CMQ Radio and began recording for Panart, the first Cuban recording company, founded by Ramón Sabat. At Radio Progreso, the Sonora

During the period that Caíto was a sailor, he frequented an eatery owned by Rogelio Martínez's father. The two men started a friendship that was to last a lifetime. It was Caíto who brought Rogelio to the group as a guitarist in 1928. Rogelio, who would later become the leader of the group, played the guitar together with Caíto and Estanislao Sureda (Laíto). Rogelio turned out to be a good talent scout and a hit producer. After fifty-seven years of leading the most popular Caribbean music band of all time, Rogelio Martínez died at the age of 93, on Sunday, May 13, 2001, in New York.

performed for an impressive thirty years. And, of course, they played in the famous Tropicana nightclub, where Celia Cruz would later meet Rogelio Martínez. The list of live performances of the Sonora Matancera is outstanding.

While performing at the Teatro Alhambra, impresario Augusto Franqui contracted the Sonora for recording with RCA Victor, which resulted in *"Matanzas," "La tierra de fuego," "De Oriente a Occidente," "Las cuatro estaciones,"* and *"Cotorrita real,"* by singer-guitarist Juan Bautista Llopis.

In 1935, the well-known trumpet player Calixto Leicea replaced Israel Goberna, and on January 6, 1944, Pedro Knight became the second trumpet. Dámaso Pérez Prado played the piano for the Sonora from 1937 until 1939, when he withdrew in order to organize his own orchestra, becoming *El Rey del Mambo* (The King of Mambo). However, the most prodigious pianist they had was Lino Frías, who was with the group from 1942 until July 1977, when he had to leave due to sickness. A pianist who marked the group because of his talent as composer and arranger during the forties was Severino Ramos (Refresquito). His arrangements were simple, but they achieved balance, and his artistic wisdom reached the heart of his audience. Another musician who also helped form the special sound quality that thrust this orchestra into the limelight was Mario Muñoz (Papaíto), who replaced Simón Espiragoza (Pinino), who in turn had replaced *timbalero* José Rosario Chávez (Manteca).

When Pedro Knight resigned his position as the orchestra's trumpet player in order to be with Celia, he was initially replaced by Chiripa and later by Saúl Torres. In 1976, another famous trumpet player joined them: Alfredo (Chocolate) Armenteros, who happened to be Benny Moré's maternal cousin.

By the time Celia joined the Sonora Matancera, the familiar voices that were heard with the group on the airwaves were Daniel Santos (*el Inquieto Anacobero*), Myrta Silva (*La Guarachera Picante*), and Bienvenido Granda (*El Bigote que Canta*), a moniker given to him by Pimentel Molina, a Radio Progreso announcer). But there is no doubt that the golden age of the orchestra began when the phenomenal *Guarachera* joined them. The Sonora Matancera made Cuban rhythms, which Celia sang in her unique style, known the world over: *guaracha, bolero, guaguancó, merengue, rumba, son, chachachá,* and even rock and roll: *El mambo hizo furor en Nueva York / pero el chachachá lo derrotó. / Ahora un nuevo ritmo apareció / y es el inquietante rock and roll. / Ven a bailar rock and roll, / ven a sentir su sabor, / con su compás / tú sentirás / una deliciosa sensación. /* (The mambo was a tremendous hit in New York / but the chachachá took over. / Now there is a new rhythm, / the exciting rock and roll. / Come and dance rock and roll, / come and feel its flavor, / with this beat / you will feel / a delicious sensation). An entire constellation of hit songs are still vivid in the collective memory and imagination of her millions of fans all over the world. One of them commented anonymously: "When the Sonora plays, everything seems more beautiful. With their music and dance, hope becomes a song, and the joy of living is renewed."

Other vocalists brought artistic quality and added prestige to the orchestra: Carlos Argentino and Leo Marini (*el Bolerista de América*), from Argentina; Alberto Beltrán (*el Negrito del Batey*), from the Dominican Republic; Nelson Pinedo (*el Almirante del Ritmo*) from Colombia; Bobby Capó and Carmen Delia Dipiní from Puerto Rico; and Toña la Negra, the only Mexican vocalist to sing with the Sonora.

Among the other popular Cuban singers with the orchestra were Benny Moré (*el Bárbaro del Ritmo*, also called El Beny), Celio González, Miguelito Valdés (Mr. Babalú), and a total of more than sixty singers who performed with the joyful repertory of the Conjunto.

During the Sonora's long trajectory, more than four thousand songs were recorded, of which a significant portion reached classic status and are still listened to around the world. And not only for the quality of the singers, because at all times Rogelio Martínez selected the best voices, but also for the specific arrangements and the lyrics that reached deeply into the popular sentiment of several generations of admirers through sixty years of history.

One reason the Sonora stayed on the charts for six decades was the strict discipline that Rogelio imposed. About this he commented, "It is very easy to gather a group of workers, but it is difficult to keep them as a unit and producing for so many years." Besides the respectful obedience and enforced punctuality of all its members, the Sonora Matancera functioned as a cooperative. Its profits were distributed in a fair manner among all its members. It was a solid motivation that bound them in an atmosphere of harmonious brotherhood that prevented them, as usually happens in other groups, from descending into a state of permanent instability. Vedette Blanquita Amaro, a *rumbera* and M.C. with the Sonora for some of its tours, explained the prevailing spirit of the orchestra: "What a beautiful fellowship there was among all of us. The group was a model of discipline, of helping each other and loving the work. There was no artistic jealousy, we were all a big loving family."

Helio Orovio, distinguished musicologist and historian of Cuban music, has been criticized for allowing—against his expressed will—the Cuban government censorship to delete from his first edition of *Diccionario enciclopédico de la música cubana* (1981) all mentions of musicians who left Cuba after 1959 (their recordings, including all of Celia's and of the Sonora's, had been prohibited on the radio and were eventually destroyed). But he had this to say about the group, as included in Umberto Valverde's *Memoria de la Sonora Matancera:* "There was something magical, a polishing, a perfection of all the popular music elements in the Sonora. It's not for nothing that it originated in Matanzas, the cradle of the *danzón,* the *danzonete,* the *mambo,* and the *rumba.* Matanzas was a forging furnace of Cuban music. Rogelio Martínez inherited the direction of the group and launched it with a discipline that other groups lacked. He had the intelligence to choose the right selections for each of his singers. Many important figures graced his concerts, from Leo Marini and Miguelito Valdés to Benny Moré (who appeared with the Sonora in the program *Cascabeles Candado*)."

During the time Celia Cruz was associated with the Sonora Matancera, her career followed a resplendent trajectory. Her diaphanous contralto voice has been considered one of the most beautiful in a country that has produced no end of marvelous musicians and famous singers. Her early songs achieved an unprecedented success for a woman singing Caribbean music with a popular orchestra. Numbers such as "*Cao cao maní picao,*" "*El yerbero moderno,*" "*Burundanga,*" "*Juancito Trucupey,*" "*Me voy a Pinar del Río,*" "*Sopa en botella,*" "*Tu voz,*" "*En el bajío,*" "*Caramelos,*" and "*Dile que por mí no tema*" had immediate and phenomenal success that kept nurturing her fame. It can be said with near certainty that anyone who has been impressed by Celia's melodic voice can remember exactly where he or she was when hearing one of her memorable renditions for the first time.

10

Celia Cruz and the Sonora Matancera

Celia began singing at Radio García Serra, then at CMQ, and later at Mil Diez (1010), but one of her first regular jobs was with Radio Cadena Suaritos. By then the Sonora Matancera was the most popular musical group on the radio, and every time she had the opportunity, she would go to see them perform. Celia's story about how she joined the Sonora Matancera is different from the story Rogelio Martínez told. As she recalled, it happened quite unexpectedly. "Mr. Sotolongo came to see me and said that he wanted me to join the Sonora Matancera. I was overjoyed. Rogelio and I had a chat, and I told him, 'Look, Rogelio, aside from the pleasure I would get working with you, I also need the job with the Sonora for economic reasons.'" Celia was still working at Radio Suaritos before she joined the Sonora, when the following news appeared in a newspaper: "Puerto Rican singer Myrta Silva is gone, and the Sonora Matancera intends to bring in another woman, possibly Celia Cruz, to take her place." When Suaritos, who owned his radio station, found out, she was immediately fired.

Celia sang all kinds of music with the Sonora Matancera. She remembers the heterogeneous LP's that were recorded then, containing a whole variety of styles so that people at home having parties without a band could play a record that included one *guaracha*, one *danzón*, one *son*, one *chachachá*, and a *bolero* or two. When she began singing with the Sonora in 1950, *chachachás* were the rage: *Tengo una muñeca que baila el chachachá / marca unos pasitos / y baila el chachachá.* She did the vocals for all those styles, but the rhythm she liked best was the *guaracha*. For boleros, the Sonora already had two singers, Bienvenido Granda and Daniel Santos. Later Celio González joined in, and he sang boleros, too, as well as other melodies. But Celia became the star singing *rumbas* and *guarachas*.

According to music writer Eloy Cepero, "The Sonora Matancera owes its fame to Celia Cruz. The orchestra was already known, but other bands were more popular. During the forties the Conjunto Casino and Conjunto Colonial were more popular. It needs to be pointed out that there were musical groups for whites and others for dark-skinned blacks, because even though people do not want to recognize this, there was a form of separation in music circles. The Conjunto Casino dominated the airwaves. Meanwhile, musical groups such as the bands led by Arsenio Rodríguez, Félix Chappotín, René Álvarez, and the Conjunto Modelo played in less affluent black clubs. Though they excelled, their success was not comparable to that achieved by Conjunto Casino. But when Celia joined the Sonora Matancera, these were the Sonora's best years.

I think of the Matancera itself as the best band Cuba ever had, without considering its singers, many of whom were not Cuban. From the beginning Celia was well received by the public, even though in the fifties some still thought that a woman did not fit in an all-male orchestra."

"For me, the Sonora Matancera is the greatest," Celia once said. "This orchestra made me famous throughout the whole world. Rogelio Martínez had faith in me even when Radio Progreso was receiving letters saying 'Get that woman out, she does not fit the Sonora,' but thanks to the many people who helped me because they had faith in me, we persisted, and persisted, and I survived,"

Manolo Fernández and his brother Adalberto, owners of Radio Progreso, shared Rogelio's admiration for the new singer, and in moments of uncertainty, supported her decisively. Celia performed with the Sonora Matancera for fifteen years, recording more than one hundred and eighty songs with the band, some of which enjoyed unprecedented success such as *"El yerberito."* Some of those early songs are still heard on radio and television programs all over the world. "I have recorded a lot of numbers that have pleased many people. Each number was well received, but there is no doubt that *'El yerberito'* has been the most famous."

On April 20, 1957 Celia traveled to the United States to receive her first Gold Record for the single *"Burundanga,"* by Cuban composer Óscar Muñoz Boufartique, her old piano teacher, which she recorded in 1953. The official ceremony was to be held at the Saint Nicholas arena in New York. For unknown reasons, there were some disturbances in the arena, and what would have been one of the happiest moments of her life never came to be. A few days later, in the company of Cortijo and his Combo, Machito and his Afro-Cubans, Tito Puente, and Vicentico Valdés, she received her well-deserved recognition.

During the fifties, still living in Havana, Celia began touring abroad, to Mexico, South America, and even to the United States. She entered the New York music scene with her debut at Teatro Puerto Rico, followed by performances at Caborrojeño and the Palladium Ballroom. Immediately following these successes, Celia received a season contract to perform at the Hollywood Palladium.

In 1960 the whole Sonora Matancera orchestra, including Celia, went into exile in Mexico. Celia and the Matancera remained in Mexico for five years before moving to the United States.

After fifteen years of performing with this orchestra, Celia concluded their shared history of countless concerts in countries around the world. "The saddest day for me was the day I left the Sonora Matancera," Celia explained. "Because my contract was not with the orchestra but with Seeco Records, which had me sing with the orchestra, not the same thing at all. And the time came when I felt uncomfortable with the Sonora, because no matter how much I recorded with the orchestra, I had to keep singing the same 'El Yerberito' and 'Burundanga.' So I told the manager of Seeco Records, Mr. Siegel, 'I am not going to record with you anymore.' Surprised, he asked, 'How come?' and he sent me a 'sello gráfico,' which today we would probably call a fax, telling me that under my contract I still had to do five more recordings. That was true, because I had been so busy touring that I had stopped recording. So I made three more recordings with him and, after the third one, he told me, 'Okay, that's enough.' Then he turned to Pedro and said to him, 'Pedro, you have also broken a relationship of fifteen years,' because he knew that it had been

Pedro who encouraged me to become independent. And Pedro was right."

The last LP Celia recorded with the Sonora for Seeco in 1965 was *Sabor y ritmo de pueblos,* a collection of numbers that was a success with Celia's fans, including *"Rinkinkalla," "La milonga de España," "Traigo para ti,"* and *"Vengan a la charanga."* Celia now found herself free then from the restrictions of Seeco Records and the Sonora Matancera. After fulfilling her commitments with the Sonora in 1965, Celia joined the orchestra of Tito Puente, who was already becoming a legend. She called him "my brother." *Luego me fui a Nueva York / en busca de otro ambiente / y al llegar tuve la suerte / de grabar con Tito Puente.* (Then I went to New York / looking for a different scene / and as soon as I arrived it was my good luck / to be recording with Tito Puente), she used to sing. As a soloist she made six recordings with *El Rey del Timbal* (the King of the Timbales). She also participated in a recording in honor of Benny Moré, with Santos Colón, José (Cheo) Feliciano, and Ismael Quintana.

With the support of Pedro, her "twin soul," although still far from her homeland, Celia was now enjoying her well-earned fame and a promise that she was now open to conquering the world with voice and talent as her only weapons. Her artistry became synonomous with the most accomplished Afro-Caribbean musicians in New York: Tito Puente, Johnny Pacheco, and Willie Colón, with whom she promoted the all-encompassing style that was gaining popularity during the seventies, called *salsa.*

A key third period in her professional career had begun, one that would ultimately crown her as The Queen of Salsa.

11

To Mexico and Beyond

fter the *Sonora Matancera* decided to go into exile in Mexico, their international careers continued to soar. As for Celia, in addition to her gigs with the Matancera, she did some work with other groups, like Memo Salamanca and Juan Bruno Tarraza, a Cuban composer and Toña la Negra's accompanist. In Mexico, Celia set about expanding her repertory. She explored her possibilities, and in the process, discovered herself. She found qualities she didn't know she had: her adaptability to various periods and audiences, and her desire to gain a wider range by working with other kinds of, and often much bigger, orchestras than the Sonora Matancera.

"The calendar has been my greatest excuse," said Rogelio Martínez, the leader of the Sonora, when a journalist asked him in 1990 about his stay in Mexico. "Look at me.

I left Cuba on July 15, 1960, to fulfill an extendable four-week contract, and the extension has lasted for more than forty years." While in Mexico, Rogelio met with Dámaso Pérez Prado. "We used to call him '*Cuello Duro*' (Stiff Collar) because he walked very upright. When Dámaso arrived in Mexico there were only five trumpet players who could play the *tessitura* he was writing for the brass section. Then the Trío Matamoros arrived, and with them came someone who was and always will be famous, Benny Moré. The Trío Matamoros returned to Cuba, but Benny Moré stayed, and began working for Pérez Prado."

In Martínez's view, "No matter what people say, there is a reality: perhaps it was not Pérez Prado who originally created the mambo, but for me he did, because one must recognize and accept the fact that the man who took the mambo beyond the Latino world to an international level was Dámaso Pérez Prado, and everything else is nonsense." For his part, singer Marco Antonio Muñiz remembers that Celia had developed a liking and affection for him while they worked together in the Teatro Blanquita in Mexico City, which produced variety comedy and musical shows of great popular appeal. At the same time, she was appearing regularly in cabarets and Mexican clubs, while also performing in concerts in cities around the world. As a token of their gratitude and admiration for the country that welcomed them so generously, the Sonora Matancera recorded the album *México, qué grande eres* in 1961, which includes a *son montuno* of the same title by Calixto Callava. Other numbers were not so memorable, like "*El aguijón*," "*Juventud del presente*," "*Mis anhelos*," "*Taco Taco*," or "*La negrita inteligente*."

In addition to this homage, Celia was able to record four other albums in Mexico, these with Memo Salamanca's orchestra. The Tico label distributed the albums in the United States under licensed agreement with the Mexican Orfeón label. Among them was *A ti, México: Con la Sonora de Memo Salamanca,* which includes numbers dedicated to that country during the first part of her exile, such as *"Afecto y cariño," "Añoranza maternal," "Rico changüí," "Potpourrí mexicano No. 2,"* and the bolero *"Cuando estoy contigo,"* by the Yucatán composer Armando Manzanero. That same year Celia's extensive tour with *bolerista* Toña la Negra helped to popularize tropical rhythms throughout Mexico. By the following year the Queen of Rumba was already among the highest rated performers in New York with her LP *La tierna, conmovedora y bamboleadora Celia Cruz,* including hit numbers like *"Virgen de la Macarena," "Yemayá," "Nostalgia habanera,"* and *"Desvelo de amor."*

Music writer Mariano Candela has suggested that without the intergenerational, transnational, and interracial popularity of Celia Cruz, Cuban music would have encountered more obstacles to popularity in the United States and Latin America. Although it is true that Afro-Cuban music was known before the revolution, particularly from the Sonora Matancera through broadcasters like CMQ, Radio Progreso, and Radio Cadena Habana, it was not until commercial recordings were distributed internationally by the Seeco label that the musical genre took off. Also instrumental in the popularity burst was the Mexican record industry's inroads into the monopoly established by American record companies.

Without the technological development marked by mass-production in the United States, the popular cultures of the Caribbean and Latin America would not have entered world markets as a profitable product. Mass production allowed this large popular output an unprecedented distribution and wider markets. Market-wise, Caribbean music had the prime advantage of its happy rhythms, making it ideal for dancing as well being enjoyable for listening. This was unique at the time.

Cuban and Mexican films were other forms of mass entertainment that helped popularize Cuban music, particularly the music of Sonora Matancera. These movies proposed a new way of looking at life. They were a mix of witty humor and spice. Moreover, they were about daily life, which helped conceptualize the imagery that strengthens popular culture. The process of this cultural dissemination had started by the mid-twentieth century with the social transformation brought about by the great migrations from the countryside to the cities. It resembled the case of jazz, which came from rural regions in the American South and gradually spread to the great cities, where it acquired a new dimension.

The New York recording industry took advantage of Cuba's disregard for copyrights as well as the island's sociopolitical isolation due to the imposed embargos, to cash in on the Latin rhythms of its most popular musicians. *Salsa* was a commercial phenomenon that came about after the Cuban Revolution when many of the island's arrangers, composers, recording tycoons, vocalists, and sundry musicians of Caribbean ancestry all wound up in New York City. A sort of fusion occurred. Starting with the Cuban *son* and *guaracha*, an enriched sense of orchestration was added to elements already developing in the United States. After boiling down the different genres, the movement assimilated jazz influences much like the Sonora Matancera had done. "No one can deny that these rhythms were made popular by Puerto Rican bands," as Celia once said.

This was the scene Celia found herself in. She tried new rhythms, a diverse repertoire that included folk music from various countries. Despite being called the Queen of Salsa, she preferred the title *Guarachera de Cuba* because the *son* and the *guaracha* were at the base of the new music. While *salsa* was a musical genre born in the United States with an international flair, Celia simply identified more with her native *son* and *guaracha*. The *salsa* movement paralleled the rise of rock music that exploded onto the cultural scene in the mid-fifties with vocalists who sang and danced like Elvis Presley. The impact of rock resonated in Latin music. Woodstock actually served as a model for the concerts organized by the Fania All Stars.

The organizers of these festival-like shows with all-star casts employed the same practices that the recording industry used to promote its records. The model adopted by these promoters provided an important vehicle for Celia Cruz, who was the only singer with real star power. In fact, credit for the many *salsa* hits with different accompanying groups that came after the seventies is rightly accorded to Celia Cruz. Celia had a highly developed musical intelligence and knew how to carefully select her numbers and the musicians who would best accompany her—often with Pedro Knight as musical consultant or director. Also in her favor was the fact that composers were creating music specifically for her, and lyrics were composed to match her personality. Many times songwriters would offer new songs to her, in the hope that she would choose to perform them. This was not routine practice in the competitive world of Latin music. Only an artist who could ensure economic success achieved this kind of distinction.

12

Miami, Friday, July 18, 2003

Her *funeral rites were performed* with choreographic precision, well rehearsed a long time before. Before dying, Celia had expressed her desire to bid farewell to Miami, a city filled with people of Cuban descent who by and large considered Celia their true idol. The coffin carrying Celia's remains arrived at Miami International Airport on Friday evening, July 18. Her fans watched as a handful of airport employees, as if motivated by some mysterious force, ran across the tarmac to the sealed coffin to touch it. The hearse then took her remains to the chapel of the *Virgen de la Caridad del Cobre*, where faithful fans waited. Miami's Assistant Bishop, Monsignor Agustín Román, delivered the requiem: "Freedom was intrinsically in your voice, and neither in its song, nor in its denunciation, could it ever be silenced."

After the ceremony, the funeral cortège headed for

the symbolic place selected for the vigil, the *Torre de la Libertad* (Tower of Liberty), an emblematic building for Cuban exiles in the center of Miami, where thousands of refugees had been processed from 1962 to 1974. Celia's body was never left alone, because her fans had gathered at the center that same night in order to be the first to say their good-byes. Not even the most daring flight of fancy could have envisioned that on Saturday morning the Miami community would flock by the thousands to Biscayne Boulevard the way they did. Despite the suffocating heat, an interminably long line of Cuban exiles, Latin Americans, and other fans waited in line to render homage to the mortal remains of the Queen. The coffin awaited them on the second floor. A gigantic, seven-story-high Cuban flag covered the facade of the building.

In a strange atmosphere that wavered somewhere between festive and mournful, the crowd shouted out *"Azúcar!"* and "Long live the Queen!," and occasionally *"Guantanamera"* sang and danced to *"La vida es un carnaval,"* and still others chose selections among her most popular songs. Julio Zabala, the well-known Dominican comedian and impersonator, aptly summoned up the spirit of the moment that Saturday in Miami: "Celia doesn't want us to be sad, she was joy personified."

More than 150,000 people showed their fervent admiration by filing past Celia's remains. Many admirers of the diva held roses, there were flags from a host of countries— Colombia, Nicaragua, the Dominican Republic, Mexico, Puerto Rico, Argentina. Many tried to protect themselves from the intense heat, sheltering themselves under hats or umbrellas decorated with Cuba's national colors—red, white, and blue. At the entrance of the building there was a flower arrangement in the shape of a Cuban flag, a map, and a pentagram arranged with chrysanthemums, together with a ribbon that read "*Azúcar!*" As the visitors ascended the stairs, a large portrait of a smiling Celia greeted them. Inside, the scent of flowers filled the air, with dozens of baskets, jars, wreaths, and bouquets of flowers in every imaginable shade.

Whenever the feeling turned somber inside, people began singing in chorus, "Celia, Celia, Celia!" and clapping their hands to the music that was playing over the building's public address system. White and lilac blossoms, her personal favorites, surrounded the open coffin. At one end stood Pedro Knight, Celia's widower, dressed in black. He was talking to friends and relatives. At the other end, was a crucifix, and next to Celia there was an image of the *Virgen de la Caridad*, patron saint of Cuba. A Cuban flag had been placed over the coffin. Celia looked very elegant in her white dress, with many of her jewels, a rosary in her well-manicured hands, fully made-up, and wearing one of her striking blond wigs. She seemed poised to go on stage with her habitual gusto, shouting *Azúcar!*

Gloria and Emilio Estefan, Colombian singer-composer Carlos Vives, Willy Chirino, Andy García, "Cachao," Don Francisco, José José, and Cristina Saralegui were among the many celebrities present.

Just before the closing of the coffin, Dolores Ramos, Celia's older sister, arrived unexpectedly, dressed in lilac (which is a mourning color in Cuba), sorrow reflected in her face. It was Saturday, and the *Nuevo Herald* from Miami had devoted an entire special edition to her with the headline: "Celia Rests in Freedom."

After nine hours, the remains of Celia Cruz were taken in a procession preceded by the *Caridad del Cobre*, toward the Catholic Church of Gesu, in the center of Miami. Mass was to be led by the Assistant Bishop Agustín Román, of Cuban extraction, and Father Alberto Cutié, among other priests. Cutié made the observation that the religious ceremony was to be a Cuban *Misa Criolla*, written in the fifties, which ended with the song *"Cuando salí de Cuba"* (When I left Cuba), a composition by Luis Aguilé. According to Father Cutié, "When I left Cuba" is "the traditional song that reminds us of the pain we suffered by leaving the island and being unable to return." The solemn ceremony closed with a few words by Pedro Knight: "With all my love and from the depth of my soul, I would like to thank you for all the sacrifices that you have made in honor of my wife."

13

The Loves of Her Life

There were simply three great loves in Celia's life: Pedro Knight, her music, and, of course, Cuba. She made a total commitment to give her audience a good show. From one city to another she lugged tons of fancy costumes. She had special shoes with steel frames that elevated her without visible support, which she ordered from Mexico, especially made for her, and all in white so that she could dye them to match her costumes. She also brought along many exotic wigs in various colors. In a dozen suitcases she carried all that she needed to transform herself on stage into a burst of joy, with the familiar cry: *Azúcar!* There are countless anecdotes from their endless tours. Pedro remembered one after her death (the country in which it happened, he has now forgotten): "There were some children between five and seven years old who recognized her and began singing. She turned to

Omer Pardillo, her personal manager, and said: 'Listen to what they are singing to me, '*La negra tiene tumbao*'!" (This black woman has the beat), which was one of her hit songs.

Celia led a happy life, and she never turned to alcohol or drugs. Her life was her music, her fans and, of course, Pedro. Celia had tons of talent, but her true brilliance came from the kind of person she was: a real human being with unique traits. There seems to be a general consensus on this. Sadly, she could never have children with Pedro and she suffered great sadness because of it. She even subjected herself to painful treatments by gynecologists specializing in fertility, but she finally resigned herself. "Seeing all the bad things that are happening in the world, I think that I could not have witnessed seeing a child of mine suffering with one of those diseases. Perhaps that is why God did not give me children. He knows what He is doing," she explained on one occasion.

If Celia had had any children, she also thought, she would have had to abandon her artistic career because, for her, children were more important than any profession, no matter how entertaining or profitable. But this extraordinary woman who was not able to be a mother was a wonderful aunt and godmother. Her sister Gladys had four children, and Celia had dozens of godchildren in various countries. The sudden death of her favorite nephew, John Paul, of hemophilia, was a hard knock that brought her deep sadness. There was a special space in her heart for all children, and she developed affection for the children of her friends and family.

Guarino Caicedo, a Colombian journalist from *El Tiempo*, Bogotá, tells the following anecdote which eloquently represents Celia's love for children. "She asked me once to accompany her on a tour of Bogotá, Barranquilla, Medellín, and Cali. I got permission from my newspaper, and joined her and her entourage. Before leaving, Celia told me, 'I want you to take along your wife and child.' Juan Pablo was not yet a year old. We were having lunch one day in the gardens of the *Hotel del Prado* in Barranquilla, and Celia took the child for a walk around the swimming pool. Later she asked me, 'Has the child been baptized?' 'Not yet,' I replied, because I was waiting until he reached the age of reason, around six or seven.

"'Blasphemy!' she exclaimed. She was mad at me for not having baptized my child. I was shaken. Then Celia asked the hotel concierge where she could find a priest, and she was told that Father Víctor Tamayo was at the cathedral. She went to the trouble of calling Father Tamayo, the Bishop of Barranquilla, and without further ado, she and Pedro Knight took the child to have him baptized that same day. So my son's baptism registration is in Barranquilla."

Since the time Celia was with the Sonora Matancera, she had a faithful friend in the New York borough of Queens whom she frequently visited, impresario Humberto Corredor. He was the owner of two record labels, Caimán and Coba, plus the popular nightclub El Abuelo Pachanguero. He has been credited with recovering Celia's birth certificate on one of his many visits to Havana, thus confirming the Diva's date of birth. She asked him not to reveal her secret, and he kept his word. Only after her death did Corredor reveal a copy of the original document that he had given to Celia. Celia was godmother to one of Humberto Corredor's children. She was always concerned about the importance of the education of her godchildren, to whom she frequently sent letters and greeting cards.

An example of Celia's zeal is clear in comments by singer

Linda Caballero (La India), who calls Celia her godmother, since "she baptized me, and when the priest was saying his blessings and pouring the water, she held me with so much love and affection. That is unforgettable. My family adores her, and Pedrito, too. They were inseparable. There are so many people who adore Pedro; he is the most decent man in the world. He never left her side, never betrayed her. That is something to be admired, loves like that do not exist anymore."

Long-term relationships are a rarity in the entertainment industry. Such a rarity were Pedro and Celia. Their closest friends say that they were very respectful of each other; they never held hands in public, but he was always discreetly behind her. And when Celia answered questions that referred to both of them, she always looked to him for confirmation. Nobody ever heard them argue or fight in public, even though she sometimes "scolded" him for silly things.

According to journalist and musical impresario Jessie Ramírez, a close friend of the family, Celia was more down to earth than Pedro. As an example, in 2001 they bought a car, a beautiful Mercedes-Benz. When they went to do their shopping at a supermarket, Celia started walking from the parking lot toward the entrance of the establishment and realized that Pedro was not beside her. Turning back, she found him sitting at the steering wheel. When she asked him whether he was coming with her, he answered that he did not wish to leave the car alone for fear something might happen to it. Celia, without getting angry, explained, "*Perucho*, if you don't get out of that car right now, by tomorrow, besides having nothing to eat, you will have no car either, because I am going to return it."

Pedro has been known to be a bit of a worrier. Ramírez, who traveled with them extensively during the times of the

Fania All Stars, told the story of one day meeting up with Pedro, who was wearing a Timex watch. Ramírez asked Pedro where was the fancy three-thousand-dollar Swiss watch that Celia had bought him for his birthday during a European tour. "Oh, but what if I wear it and I get assaulted?" Celia matter-of-factly quipped, "Hey, *Perucho*, who is going to steal that watch from you, if you always travel in the limousine with me, *chico*." That is how it was with Celia and Pedro.

The couple always had words of high praise for each other. They expressed their mutual admiration at every opportunity. Celia, for instance, used to say, "Pedro has been and will always be the most handsome and elegant man I have ever met. He is my life, my eternal love. Without him I would never have existed." When she was asked which had been her greatest success, her answer was not unexpected at all: "Having been able to find a man like Pedro, who thinks like me, even though he has a harsher character and does not speak much. I don't even know how he managed to court me; but he is very supportive of everything, that has been my real success. In today's environment, to have kept our marriage together, without ever being apart for forty years, that is a real triumph."

As for Pedro, he never tires of affirming, "Celia has been more than very courageous. Her vitality still perplexes me. There were times when she confessed to feeling sick before a performance. But when I expected her to be resting on a reclining chair or in her hotel bed, there she was on stage. Her strength was incredible. I won't forget a particular presentation in Spain when she had a fractured toe. It was impossible to cancel the show because we didn't know how the public would have reacted. But out of sheer spunk, she sang and danced as never before. One had to see her to believe it!"

Wherever they traveled, Celia carried all of her husband's medications in a small suitcase. Pedro is a diabetic and requires insulin injections. Because of his diabetes, she paid a lot of attention to his diet: no sugar, fats, or carbohydrates. In the summer of 2002, Celia and Pedro celebrated their fortieth wedding anniversary with a fiesta in Madrid organized by the famous singer Lolita (daughter of Lola Flores). By October of that year Pedro required emergency surgery for colon problems. She always took good care of him. Later, when Celia fell ill and was lying in bed, she asked her close friends, "Please, take good care of Pedro, make sure he takes all his medications."

It was Celia's custom never to travel alone to her professional commitments, first when she was with the Sonora Matancera, afterward as an independent soloist, and later with the Fania All Stars. The only time that Pedro did not accompany her was on a trip in 2001. As they approached the airport, on the way to Argentina to promote an album, Pedro's diabetes made him ill. Celia had to travel alone to Argentina and Mexico. But this was an exceptional case, which could not be helped. At other times, when Pedro had gotten sick in foreign cities, he usually remained in his hotel room while Celia performed.

In 1990, the couple finally bought a townhouse in Fort Lee, New Jersey, just across the George Washington Bridge from Manhattan. They had spent decades living in hotel rooms and rented apartments in both Manhattan and Queens. Celia and Pedro's home had four floors, an interior patio full of white orchids, and a garage at street level for four automobiles. The furniture was all white, and on the second floor there was a living room, something like a den, with a piano and some of Celia's photos. The library was a cozy space where her many trophies, diplomas, "keys to cities," and other decorations and awards were kept. On the third floor was the sitting room and a large dining room; on the fourth and last floor, the three bedrooms. The dwelling had an elevator that, curiously, they never took together, just in case it should go out of order, though as an emergency measure, they had a telephone installed in its interior to be able to call for help in case a quick rescue was necessary (Celia was very punctual and could not stand being delayed). She was happy with her home in that quiet suburb in New Jersey. "This home belongs to Pedro and me. Here I welcome my relatives and some friends," she once said, "but the truth is that until we moved here, I had never enjoyed a home so much, or this beautiful man, whom I must take very good care of."

At the beginning of 2003, the couple had to sell a deluxe apartment they owned in the Aventura district in Miami to help pay for the mounting hospital and doctor bills from Celia's illness. They also had to leave their townhouse in Fort Lee and move to a penthouse not far from their former home. As fate would have it, Celia lived only three months in her new home. In order to help with the onerous tasks of moving and of taking care of Celia during her illness, she had invited her cousin Nenita and her daughter, Silvia, from Havana. They were present at a celebration in Celia's honor organized by Telemundo in Miami Beach in March 2003. Nenita had faithfully accompanied Celia on her first tours, and she came from Havana with her daughter Silvia, who was a nurse by profession.

After the move, Nenita and Silvia spent three months taking care of domestic chores and, day and night, watching over sick Celia until they returned to Cuba in May, two months before La Guarachera passed away. In return for their care and hard work during the final stages of Celia's illness, at the time of saying good-bye, Pedro handed them $500. They are still smarting at having been treated with such disregard, which they attribute to Pedro Knight's legendary stinginess. They were also taken aback that, contrary to Celia's explicit wishes to include them in her last will and testament (as well as her sister Dolores, her niece Lolina, and the rest of her family, all having urgent needs living in Cuba), their names were struck from that document at the last minute, making Pedro the universal and sole heir of all her properties and royalties. It seems more than possible that Celia did not want to send her dollars to Cuba.

14

Celia and Pedro: A Love Story

Todo el mundo me pregunta / Celia, ¿cuál es el secreto / de estar unida tanto tiempo / al hombre de tu corazón? / Y yo siempre les respondo / que yo tengo mi receta / y aunque sea muy discreta, / sé triunfar en el amor: / Una taza de cariño, un chinchín de pimentón; / revolverlo con ternura / y dar besitos a montón, / una pizca de alegría, / un costal de comprensión; / con salero y santería / yo conquisté su corazón. / Y todas las noches / sin falta / yo le pongo sazón, / son son, le pongo sazón / yo le pongo sazón a mi negrito, pongo sazón. / Lo mantengo entretenido / siempre dándole algo nuevo. / Le cambio de color de pelo / como cambiar de pantalón, / tacón alto o / falda corta. / Todo por mi cariñito. / Siempre le digo, "mi amorcito, / papi, tú eres el mejor." / Yo me siento muy dichosa / de tenerlo tantos años; / se va un minuto y ya lo extraño. / Le doy gracias al Señor…/ Con amor y pasión le doy mi corazón.

Born in Matanzas in 1922, Pedro was about three years older than Celia. The oldest of four brothers, Pedro was the son of clarinetist Orozco Piedra Knight and Amalia Caraballo. He was tall, strongly built, swarthy, and very attractive. He earned his living as a typesetter at a local newspaper, but he loved music above all, and taught himself to play the trumpet. One day, he decided to make a radical change in his life.

He joined the Sonora Matancera when its founder, Valentín Cané, decided to add a second trumpet, which was something combos were doing in those days. Pedro was not the first trumpeter asked to join. Valentín first called Oswaldo Díaz, the son of Aniceto Díaz, who created the *danzonete* and conducted the Matanzas Municipal Band. However, Oswaldo's stay with the Sonora was brief, as he was soon called away to join his father's band. Aniceto recommended Pedro, whom he considered an excellent trumpet player, as a replacement for his son. And thus the typesetter joined the Sonora on January 6, 1944. Pedro played so well with the first trumpet, Maestro Calixto Leicea, that they sounded like a single fanfare.

His musical talent became clear when he composed, with *bolerista* Leopoldo Ulloa, the *guaracha* "*El corneta*": *Te metiste a soldado / y ahora tienes que aprender /* (The Bugle Player: You became a soldier / and now you have to learn). It had two trumpet solos, and became popular when sung by Daniel Santos, who recorded it with the Sonora Matancera in 1953, under the Seeco label.

/ [*"Sazón"*]. (Everybody asks me, / Celia, what is the secret / that keeps you and the man you love / together for such a long time? / And I always answer / that I have my recipe, / and though I am very discreet, / I know how to triumph in love. / A cup of affection, a sprinkling of seasoning; / stir everything with tenderness / and add a lot of kisses, / a bit of joy, / a lot of understanding; / with sassiness and santería / I won his heart. / And every night without fail / I add more seasoning, / *sea son*, I add seasoning, / I add seasoning for my *negrito*, / add seasoning. / I keep him entertained, / always giving him something new. / I change the color of my hair for him, / just like changing into another pair of pants, / or high heels, / or shorter skirt. / I do everything for my love. / I always tell him, "Love of my heart, / honey, you are the best."/ I feel very lucky / for having him so many years; / only one minute away, and I already miss him. / I thank the Lord..../ With love and passion, I give him my heart.... [from "*Sazón*" (Seasoning)].

Celia's love life has been a secret well kept by those close to her. As Héctor Ramírez Bedoya revealed in his *Historia de la Sonora Matancera y sus estrellas* (*History of the Sonora Matancera and its Stars*, 1996), Celia was engaged for a while to Alfredo León, a young bass player and the son of Bienvenido León, member of the noted Septeto Nacional. An old photo of Celia, wearing a full, flowery skirt and singing into a microphone, shows Alfredo accompanying her on the *tumbadora*. Bedoya also comments that in 1958, when the Sonora was playing in the Caracas carnival in Venezuela, it had three singers: Nelson Pinedo, Carlos Argentino, and Celia Cruz. "At a certain exalted moment, Carlos Argentino (el Ruso) asked Celia to marry him. The proposal was so gossamer and wild that it just floated about. But it happened, it's true that it happened," added the well-documented historian. To all appearances, this resembles some busybody's gossip more than a verifiable, real event, though the incident has neither been denied nor confirmed by any reliable source.

It could be that the supposed romance between Carlos Argentino and Celia Cruz never happened, but the love story between Celia and Pedro Knight is indeed true. It was Pedro who welcomed the young singer that fateful day of August 3, 1950, when she arrived early for her first rehearsal with the Sonora at the Radio Progreso studios. Over the course of time, a deep friendship developed between them, working together day after day in concerts, tours, recordings, festivals, and all types of orchestra activities for fifteen years.

How Celia and Pedro fell in love is a modern-day fairy tale. Theirs was an affection that grew out of friendship, developing slowly until eventually it led them to the altar. As Pedro tells it, "We got to know each other while working with the Sonora, and became fast friends. There is no way to say when our romance started. Celia was a sensible, reliable young woman, and in time our friendship turned to love. Neither of us thought that we were going to end up getting married one day, but that's what happened. That is why, when she wants to annoy me, she tells me, 'I said yes to the judge, I have not yet said yes to you.' Celia is a very generous woman; her principal character trait is her happy disposition, always trying to find some humor. We get along very well: we don't argue, and neither of us is the boss. When we engage in some business, we don't blame each other if anything goes wrong. She is a sensational wife. I'll even tell you this, she is always worrying about me, and when we are in a hotel, my underwear never goes to the laundry, she washes it herself and hangs it to dry in the bathroom. She takes so much care of my things that she even picks the clothes I am to wear every day and the tie that matches my suit. And I try to please her because I know she does everything for my benefit."

Celia, in turn, said that when she joined the Sonora, "Pedro was the only person who took care of me, who helped me with the musical arrangements. When I arrived, he took the scores and distributed them, and that was the beginning of a very beautiful friendship between us. Pedro has many good qualities, but his gentlemanliness has always captivated me. He still opens the car door for me, and he makes my coffee every morning, and if he doesn't, I don't have any, because I like him to pamper me." Celia attributed her happy marriage of more than four decades to "a particular factor: constant communication. Besides understanding, mutual respect, and a lot of spice, Pedro and I are always talking about our things."

When Celia and Pedro Knight met, he was still married to his first wife, with whom he had six children. A year after Celia joined the Sonora, in 1950, Pedro obtained his divorce. Their courtship had been very discreet, but one day Rogelio Martínez heard about the blossoming romance from one of the orchestra members. "I had no reason to object," he said, "Celia was a very sensible person, and they had behaved decorously." For a time Pedro had pressed for marriage, but Celia refused, arguing that he had a reputation as a ladies' man. He defended himself, saying that it was just "malicious gossip."

After a ten-year courtship, Pedro finally convinced Celia to marry him. They were married on Saturday, July 14, 1962, in a simple ceremony before a Connecticut judge. Singer Rolando Laserie was their best man; his wife, Tita Borggiano, was the matron of honor; and Laserie's manager, Catalino Rolón, a witness. By then Celia was already thirty-six and Pedro thirty-nine. Because Celia was still in mourning over the death of her mother, Ollita, there was no party or honeymoon. Their marriage took place a short time after the death of her mother, a moment she could not share with her family because the Cuban government did not allow her to reenter her country. Her father had already died, after a long illness. So Pedro, according to Celia, replaced both her mother and her father.

According to Mexican singer Marco Antonio Muñiz, Celia and Pedro were also married in a simple but moving civil ceremony on the stage of the Teatro Blanquita in Mexico City, where Celia performed in 1962 and 1963, with all the cast members as witnesses. They had professional commitments that could not be postponed and, again, they were not able to take a honeymoon trip.

Twenty-five years later, in 1987, Celia and Pedro renewed their marriage vows in a Catholic ceremony with a cooperative priest, overcoming what seemed insurmountable obstacles. Two or three churches rejected their wish for the Catholic service because they could not produce Baptism certificates. Their certificates were in Cuba, and it was almost impossible to obtain them.

Tita Borggiano, now Laserie's widow, remembered when she and her husband first met Celia and Pedro in New York as exiles. Both couples lived in the same building in Manhattan. When they moved, their apartments were not only in the same building but on the same floor. The two couples established a very close personal and professional relationship. They traveled together on several occasions when Rolando was featured in the same shows as Celia. Tita remembers that Pedro affectionately called Celia *Negrita*.

Celia's "blue prince" is an easygoing man, cheerful, honest, good-natured. He is tall, elegant and conservative in dress, with long, thick sideburns and a white head of hair that imparts an attractive tone to his reddish-brown complexion. Celia affectionately gave him the nickname Cottontop, though sometimes she called him *Perucho*.

Celia always took her profession very seriously, and was totally devoted to her career. Her husband became her perpetual, loving shadow, occasionally prone to fits of unjustified jealousy. Pedro willingly put his trumpet to rest on Sunday, April 30, 1967, two years after Celia left the Sonora, canceling her contract with Seeco, and signed up with Tico Records. He wanted to be with her, to promote and protect Celia's career, and to make her not only the most famous interpreter of *salsa*, but also of *guarachas*, *sones*, and *boleros*. He always encouraged her to undertake musical adventures that might come her way, with the understanding that he would be there to lead the orchestras that were to accompany her presentations.

Celia never denied her dependence on her husband, and in one interview she declared, "Pedro is my manager and my spiritual advisor. He even taught me how to cook, and is my most severe critic. He is mindful of everything. It was a great relief for me, a true comforting experience, to enjoy his support and his company."

Joined by their talent, their music, and their love for each other, Celia and Pedro traveled the world taking their music to the most remote corners, where she was always appreciated and applauded. Sadly, though, her husband admits, "We have traveled around the world but we do not know it; it was always the same: from the airport to the hotel, and from the hotel to the stage." Celia was so dedicated to her work and held her public in such regard that she forced herself to limit her activities. "She didn't keep this a secret," Pedro comments, "she took very good care of herself. She imposed restrictions on her private life. For instance, she did not go to the beach, afraid of getting sick and then having someone say that because of going out to have a good time, she could not do what she was supposed to. When she liked a place we toured, she used to tell me, '*Mi negro*, bring me here again when we are on vacation.' She was always in a good mood and liked to joke around. Very few things bothered her really, aside from being lied to."

In many interviews throughout her life, Celia explained their secret to keeping a happy, stable marriage. Her simple, though not superficial, prescription for a happy married life can be easily summarized by a few philosophical principles and rules of conduct. According to Pedro and Celia, the most important ingredient to a happy marriage is communication. One of the first requests Pedro made of Celia after marriage was that she remain open with him about anything that upset her. If he did something that she did not like, he wanted her to tell him so that he could correct it. This became a steadfast rule in their relationship. Despite their having many things in common, mistakes were inevitable, but their openness and willingness to sit and talk it out until they found a solution set the course right. Celia never tired of insisting on the need to exchange ideas, opinions, or criticisms as the best way to keep a well-balanced relationship.

An important factor was to do everything by mutual accord. Celia remembered buying a twelve-story building in Miami that turned into a total fiasco. The manager of the building doctored the numbers and stole a substantial amount of money. Because Pedro and Celia had agreed on buying the building as an investment, they did not blame each other. Rather, they learned a valuable lesson together that served to strengthen their marriage.

Celia said that it is necessary for couples to be like an

open book to each other because the moment that they begin to lie and to hide their feelings, people become uncomfortable and insecure to the point of reaching a state of anger that will harm any relationship. Neither of them ever left home after an argument, or kept silent for more than twenty-four hours.

Pedro took care of fixing things at home, like carpentry, or making coffee, while she cooked or washed dishes in the kitchen. Most of the time, Pedro did the shopping at the supermarket, and Celia cooked, even though at times meals could be served well past midnight. She considered it a pleasure to cook for Pedro in the same way that he enjoyed helping her. She always followed her mother's advice. Ollita had taught her what roles a man and woman should take in the home, and with this Celia was happy. Celia never liked that in the United States the man sometimes did a wife's work, because that was not what she had learned in Cuba. She never criticized this type of behavior, but she did not follow it. They kept their solidarity at all times. Neither Celia nor Pedro paid attention to celebrations such as Valentine's Day because each day was a source of celebration for them. If Pedro gave her a gift, she accepted it gladly so that he would feel happy about it. In turn, she would, without any reason, come up with a gift for him, like a dozen neckties that she happened to see. The gifts always came in earnest and without motivation. In this way, any day was a good day for the happy couple to celebrate their love and friendship.

On vacations, it was enough for them to be together to have a good time. They were never bored when traveling on their own because they knew how to take advantage of their spare time. A good example of their marital harmony can be found in this story: In difficult times when they had only one television set at home and Pedro was watching a football game, Celia would never change the channel in order to watch a boxing match, which she liked best. And if she was watching two boxers in the ring, Pedro would never change to a different channel.

Mutual respect and consideration for the decisions and preferences of the other were undoubtedly a crucial factor in the long and amiable life together that brought forty-one years of joy to Celia and Pedro. These are the little things that most people overlook, but to Celia and Pedro they were of capital importance to keeping a relationship healthy.

When Celia became sick, Pedro's worry consumed him. He was afraid that *"su negra"* could leave him forever. A feeling of anguish that would not let him breathe kept him alert to any of her movements. After she became ill he would not let her out of his sight. When the medical diagnosis was revealed and it was discovered that Celia had a malignant tumor growing in her brain, the volcanic, emotional Celia blurted out, "Doctor, take it out!" That was December 5, 2002. Later at home, she proudly told one of her closest friends, "I didn't shed even a tear!" Pedro Knight stood by her side every minute after the delicate six-hour surgery at the Columbia University Presbyterian Hospital in Manhattan. At that moment, Celia, the eternal optimist, was sure everything would turn out all right.

Some time before, Celia had a knee operation. But now, this was decidedly more serious. In fact, it was the second operation the singer had undergone in thirty days. At the Hackensack Hospital in New Jersey she had undergone another operation for cancer in which her left breast was removed. She was recovering when she had to return to work to promote her album *La negra tiene tumbao*. For some time she had stopped wearing those steel-frame shoes that were her signature. But she was always full of joy, always positive. The world got to know her playful laughter, her music, and her chant, *Azúcar!*, but could only imagine her tears.

"*La negra más cumbanchera del solar*" (The most fun-loving, outgoing black woman in the tenement), the same one that had shaken world stages, was waning at seventy-seven years old, preparing to join "the celestial choir from the Matancera," where her old colleagues who had parted before were waiting. Pedro was sad and depressed, but ever vigilant by the side of his dearly beloved life partner.

Two days before she died was the couple's forty-first wedding anniversary. With loving tenderness, holding her hand almost without touching her, he kissed her forehead and reminded her of the date. Celia responded with tears in her saddened eyes.

Since the beginning of 2002 there had been rumors that Celia was seriously ill, and even that she had died. A Miami radio station once interrupted its regular programming to give the breaking news that paralyzed the city. "Our Celia Cruz has died," said the radio announcer's voice in a mournful tone.

The news spread around the world in a matter of minutes, leaving those who heard it shuddering. As was learned later, the announcement had been a false rumor. Even so, millions of her fans and lovers of *salsa* were stirred emotionally to know that the most loved feminine voice of this joyous music was about to be silenced. Perhaps the most alarming thing was that for the third time in six months, the rumor had acquired such urgency. It was no secret that the health of *La Guarachera de Cuba* had undergone serious setbacks during previous months, but nobody imagined a fatal outcome after all the false alarmists who, like vultures carrying bad omens, had been announcing her sad departure from this earth.

Wanting to counteract the fake news, though without quite succeeding, the Diva circulated a letter on December 9, 2002, asking her fans to respect her privacy, which read like this:

Only a few words to express my most sincere appreciation for your concern about the latest developments regarding my health.

At this moment I am going through the process of recovering from surgery and facing a situation that once in a while we human beings have to face.

Though my life has always been a carnival show and an open book for so many of you, in these moments I humbly beg you to respect my privacy and that of my loved ones.

Your prayers and messages of solidarity have been proof of your affection and they are the energizer that accompanies me day by day, and gives me courage to face this new challenge in this period of my life. Thanks for the unconditional support you have given me throughout all these years, for having received me with open arms and given me the opportunity to bring joy to your hearts through my music.

During this rest period I beg all of you for your cooperation, with the understanding that it is a part of my personal life that I wish to have treated precisely in that way, privately.

In the meantime, I wish you all a merry Christmas and a happy New Year full of health, peace, and prosperity.

Until we meet again, your friend, always,
CELIA CRUZ

"Celia had elevated her art to the highest level; her sense of rhythm was the most developed, her clarion voice was incredibly well-tuned and clear, and her talent for improvisation was tremendous," said Cesar Pagano, music writer and journalist. In March 2003, Miami had organized a gigantic event in honor of its most cherished singer at the Jackie Gleason Theater in Miami Beach, where the list of attendees included many big names in music from Latin America, the Caribbean, and the United States. Celia arrived dressed in gray, looking happy and healthy, with a bouquet of red roses in her hands. "I had no idea people loved me that much, commented the immortal Celia a little while before the gala performance began, which was telecast live by Univision. Her friend and compatriot Gloria Estefan, Mexican star Paulina Rubio, Gloria Gaynor from the States, and José Feliciano from Puerto Rico were some of the artists who sang the songs Celia had made famous.

Celia had thought many times, and told the press, that she was going to die on the stage. "My life is to sing, and I don't intend to retire. I am planning to die on the stage like my dear friend Miguelito Valdés (Mister Babalú), who died according to his own design, singing in Bogotá, Colombia. I might have a headache, but when the time comes to go onstage, it disappears," she had declared to a journalist, and no star had ever achieved such virtuosity, much less her popularity.

However, fate decreed that she die in bed, serene, away from the bright stage lights and nightclubs, the multitudes in the stadiums, the noisy merrymaking of the carnival, the delirious applause of her fans, the explosive flashes of the paparazzi, and far away from the sugarcane plantations, the sugar-like beach sands, the blue skies of her loved Caribbean homeland.

Shortly before dying, Celia stopped her chemotherapy treatments because she felt they were no longer of use. She had been under medical care for months, after the operation for removal of a breast cyst that turned out to be cancerous, and after her brain surgery. She had numerous health setbacks in the final weeks that caused her to stay in bed her last days.

On Wednesday, July 16, 2003, surrounded by her adored Cottontop and some family members, she died at 5:15 in the afternoon. She had been in a coma since the day before. In his statement to the press, Pedro, in his habitual laconic style, just said, "She died in peace and without pain. She only stopped breathing, and was gone."

Johnny Pacheco, the famous flutist and friend of the couple, confided that when Celia stopped breathing, her husband Pedro Knight said, "I want to die," and Johnny answered him, "Pedro, you cannot die now."

After the monumental display of sympathy accorded the undisputed Queen in Miami and in New York, her widower confessed that during those days of infinite sadness, he consoled himself with "the love for Celia that all Latin Americans in the United States had expressed." However, a day after her demise, he seemed confused and disoriented. Pedro Knight was very affected by the death of his inseparable companion. He seemed lost in deep, moving nostalgia. In the midst of his pain, he remembered that he had been *"la niña de los ojos de esa mujer"* (the apple of the eye of that woman). "She loved me, and I loved her. I feel deeply sorry she is no longer with me. I am going to miss her terribly. The sadness I feel today will be with me for who knows how long. I would say that if there are twenty-four hours in one day, we were together for twenty-five." His gaze was lost in reminiscence of their happier

Another of the great Cuban musicians, her colleague, *sonero* Francisco Repilado, better known as *Compay Segundo*, preceded Celia in death by two days. It seems Celia never knew, because her husband kept it secret. Compay Segundo had been born in Siboney, on the other end of the island of Cuba, in 1907. He was always accompanied by his music. However, in order to make a living he worked in a barbershop and in a cigar factory, while taking part in orchestras and combos, playing the clarinet or the *tres*, as in the duet of Los Compadres, with Lorenzo Hierrezuelo (*Compay Primo*). Repilado composed more than one hundred songs, among them "*Chan chan*" and "*Macusa*." He also designed a musical instrument for himself that he named "*armónico*," a hybrid between a guitar and a *tres*. He had come to fame in the world of music late in life, thanks to the research on old Cuban music conducted by the American guitar player Ry Cooder. Ry's work resulted in the popular film documentary *Buena Vista Social Club*, directed by Wim Wenders, from Germany, and in the great soundtrack album that won a Grammy Award for the best Caribbean album of 1998.

days. His first statements were to thank the media for their support. "I have been watching all the good things from Celia that the media have been showing around the whole country and in Spain," the musician explained, "and I am grateful for the generous displays they have dedicated to my dear Celia."

A few days after her funeral, when Pedro returned home, he told Luis Falcón, a young admirer of Celia's and ex-president of the Queen of Salsa Fan Club of Miami, and whom she had sort of adopted, "Look, I went to fix her breakfast, but she is no more." For many years, Pedro took Celia's breakfast to her bed, and automatically he had continued with his daily routine, which fate had broken forever. And Falcón could only wonder, "What else can we expect from a man who is not used to moving in a world without her!"

15

New York, Tuesday, July 22, 2003

The day of the funeral, the skies were overcast and the rain blended with the tears accompanying the singing of the hundreds of people converging on the funeral home to bid farewell to Celia Cruz. It was a concert under the rain. That is the best way to describe the last good-bye from the hundreds of Celia's New York fans at the Woodlawn Cemetery in the Bronx, on Tuesday, July 22. The rain did not dampen the enthusiasm of the fans lined up along Fifth Avenue. The loud thunder resounded right before arrival of her funeral cortège like a special effect for her last appearance. Since early morning a curious crowd stood by the main entrance to the cemetery in order to render a last homage to the Queen of Salsa.

People came with radios, flags, umbrellas, even autographed photos, and they waited patiently for the funeral carriage to arrive. "Hurry up, it's going to rain, but it's going to rain sugar!" José Vargas said in a rueful tone. The music *La Guarachera de Cuba* had interpreted could be heard everywhere, and there was an air of joy as well as of sad resignation. Some were singing her most popular hits, some were incessantly chanting "Celia...Celia..." while others were crying and laughing at the same time. Across the street from the cemetery, from the Woodlawn Café, customers were watching the funeral and listening to the tireless rhythm of "*La negra tiene tumbao.*"

By 4:30 the hundreds of fans entering the cemetery had become thousands. The policemen watching over the multitude seemed confused by the crowds and their behavior. When the first strains of the number "*Siempre viviré*" (I'll Live Forever) were heard through the public address system, the crowd responded with a deafening roar, some sobbing more intensely or shedding tears. The funeral carriage finally entered the cemetery, amid shouts, applause, and signs of dismay. Relatives, politicians, artists, and Pedro Knight stood under a green awning to protect themselves from the rain. Then there was a short funeral prayer, and with their own prayers and songs, the people bid farewell to Celia Cruz.

16

"Por si acaso no regreso":
In Case I Don't Return

On January 1, 1959, after three years in the Sierra Maestra, Fidel Castro's revolutionary guerrillas triumphed over Fulgencio Batista's dictatorship. The political, economic, cultural, and social changes were immediately felt. The new government assumed a communist ideology that in a short time polarized Cuban society into two opposing factions. In part, the political arguments for and against the new regime created an atmosphere of insecurity that contributed to the Cuban exodus that settled mostly in Miami, but also in New York, as well as in Puerto Rico and many other countries. The U.S. government supported the fight against the Cuban Revolution, and in April 1961 there was a failed invasion of the Bay of Pigs. The campaign against the new government of Fidel Castro, plus the danger of nuclear war, posed by the installation of remotely controled atomic missiles in Cuban territory in 1962, resulted in the imposition of a paralyzing embargo of goods and tourist services that isolated Cuba from the rest of the world. Aside from a few neutral countries and the socialist block in Asia and Eastern Europe, Cuba was alone. In addition, restrictions were placed on international travel for all Cubans. Authorization was needed even for domestic travel.

One of the first casualties of this transformation was the music world in Cuba. As Carlos Puebla sings, *Y en eso llegó Fidel, / y se acabó la diversión. / Llegó el Comandante y mandó parar ...* / (And then came Fidel, / and the fun was over. / The *Comandante* arrived and ordered a halt.../) Political corruption, which had encouraged tourists and visitors to enjoy entertainment and ephemeral pleasures, like casino gambling (managed by the mafia) and prostitution, while the masses struggled in poverty and ignorance, was over.

As radio stations, traditionally devoted to musical programming, became state property, they focused more on political and social issues. And as the government took over the radio waves, they also took over the television channels. With the exodus of the upper and middle classes and the absence of tourists interested in Havana's legendary entertainment world, nightclubs progressively started to close. The only exception was the Tropicana nightclub. Given this reality, engagements for musicians and singers became increasingly scarce, and tours abroad as well domestic ones became much more difficult. The Sonora Matancera managed to continue recording with their usual singers, Carlos Argentino, Celio González, and Celia Cruz.

It made sense that in the beginning the Sonora Matancera and Celia Cruz sympathized with the process of reforms

In June 1959, Radio Cadena Habana awarded the prestigious Wurlitzer prize to the Sonora Matancera as the best musical group in Latin America. Despite the initial discontent of many Cuban entertainers who sought, by any means, contracts abroad so that they could leave, some decided to stay. They stayed for family ties or in the hope of better times that might come after the country went through its period of change. Among those who stayed were Celeste Mendoza (Queen of the *Guaguancó*), the duo of Celina and Reutilio, Los Compadres, Félix Chappotín, Joseíto Fernández, the Trío Matamoros, Omara Portuondo, Orquesta Aragón, Barbarito Diez, and Elena Burke (selected as the best singer in Cuba, 1958-59), only to mention the most popular.

Opting for exile were such well-known figures as Rogelio Martínez and his Sonora Matancera with Las Mulatas de Fuego and Celia Cruz, Fernando Albuerne, Xiomara Alfaro, Blanquita Amaro, Olga Guillot, comedians Garrido y Piñero, Rolando Laserie, Bobby Collazo, Osvaldo Farrés, Eduardo Davidson. Leaving the country a few years later were Bienvenido Granda, Los Guaracheros de Oriente, "Cachao" López, Bebo Valdés, La Lupe, Chocolate Armenteros, and more recently, Irakere's Paquito D'Rivera.

occurring on the island. In fact, *La Guarachera de Cuba* sang a number within the context of these transformations with the Sonora on CMQ radio in 1959. *Guajiro, ya llegó tu día, / guajiro, ya llegó tu día. / Para qué tantos con tanto / y por qué tantos sin nada, / si esta es la tierra sagrada / porque Dios mandó a Fidel. /* (Peasant, your day has come. / For what reason do so many have so much / and why do so many have nothing, / if this is the sacred land / because God sent Fidel).

The beginning preparations for exile of the Sonora Matancera happened on December 12, 1959, when Rogelio Martínez went to Mexico City in order to sign a contract with Hernández Zabala's Teatro Lírico and Pepe León's Casino Terraza. On May 10, 1960, they recorded their last numbers in Cuba. Included were *"Mi cocodrilo verde"* (which alluded to the reptile shape of the island), *"No me mires más,"* *"Caramelos,"* *"Ya te lo dije,"* *"Mágica luna,"* *"Báchame,"* *"El heladero,"* *"Suena el cuero,"* and *"Pregones de San Cristóbal."* On July 15, 1960, all the members of the Sonora Matancera, together with Celia Cruz and the group of dancers Las Mulatas de Fuego, went into exile in an act of musical solidarity. They left behind family, friends, properties, full moon evenings on the Malecón, the warm Varadero beaches, and the friendly chats at the Bodeguita del Medio. They lived in hopes of returning someday, a day that for the *Guarachera* in her long exile never materialized. According to Rogelio Martínez, on the flight to Mexico City she had a foreboding that turned out to be prophetic: "This is a trip of no return."

Once her income in Cuba was sufficient, Celia had left her Santos Suárez neighborhood and moved, with her cousin Nenita, to an apartment in the Pontón district, near Infanta Street. Later they moved to Calle 126 and Avenida 87, in Marianao. After becoming famous and coming into some money, Celia had a house built at Calle Terraza #110, in the Havana neighborhood of Lawton, where she lived with her family from March 1954 until she left the country in 1960. Some of her relatives still live there and maintain a room exactly as she left it, with photos, awards, and trophies.

With her earnings, Celia also acquired before the Revolution a small, four-apartment building and two lots where she was planning to build houses in the modest Lawton and Luyanó neighborhoods. Although her economic condition had improved, she was not considered wealthy.

There was no recorded threat or condemnation by the revolutionary government against Celia. She had not lost these properties yet because the law of urban reform had not come into effect by the time she left. She claimed certain violations of basic human rights and restrictions on traveling both domestically and abroad without specific authorization. She also added that she had left Cuba with the intention of making more money so that her mother could eat whatever she wanted. But her mother died in Cuba while Celia was in exile, and Celia commented: "I was not allowed to go bury my mother, who brought me into this world, and who said to me, opposing my father, 'Yes, be a singer, go on with it, I support you.' I was never allowed to visit her tomb in Cuba. Never," she insisted, "I will never forgive Fidel for that, because our mother and father are the greatest treasure we have."

"I would like to return to Cuba when the present regime is no longer in power," Celia always declared. "I saw Fidel two or three times, from afar. I never ran to have my picture taken with him. I am not a communist, and neither do I like communism. That is why I left Cuba. But I don't wrap my art in a political flag. Those who hear me sing could hold whatever political view. I don't sing anything that offends anyone. That is why it hurts me to have been banned in Cuba, and to have my music restricted for so long. I love my country dearly, but I don't like the people who are governing it. I do not know anything about politics, my life is just singing."

Celia's well-known dream was to sing in a Cuba free of communism, and perhaps this could be the only disappointment she carried to her grave. To die far away from her country was very painful for this singer who so wholeheartedly loved the island that she hailed from.

However, international critics argued that, apart from her great qualifications, she was accused of political intolerance, and this alienated her from her public on several occasions. She did not accept decisions made by impresarios who, taking advantage of her name as a draw at the box office, contracted Cuban orchestras or singers to appear on the same stage with her. Not only did she refuse to go up on the boards, but people say she exploded in bouts of anger. And taking advantage of her Diva position, she forced those impresarios to cancel or postpone contracts with artists who supported Fidel's ideas, and who would take the dollars they earned performing with her to him. The Cuban exile community applauded her indignation as part of the campaign against the revolutionary government, but they did not seem to realize that in the same way they rejected the Cuban regime, there were people in other parts of the world who admired it. Such an attitude cost Celia more than one fan and some fallings-out with people who loved her music but despised her intransigent position, especially those from generations born after the sixties who were able to consider both the achievements and the failures of the Cuban Revolution.

There is a concrete instance described by music writer Rafael Bassi Labarrera. On August 6, 1980, the Fania All Stars were engaged to perform in the Romelio Martínez Stadium in Barranquilla (Colombia). Also touring the country at the time was the Cuban orchestra Rumbavana, one of the musical groups that had come to participate in the festival organized by the newspaper *Voz Proletaria del Partido Comunista*. They happened to be in that city, and the impresario tried to make a smart commercial deal by including the orchestra in the same program. According to journalist Markoté Barros, who was present during the incident, Celia came to see the impresario after the rehearsal, and literally said to him: "Capi, what were you thinking? Are you from another planet? You better know that this 'worm' (the word used by the Cuban government to describe those who had left the country) will not climb on those boards together with that orchestra hanging around over there." The orchestra had been invited to Colombia by the *Voz Proletaria del Partido Comunista*. Impresario Captain Visbal tried to explain to her that his decision had nothing to do with politics, but she answered, "The simple fact is that I won't perform then." Needless to say, the Orchesta Rumbavana did not appear in that concert.

Carnival time every year in Barranquilla usually includes in its program a festival of orchestras. In 1994, one of those invited from around the world was the Cuban group Los Van Van, with Juan Formell. Another one of the invited stars, and a big festival attraction, was Celia Cruz, who was going to perform in several dance halls. Celia had announced that she was boycotting the festival by refusing to share the stage with her countrymen from Revolutionary Cuba. The organizers commissioned Pablo Gabriel Obregón and Marciano Puche, two distinguished citizens with connections to the Mario Santo Domingo Foundation, to go see her at the Hotel Del Prado where she was staying. The men tried to convince her to perform, by public demand, but Celia would not even see them. By then, Fidel's need for dollars had forced him to legalize the dollar as Cuban currency. This act divided the country into those who had access to dollars and those who possessed the almost worthless Cuban pesos.

In Madrid, a similar case occurred in 1990 when Celia forced the organizers of a festival to choose between her and a Cuban group with popular *salsero* Isaac Delgado. Obviously, in spite of various public protests, the impresarios had no other option but to choose Celia.

Some observers saw her conduct as a demonstration of unshakable integrity. Others, in spite of the fact that her records were banned in Cuba, felt her defiance signaled an intransigent attitude. They believed that with the standing she had achieved on an international level, she could have played a conciliatory part, promoting a dialogue between the musicians and singers in exile and those living on the island.

In April 1997 there was another similar incident in which Celia caused a commotion within the Hispanic community in the United States, with repercussions elsewhere. Some major newspapers had published a photo that showed Andy Montañez warmly embracing and welcoming to Puerto Rico the famous singer of the Cuban Revolutionary *nueva trova*, Silvio Rodríguez. Celia refused to participate in a concert sharing the stage with Montañez. In her defense it could be stated that, had she done so, the radical Cuban community in Miami, great admirers of her music, would not have easily forgiven her.

After this incident, the Kiwanis Club of Little Havana vetoed and canceled the participation of the Puerto Rican singer in the Carnaval de la Calle Ocho, held every year in Miami, in which he was going to act as Grand Marshall. Montañez considered the decision unconstitutional. "I don't look at Silvio Rodríguez politically. I am not political. I admire Silvio as a singer and poet. And I represent Puerto Rico as an artist," he commented. "I am not interested in the political affiliation. I am only interested in whether the person is a good singer."

It was not the first time Montañez was involved in a controversy like this. In 1989, he was one of three singers excluded from the Miami Carnival because he had performed in Cuba when he was with the Venezuelan group Dimensión Latina. Also excluded was singer-composer Denise de Kalaff, who sued the Kiwanis Club for damages. A judge awarded her three million dollars in compensation. About this incident, Celia Cruz said that she understood the decision by the Cuban exile community because "Andy Montañez had wounded their sensibilities."

Along the same vein, by mid August 1997 some Puerto Rican radio stations began a campaign—claimed to be without the approval of Montañez—that attempted to boycott the *Guarachera de Cuba*, who was on the program to participate in the first World Salsa Festival in San Juan. The festival also included the Sonora Ponceña, the Colombian group Son de Azúcar, José Alberto (el Canario), Óscar D'León, Gilberto Santa Rosa, and the scheduled special encounter between Cano Estremera and Bobby Valentín. The boycott was effective, and the organizers were forced to cancel Celia's performance. With some numbers from the album of boleros they had just recorded together, Andy Montañez and Ismael Miranda were engaged in her place.

The Puerto Rican *salseros* never forgave the Kiwanis's affront, or Celia's political intolerance. On Saturday, April 29, 2000, the Fania All Stars were engaged for a concert before thousands of people in the Blithorn Coliseum in San Juan. Cheo Feliciano, who had been in Cuba recently and had come with praises about the island, had the difficult responsibility of presenting the Queen of Salsa. With his well-known gentility, he prepared an introduction for the star of the show. According to Larry Harlow, people there had advised Celia before she was called to the stage to make an apology for her past behavior, and she had agreed. Pedro Knight, however, even more reactionary than Celia, convinced her that she could not do such a thing. They suffered the consequences of a hostile audience ready to antagonize her and disrupt her performance. It resulted in one of the most humiliating moments in all of her artistic career.

Celia was received with mild applause, immediately drowned by angry boos and shouts of "Out!" and "We want Andy." Disregarding the shouting, Celia controlled herself and began singing "*Cúcala*," but a large portion of the public continued with their catcalls until the singer, who was the closing act for the evening, finished her song, and said with her characteristic generosity: "Thanks, I love you very much!"

At that moment, Maestro Johnny Pacheco signaled to the orchestra, and the beginning strains of "*Químbara*" were heard, but the audience was still shouting their un-yielding disapproval of Celia's presence in Puerto Rico. When she finished the number, she left the stage crying and did not return to join all the invited vocalists in the improvisations on "*Quítate tú*," the final number of the concert. Montañez, however, said that he did not approve of the lamentable incident, and expressed his respect and admiration for Celia.

Celia defended herself by arguing that Montañez had planned the entire thing. In an interview on the Internet with journalist Néstor Louis, she commented, "That was gossip that was started by Andy Montañez. Gossip that I prefer not to discuss. I would love for this rumor to be resolved in an honest and truthful way. To speak of a man that claims I spoke ill of him and his country and can't exactly repeat what he claims I said, does not deserve a statement from me.

If he tells me, 'Celia, you said this about Puerto Rico' or produced recorded evidence of my making a negative commen-
tary about Puerto Rico and its people, then he would have
earned my apology. I love Puerto Rico and its people, and I
will admit that there was an incident with the Fania All Stars
in Puerto Rico, but people reacted to gossip without knowing the truth. I cannot blame them for what happened that
day. This is the only blemish in my long career and it should
never have happened with a rumor someone spread. I am
not about gossip or controversy. I have lived my life and
carried my career cleanly, and it doesn't make any sense for
me to further address that situation." With those words Celia closed the argument. It was a source of grief for her and
of discomfort for her countless fans in Puerto Rico. Néstor
Louis also said that "The average fan on the street, industry
insiders, and musical comrades credit her with being the nicest lady in music."

The affection of Puerto Rico for Andy Montañez (el
Niño de Trastalleres) is better understood if we consider
that he was a member of El Gran Combo, the insignia
salsa orchestra in Puerto Rico from 1962 to 1976. For
fifteen years his imposing voice was heard on twenty-seven
albums that included many hit numbers. Later, he joined
the Venezuelan orchestra Dimensión Latina, with which he
visited Cuba and performed until 1980, when he became
an independent soloist. He has made many recordings and
gained well-deserved recognition. These were some of the
reasons for the nationalistic discord when his appearance
was canceled in Miami for embracing a guest and veteran
trovero from Cuba.

But for many other exiled Cubans, Celia was a symbol
of anti-Castro feelings, with access to world forums and
international mass-media communication. No matter

what corner of the world she found herself in, she always expressed her yearning for a "free Cuba." And she took advantage of opportunities to express her opinion against the Cuban regime. In the Concert of the Americas held in 1994 in Miami during the Summit Meeting of Latin American Presidents, Celia closed her presentation thus: "Honorable presidents, please don't do anything to help Fidel. We want a Cuba free of Communism."

17

Celia Cruz: The Undisputed Symbol of Afro-Cubanism

Celia was any music promoter's dream because of the added value she brought to every contract. She offered more than just interesting musical interpretations: Celia transformed herself into a stage image that projected well beyond any performance. Her magic included a distinctive orchestra sound, staging, scenery and props, backup choruses, and a lot of color and special effects. Besides the power of her engaging voice, that black woman with her beat (*tumbao*) and her big red lips (*bemba colorá*) made waves with her imaginative costumes. Some were quite wild and exuberant, sprinkled with sequins or adorned with colored feathers; her nails were silver or had original designs; her favorite costume jewelry was showy: necklaces, chokers, pendants, earrings, wrist and upper-arm bracelets, big fancy rings; and her makeup was striking, with thick, fake eyelashes and brightly shaded eyelids.

Celia was very fond of sunglasses. They had to be prescriptions and she ordered them in exaggerated sizes and adorned with small, bright-colored stones to make them more festive. She tried, out of vanity, not to appear in public wearing reading glasses, and later wore contact lenses both for her shows and daily life. Her favorite perfume was by Guerlain, which she wore discreetly, but she was not opposed to trying other fragrances, whether bought or received as gifts from friends. For her presentations Celia had advisors and makeup artists always watching over her appearance, even to the most minimal details, such as the manicure of her beautiful hands.

Wigs were the second most important prop for Celia in the creation of her image. Besides Queen of Salsa, she could also be considered Queen of Wigs. She had them in every color—though she preferred blond or silver—and every style, to cover her curly hair. This artist with the chameleon image confided that her collection of wigs was not extravagant, that it seemed so only because they were coiffed in different styles each time. To avoid wasting whole days at the beauty salon and having to sleep in uncomfortable positions in order to coddle her hairdo, she had come up with the idea of wigs. During her travels to distant places she always visited wig stores in search of new styles. In later years, though, she got wigs from a specialized wig factory in Los Angeles that sent her a catalog of original exclusive models to choose from. Celia became so knowledgeable about wigs that, at some point, she thought of launching her own line of wigs, but she was always so overcommitted that her idea never materialized.

Celia's characteristic humor allowed her to give good

interviews and to answer questions with originality. On one occasion, while having dinner in Cali (Colombia), at the home of her friend and compatriot José Pardo Llada, she was asked where she spent all the money she was making. Laughing out loud, Celia said, "On wigs, my darling, on wigs. I have spent a fortune on wigs. I have them in all colors and in all styles." She initially had them in natural hair, but they were too burdensome to be carried around in boxes. Later her wigs were synthetic and thus much easier to transport. She would simply turn them inside out, tuck them into a suitcase, and when she got to any city, she would shake them out and they were ready to be worn. Wigs were one of her stage trademarks.

Besides her visual repertory, Celia counted on her mastery of the art of *soneo* or improvisation, which she did with great skill. She also depended heavily on her good memory, which often allowed her to perform numbers without rehearsal. In the Big Apple, she became the unquestionable icon for Afro-Cuban music, without overlooking her Latin side. All rhythms converged in New York, with musicians and vocalists from various Caribbean regions, Latin America, or first-generation Americans with Hispanic ancestry. Despite living in exile for more than forty years in the postmodern world of globalization and cultural assimilation, the tropical diva never forgot her humble origins, which were well rooted in the Cuban traditions. Celia Cruz owed her enormous popularity in the immigrant community to the essential elements of her distant homeland, represented with great joy in her melodies.

For instance, in her song *"Yo soy la voz"* (I Am the Voice), Celia enumerates all that her voice evokes: her origins, the tropical flavor of the *son*, coffee, and molasses. Perhaps without conscious intent, her trademark cry

"Azúcar!" is also a historical reference to the culture of the sugar mills in Cuba, the economy of slavery, the heritage and the dynamics of the Afro-Spanish crossbreeding which is the source of the popular rhythms that catapulted her to fame in the fifties.

Azúcar negra (Black Sugar), by Mario Díaz, is the title of her 1993 album and is one of her favorite numbers. It begins with a ceremonial rolling of drums that metaphorically alludes to her ancestry: *Soy dulce como el melao, / alegre como el tambor, / llevo el rítmico tumbao / de África en el corazón. / Hija de una isla rica, / mi sangre es azúcar negra, / es amor y es musical. / Azúcar negra, cuánto me gusta y me alegra.* (I am sweet like syrup, / joyful like the drum, / I have the rhythm / of Africa in my heart. / Daughter of a rich island, / my blood is black sugar, / it's love and it's musical. / Black sugar, how I like it, and what joy it brings me.)

In the United States, Celia extended her Afro-Cuban traditions to include the characteristics of the Afro-American community, which at the moment of her arrival in the sixties (the time of the Civil Rights Movement) was organizing into civil disobedience protest. The Goddess of the Rumba, as singer Bienvenido Granda called her, transformed her personal appearance to assume her blackness. It was her hair that became one of the first symbols of "black is beautiful." She wore a splendid afro on the cover of the album *Recordando el pasado*, with Johnny Pacheco (1976).

Reaffirming her ethnic heritage in the seventies, Celia sometimes performed in concerts wearing multicolor beads in many thin braids—a style popularized by Bo Derek—which made her look like an African princess (as on the cover of her album *Celia y Willie*, 1981). Over time, Celia had to abandon braiding her hair because with per-

An important element of Celia's music was her Afro-Cuban heritage. It was through her singing, along with the popular tradition of street vendors, street jargon, black poetry, and even the lyrics in the Lucumí language that she sang devotedly to Yoruba deities as in "*Lalle Lalle*," a *guaguancó* by J.C. Fumero (1961), and "*Changó tá vení*," a *guaracha* by Justi Barreto (1965). From her first themes with the Sonora Matancera, her intention to reclaim her roots was evident, with numbers like "*El yerbero moderno*," "*Caramelos*," "*Burundanga*," "*Herencia africana*," "*Pregones de San Cristóbal*," her anthology in two volumes, *Homenaje a los santos*, and so many others. They are all eloquent testimonies of the African musical heritage present in her artistic career. Just as the sound of a drum is a call for celebration, songs like "*Químbara*," by Junior Cepeda, have the evocative power that incites all to dance: *Químbara, químbara, cumbanbinbabá, / químbara, químbara, cumbanbinbabá, / Químbara, químbara, cumbanbinbabá, / La rumba me está llamando. / Bongó, dile que ya voy, / que me espere un momentico / mientras canto un guaguancó / Dile que no es un desprecio, / pues vive en mi corazón. / Mi vida, mi vida, mi vida es tan sólo eso, / rumba buena y guaguancó, /.* (... / The rumba is calling me. / Bongo, tell her I'm coming, / tell her to wait just a moment / while I sing a *guaguancó*. / Tell her it's not an insult, / because she lives in my heart. / My life, my life is only for that, / good rumba and *guaguancó*). An interesting side note is that Celia fought tenaciously to convince the Fania Records executives to include this joyous number in the LP, and it surprisingly became one of the most requested numbers in the Fania All Stars concerts.

spiration, her natural hair shrank, while the artificial fibers remained straight, creating a fake look. Celia wore this style as a symbol of solidarity during the early seventies, a time characterized by political strife, and of the opposition to Anglo-Saxon, white superiority. It was during this era in New York City that groups like the Black Panthers and the Young Lords were formed (the latter was a combative group of Puerto Rican militants from East Harlem, known in New York as El Barrio, or the Neighborhood).

Celia's trademark, *Azúcar!*, with which she began each concert, was adopted as the exclusive slogan of the world of *salsa*. Celia told the story many times about the origin of *Azúcar!* She was performing at the Montmartre in Miami when her friend Raúl González and his wife invited her and Pedro to dinner. They went to a restaurant, and after dinner the waiter inquired if she wanted her coffee with sugar or without. She told him that if he was Cuban, he should know that the bitter Cuban coffee must be served with "*azúcar,* of course, with *azúcar.*" She began telling that story in her concerts, but she grew tired of it, "it had become old hat." Then, at one presentation, her dressing room was above the stage, and with the microphone in her hand, she went down the stairs singing "*Tu voz,*" when suddenly she cried "*Azúcar!*" and then continued singing her number. Later, while singing with Memo Salamanca's Sonora in Mexico, she recorded the album *Nuevos éxitos de Celia Cruz* (Celia Cruz's New Hits). In one of the numbers, "*Te solté la rienda*" (I Set You Free), she cried "*Azúcar!*" for the first time on a record. With the good sense of humor that was her signature, one day she quipped, "I think that because of my shouting *azúcar* so often, Pedro got diabetes."

From then on, her cry of "*Azúcar!*" was like an electrical discharge. Nobody else could capture so well its Cuban flavor and give this word all the connotations of her island: the joy and sweetness of its main agricultural product. It became so embedded into her artistic personality that on occasion she declared: "The day I die, I want to say good-bye with '*Azúcar!*', but only God knows when that day will be." Her cry assured the uplifting of spirits of her most unprepared spectators, who would immediately start to dance, joyously uninhibited. It was the royal decree for the fiesta to start, with the sound of drums and trumpets in the background.

Celia's unique voice, with its deep Afro-Caribbean roots, crossed over every barrier, from her country of residence, the United States, to the ends of the world. Her most popular hits have the power of a rumba hymn that her public sings wholeheartedly in chorus with her. In some of her hits, the composers wrote the lyrics of their melodies with her, such as Marisela Verena, whose "*Diagnóstico*" seems to have been created to measure for the *Guarachera*. For more than four decades of exile she always carried her Caribbean island in her heart: *Yo tengo azúcar, llevo la clave. / Yo tengo el son en el corazón. / Yo tengo azúcar, yo tengo son, / yo tengo a Cuba en el corazón.* (I have sugar, I have the beat. / I have the *son* in my heart. / I have sugar, I have *son*, / I have Cuba in my heart.) And to the rhythm of her cry, *Azúcar!*, Celia Cruz became a legend in Caribbean music to the joy of all her fans. One can only wonder exactly when in her life did Celia realize that she had become a legend.

18

The Blossoming Queen and Her Court

To some observers of her professional trajectory, from the sixties till her death, half of the salsa music is pure Celia and the other half belongs to all the other musicians: *salseros, soneros, guaracheros, merengueros,* or *boleristas.* These other genres included well-known names like Francisco Repilado (Compay Segundo), Myrta Silva, Eddie Palmieri, Omara Portuondo, Willie Colón, Graciela Pérez (Machito's sister), Gilberto Santa Rosa, Rubén Blades, La Lupe, Henry Fiol, Tito Puente, Elena Burke, Papo Lucca, Justo Betancourt, Olga Guillot, Pete (el Conde) Rodríguez, Héctor Lavoe or, most recently, La India, Marc Anthony, Olga Tañón, and Víctor Manuelle.

Other female figures in *salsa,* like Yolandita Rivera or Carolina Laó, either with the Orquesta Alquimia (echoes of the Sonora Matancera) or as soloists, made recordings that never attained Celia's impact. But one must recognize that without Celia, they would have been totally overlooked.

Some musicians and performers did not outlive the peak of their popularity or remained in the classic genres, like the Cuban *guaracha* or the romantic *bolero* that the combos played during the forties and fifties. Some simply settled themselves comfortably in their most popular hits, ignoring all innovations and challenges, while Celia worked at developing her art. Jumping into the modern musical groups after the seventies, she soon adapted to the new movements, like *salsa*, with the Fania All Stars in the vanguard. Afterward, other young rhythms guaranteed her a wide spectrum of admirers. She sang *"La negra tiene tumbao"* by Venezuelan-Colombian composer Fernando Osorio, and arrangements by a young New York musician, Sergio George, both of whom attempted to renovate *salsa* with postmodern airs, sometimes adding typical musical instruments from Cuba like the *timba*. Let's not forget that, in fact, *salsa* is a conglomerate of Caribbean genres. *Salsa* owes much to Celia Cruz, particularly in her last recordings in which she strove to adopt more modern rhythms. In this sense, she was one of the first to blaze the trail that Latin music would eventually follow.

After withdrawing from the Sonora Matancera in 1965, Celia became a soloist dependent only on her limpid record as a performer with a unique, experienced voice and an unquestionable prestige. Before changing to a new recording label, however, she did a record entitled *Canciones que yo quería haber grabado primero* (Songs I Would Have Liked to Be the First One to Record), with René Hernández and his orchestra and musical production by Vicentico Valdés, for the Seeco label.

Before reaching this point, the *Guarachera del Mundo* had to overcome many obstacles on the way to success. Among them were fads that had altered the musical tastes of millions of young fans. The closeness of the Latin musicians to the rhythm and blues then dominant in Harlem contributed to the development of the *bugalú* that fused R & B and Latin rhythms. The boogaloo then became a commercial phenomenon that monopolized the musical scene as long as it lasted. Among the great boogaloo hits were *"El watusi"* by Ray Barretto, which sold a million copies in 1962. As a rock-and-roll piece, it was known as "Wah Wah Watusi" by the Orlons; "Bang Bang" by Joe Cuba; and "Watermelon Man" by Mongo Santamaría (*el Maestro de la Conga*). By the end of the sixties, the boogaloo was history.

After the Cuban Revolution in 1959, it became difficult for Cuban musicians to tour in the United States or abroad. To fill the empty space left by the quarantined Cuban musicians, *charangas* were organized with a band format in which traditional Cuban instruments, including flute, violins, bass, *güiro*, and *timbales criollos* (replacing trumpets and saxophones), were used. Eddie Palmieri, Charlie Palmieri's younger brother, founded his first *charanga*, La Perfecta, in 1961. Johnny Pacheco, who was a percussionist with Tito Puente and later flutist with Charlie Palmieri's band, also became independent in order to create his own combo, popularizing the *pachanga* in New York City by the end of 1963. His first album, *Pacheco y su Charanga*, became one of the best-selling albums in this genre.

In the sixties the *pachanga,* with its energetic, fast dance rhythms played by the then popular *charangas,* could be heard in every club in Manhattan and the Bronx. "*La pachanga,*" by Cuban composer Claudio Davidson (later

When Celia arrived in New York, she worked briefly with Tito Rodríguez and an orchestra of new musicians. They performed at the Palladium Ballroom. The Palladium was a club on Fifty-third Street and Broadway that, from the time of its opening in 1946, enjoyed a period of splendor for Latin music in New York. Tommy Morton, its owner, brought the popular Machito's Orchestra and his Afro-Cubans, who dominated the musical scene, under the direction of Mario Bauzá, a versatile musician who has been credited with being one of the first to achieve a fusion between Afro-Cuban music and American jazz that came to be known as *Cubop*. For his part, Frank Grillo (Machito) was the legitimate representative of Afro-Cuban music in the United States. He was a natural *sonero* from Havana who had come to the States in 1937 and had attained real success. Machito recorded with famous bandleaders like Xavier Cugat before creating his own orchestra, which played for the first time at the Club Cuba of New York in 1940. His female vocalist was his sister Graciela, who obtained a well-deserved celebrity. The Palladium Ballroom later became known as the Home of the Mambo, and Latin music began to acquire popularity thanks to the bands playing there, including those of Noro Morales, José Curbelo, and, of course, The Picadilly Boys under the baton of Tito Puente on the *timbales* or the vibraphone. It was his first experience as a bandleader.

known as Eduardo Davidson), had been recorded in Havana with the Orquesta Sublime in 1959. It was a rhythm with connections to the *merengue dominicano* that the Sonora Matancera had also adopted in the voice of Carlos Argentino, who recorded it for the Seeco label.

In 1960 Celia Cruz had recorded "*Vamos todos de*

pachanga" by Lino Frías. Later, in Buenos Aires, Argentino composed a dozen *pachangas*, among them: "*La pachanga del fútbol*," "*La pachanga de los pibes*," "*Gaucho pachanguero*," and "*La pachanga cantonera*." They became so popular in his native country that he was nicknamed "the King of the Pachanga."

In New York City, Tito Puente worked with Rolando Laserie to make Davidson's original *pachanga* into one of the greatest hits of the sixties. Parallel to the reappearance of the *charanga* bands, the nostalgia of the Cuban community in the New York area gave rise to bands called *típicas*, which replaced the strings and flute of the *charangas* with two trumpets, sometimes adding a trombone, thus creating a fusion of jazz, more advanced improvisational techniques, and traditional folk themes.

Celia's musical path took her from her difficult years in the sixties, when Caribbean music struggled to survive the onslaught of rock, particularly with the incredible popularity of singers like Elvis Presley, The Rolling Stones, and The Beatles, until her star soared again after 1974 with the Fania All Stars and her universal recognition as Queen of Salsa.

19

Celia and Tito: The Birth of Salsa

Celia worked on developing her craft before settling in the United States, where she embarked on a different path with Tito Puente. It was true that she did not yet have the promotion her recordings deserved, but she was enjoying some isolated triumphs. In any case, a new world dimension opened up for her that confirmed and expanded her considerably during the time she was associated with the Fania All Stars. The group played the kind of music known as *salsa* and during her immigrant days she performed with many other *salseros*, such as Johnny Pacheco, Willie Colón, Ray Barretto, Charlie Palmieri, Rubén Blades, and Papo Lucca with the Sonora Ponceña.

There was a process to be followed before becoming the top world figure, recognized in film, soap operas, and concerts that span five continents. It proceeded by Celia's singing and innovating with astounding facility and catching up with the times so well that she eventually recorded with rock and rap groups. Not all of these ventures may have been her best, or the best balanced from a musical point of view, but they were still incredible feats for one her age. They demonstrated an openess and a desire to be contemporary, not to be left behind in the polyphonic waves that were happening at the moment.

In 1966 Celia signed an advantageous contract with Tico Records, where she found common ground with another member of the music royals: *El Rey del Timbal*, Tito Puente. Celia had met him at a party in her honor on one of her visits to New York during the fifties. They talked about their careers, their interests, their preferences, and they exchanged addresses. Some time later, the musical impresario Gaspar Pumarejo—a pioneer in Cuban television—invited Tito to perform on the island. There Celia and Tito met again, and a friendship blossomed that was to last a lifetime, only to grow stronger while they worked together for Tico Records. Celia always held Tito in high regard. "For me," she said when he died on May 21, 2001, "he was the gentleman of the stage. His friendship, his affection, and the way he made me feel are things I will always cherish in my heart."

It is fair to say that Celia Cruz and Tito Puente were among those few artists who had a momentous influence on the development of Latin music in the United States and worldwide. Tito brought his magical musical arrangements and original style, and Celia brought magnificent performances and her unforgettable personality. Their first LP was *Cuba and Puerto Rico Son* in 1966. Even without much promotion, Celia and Tito's early recordings enjoyed some commercial success. Their greatest achievement was

With Tito's arrangements, Celia's act started to have a big band sound. Other recordings followed: *Quimbo, Quimbumbia* in 1969, *Etc. Etc. Etc.* in 1970, both *Alma con alma* and *Celia Cruz y Tito Puente en España* in 1971, *Algo especial para recordar* in 1972, and *Homenaje a Benny Moré, Vol.3* in 1985. These albums gave rise to some hits, such as *"Ritmo gitano," "Desencanto," "Acuario," "Preferí perderte,"* and *"Changó tá vení"* (by 1977, they had recorded together the percussionist's hundredth recording, *"Celia y Tito,"* in which Puente does not sing, but plays the *timbal* in a duet with Celia). With these recordings Celia opened up an international dimension to her work, which later culminated in her work with the Fania All Stars.

to attract the interest of the English-speaking world, both in the U.S. and Europe, where Caribbean music was just catching on. The phenomenon was later known as The Seventies *Salsa*.

After the *mambo* craze had swept the musical landscape, after rock and roll, *chachachá*, boogaloo, and *pachanga*—which monopolized urban tastes during the sixties—began to wane, a new rhythm emerged. This rhythm had been cooking in the Latin clubs of Manhattan and the Bronx. It was not really new; rather it was a new instrumentation of known Cuban themes created by exceptional musicians and vocalists. Their efforts rendered an innovated fusion, a unique musical sound—*Salsa*. *Salsa* surged with unexpected vigor, surprising everyone, including the founding musicians.

With the breakup of the Beatles, the death of Elvis Presley, the excesses of hard rock, and the gradual disappearance of each successive musical fad toward the beginning of the seventies, young Latinos in New York, New Jersey, Miami, and other large industrial cities in the States began to take an interest in their roots. *Salsa* became the musical symbol that unified them into one cultural and ethnic community. The prodigal return of native music under the generic name *salsa* brought changes to dancing styles in New York, Puerto Rico, Colombia, Venezuela, and other Latin American areas. In the same way, it contributed to the death of New York disco, which was more for spectacle.

Celia's induction into the world of *salsa* occurred in an opera format. She made her debut in the so-called *salsa*-opera *Hommy*, composed by pianist Larry Harlow, and based on the successful rock opera *Tommy*, originally sung by Roger Daltrey with The Who. *Hommy* was organized by the Fania label, with Celia in the lead role of Gracia Divina. It was performed at Carnegie Hall on March 29, 1973. That same year *Hommy* was performed in San Juan, Puerto Rico, with equal audience approval. Still under contract with Tico Records, Celia obtained permission to record (in just twenty minutes, which was record time) *Hommy, Hommy, Gracia Divina, / no me importa, Hommy, lo que pasó por ti /* (Hommy, Hommy, Divine Grace, / I don't care, Hommy, what you were thinking). This song was based on a chorus or refrain with the inspiration provided by *La Guarachera de Cuba*, because Jerry Masucci, owner of Fania Records, was a good friend of Morris Levy, the manager of Tico Records. Celia's participation in this musical production organized by Fania made her a favorite of music lovers. The *salsa*-opera *Hommy* was a hit that contributed to the consolidation and popularity of *salsa* at a crucial point in its development. It introduced Celia to a new generation of fans.

Suddenly, the name *salsa* became a household word.

Several theories attempted to explain the origin of the name. It has been said that it began with the *son* "*Échale salsita*" (1933) by the Septeto Nacional. *Salsita* was also a cry used in Cuba to energize musicians playing. Some attribute its nomenclature to Izzy Sanabria, who used the term when he presented one of the first concerts of the Fania All Stars. Others point to Cal Tjader's hit record *Soul Sauce*, which had a bottle of Louisiana hot sauce on its cover. It does not matter how the name came about; the fact is that in a short time the term *salsa* had become so popular that Latin musicians, even those who rejected the term, had to jump on the bandwagon of this new, hybrid style.

Musicians who had been around for a long time thought this name was merely a marketing ploy, and resented that their music now had another name. Tito Puente was one of the first to criticize the name. "There is no such thing as *salsa* music," he explained when asked about it. "This is a new name for the music we have been playing all along. The *mambo* or the *chachachá* is now called *salsa*. *Salsa* is something you eat; you don't listen to it or dance to it. However, the new word has become so popular that people ask me to play *salsa*....Latin music got that name to make it 'hot,' to make it exciting. It's a word everyone can pronounce. In my concerts I always announce: 'Now we are going to play...*salsa*!' and people are happy. And it's the same *mambo* I have been playing for forty years."

Composer Sergio George also thought it was a marketing device. "For better or worse, the music needed a name. Why not *salsa*? *Guaracha*? I would not call what I am doing now *guaracha* or *son* or *mambo*. *Salsa* is a good term because this music is precisely that, a mixture, a *sofrito* used for seasoning, with a mix of different ingredients." And that is what it is, a mix of traditional and happy folk rhythms

The real force behind *Hommy* was Larry Harlow, a Jewish pianist and all-around musician born in Brooklyn in 1930. He grew up in East Harlem, known as El Barrio by many Puerto Rican immigrants who settled there when the exodus from the island started after World War II. Larry, whose real name was Lawrence Ira Kahn, had formal musical training and played several instruments. His first love was jazz, but as he said, "If you were not black, you couldn't play jazz." He also had been fascinated by the Latin music played by Tito Puente, Charlie Palmieri, and Tito Rodríguez that he heard in his neighborhood, though he was so young he could not be admitted at the Palladium to hear them. So he joined the Latin band of Hugo Dickens, an African-American. Eventually he organized his own band in 1967 with a very young vocalist, Ismael Miranda, who was only eighteen. Among his most popular hits with his star singer Miranda are *"El malecón,"* *"¡Abran paso!"* and *"Tributo a Arsenio Rodríguez,"* honoring the much-admired innovator of Afro-Cuban music who died in late 1970. After Miranda left to become independent, Harlow devoted himself to the orchestration and production of his *salsa*-opera. This interest came from his family: his mother was an opera singer, and his father a professional bass player.

Harlow, affectionately nicknamed *"El Judío Maravilloso"* (The Marvelous Jew), was the first artist signed by Fania. He had met Jerry Masucci in Havana, where Larry had gone to study Cuban music and also *Santería,* becoming a "child of Ochún."

The Latin *salsa*-opera Harlow directed was written and co-produced by Genaro (Henry) Alvarez. In the studio album, as well as onstage at Carnegie Hall, Celia Cruz sang the role of Gracia Divina, joined by a constellation of Fania Stars, including José (Cheo) Feliciano, Adalberto

Santiago, Justo Betancourt, Pete (el Conde) Rodríguez, and Henry Álvarez as narrator.

Larry Harlow has also been credited with introducing the trumpet/trombone sound to salsa along with the *batá* drums from Cuba, and with the idea for the documentary *Our Latin Thing*, plus the historical live recording of the Fania All Stars concert at the Cheetah Club in New York in 1972.

that include *son, guaracha, chachachá, guaguancó, guajira, rumba, bomba, plena, merengue dominicano, cumbia colombiana*, and even the *bolero* and Brazilian rhythms. The name *salsa* thrust this kind of music into a wider popularity making it accessible to people who knew nothing about *guarachas, son montunos,* or *guaguancós.*

Celia commented on this debate in 1997 when she stated, "*Salsa* is only my Cuban music, variations of the same. A different name was needed to update it and make it succeed. *Salsa* originated when the big Cuban orchestras were not allowed to travel to the United States. It so happened then that our music started to become marginal, and the name *salsa* appeared. Nothing else had changed. It was Cuban music with some innovations, such as adding electronic instruments." *La Guarachera* also said, "The Sonora Matancera never used electronic instruments until the last minute, when they added an electric bass. It is also true that many of the musicians and arrangers of today were born in other places, like Puerto Rico or New York. Tito Puente, for example, has had jazz influences and is playing *salsa*. However, that is not my style, I will continue with my Cuban music till the end. You can call it *salsa*, or you can call it whatever you want. No matter where I am, whether in Mexico, or Venezuela, or Spain, or Argentina, my accent will always be Cuban."

20

Latin Music Before Salsa

The antecedents of the salsa movement are the *son* and the *guaracha*, which both originated in Cuba. There was also a variation of the *son* in Puerto Rico that probably traced its heritage from the first immigrants to Puerto Rico from Cuba. One can hear this in the melodies of Rafael Cortijo as well as Ismael Rivera and his Cachimbos. According to Fabio Betancur, author of *Sin clave y bongó no hay son*, Arsenio Rodríguez, *el Ciego Maravilloso* (The Marvelous Blind Man), was an innovator of tonalities, besides being a virtuoso on the *tres*, and he is credited with being one of the originators of the *salsa* sound. For those who doubt the strength of improvisation in the *son* and the *rumba*, the writer and scholar Leonardo Acosta remembers how Arsenio used to improvise on the electric *tres* that he invented: "The rhythm is of the traditional *son*, but with the distinction that he does instrumentals without lyrics." The jam-session, or impro-visation, has an influence in the world of Cuban musicians like Israel (Cachao) López. As in the *son* and in jazz, an im-portant characteristic of *salsa* music is improvisation, and Celia Cruz was a great *sonera,* very deft at improvising.

The *son* has a long history, going back to the end of the nineteenth century in the eastern part of the island, particu-larly in Santiago de Cuba, the city of Manzanillo, and the Guantánamo region. It became popular during the carnival in Santiago, in 1892, with a *tresero* by the name of Nené Manfugás. The *tres,* as indicated by its name, is an instru-ment with three double strings. It is the traditional symbol of the *son.* Composer Ignacio Piñeiro—a double bass player from Havana, born in 1888—turned the *son* into a national tradition with his Septeto Nacional. He did this by creating a fusion between the *son* and the *canto guajiro* (from the countryside or the mountains), to form the *son-guajiro* that reached its best expression in "*Guantanamera,*" composed by Joseíto Fernández. Celia sang many *son montunos* with the Sonora Matancera, such as "*Ven, Bernabé*" by Ortega-Lara (1956), "*Tamborilero*" by Evelio Landa (1960), "*Ca-pricho navideño*" and "*Caramelos,*" both by Roberto Puente (1960), and "*Lamento de amor*" by Lourdes López (1961).

The *guaracha* also played a crucial part in the develop-ment of *salsa.* It was one of the most popular genres in Cuba with an unknown ethnic origin. Its lyrics resemble the picaresque ballads of the *Cancionero* from sixteenth-century Spain. *La guaracha-son* became part of the Cuban musical tradition, as well the so-called *son trovadoresco* (with poetic lyrics). The important performances were by the Trío Matamoros and the Dúo Los Compadres, with Lorenzo Hierrezuelo (Compay Primo), first voice and guitar, while Francisco Repilado (Compay Segundo) who was his cousin, and the second voice, accompanied by the *tres* or the *laúd* (lute). Hierrezuelos was noted for his duets with María Teresa Vera, a popular vocalist in the traditional *trova* style, which had a modified revival during the twentieth century. Los Compadres, organized in 1945, played a faster *son* with less emphasis on percussion and no *conga* drum (*tumbadora*), conveying a happier mood than that of the the *conjuntos* of that time, though for their recordings they added bass, *güiro,* and *bongó.*

In turn, the Trío Matamoros is undoubtedly the most eloquent exponent of the *son trovadoresco* of all time. Founded in 1925, the trio made their first recordings in 1928, within the *sonero* movement that enjoyed such an extensive impact among harmonic string groups. The Trío was formed by Miguel Matamoros, composer, guitar, and voice; Rafael Cueto, guitar and third voice; and Siro Rodrí-guez, second voice, *clavero,* and *maraquero.* Some of their most famous *sones* are the unforgettable *"Son de la loma"* (They Are from the Hills), which says: *Mamá, yo quiero saber, / ¿de dónde son los cantantes? / Los encuentro tan galantes / y los quiero conocer, / con su trova fascinante, / que me la quiero aprender* (Mother, I want to know, / where are these singers from? / I find them very gallant / and I want to meet them, / with their fascinating song, / which I want to learn) and *"El que siembra su maíz"* (He Who Plants His Own Corn). The Trío Matamoros exerted a fundamental influence on the development of the *son* that later shows up in certain elements of *salsa* after the seventies.

"Besides their style and their arrangements," Betancur goes on to explain, "the constellation of Cuban soloists like Bienvenido Granda, Celio González, and the presti-gious Celia Cruz will join a bunch of other multinational vocalists such as Daniel Santos, Alberto Beltrán, Nelson Pinedo, Víctor Piñero, and other singers, to the virtuoso musicianship of pianist Lino Frías and percussionist Mario Muñoz (Papaíto), forming a bridge out of this *guaracha* group [Sonora Matancera] between the *son* and *salsa*, and the Cuban genres—now complemented by *merengues, porros, boleros, salves,* and the rest from other countries— making one think of a Cubanization of the Caribbean region." And it was precisely in the Caribbean communities in the United States, as well as regions bordering on the Caribbean Sea (the Antilles, Mexico, Venezuela, Colombia, and Central America), that Celia was most loved and most recognized. However, she was equally adored in Spain, the rest of Latin America, and the rest of the world from Africa to Japan and the lands in between.

21

The Birth of the Fania All Stars

Fania was really composed of two entities. One was Fania Records, which featured the youngest and most talented artists playing Latin music in New York and Puerto Rico. The other was Fania All Stars, which was a group of famous musicians and vocalists contracted for gigantic concert productions all over the world, from the United States, Europe, and Africa, to Latin American countries, and even some places in Asia. These concerts were then used to make documentaries, television programs, and live recordings. With the last, Fania planted the seeds for salsa's immense popularity, introducing the new sound to millions of spectators who then went out to buy their recordings. It was a neat deal. The idea for this phenomenal project was the brainchild of Jerry Masucci, an Italian-American ex-policeman and law school graduate, and Johnny Pacheco, a Dominican musician. The idea was born on March 23, 1963, during a party at Masucci's home.

The name Fania (without an accent mark) was taken from a *son montuno*, *"Fanía Funché,"* by Cuban composer Reinaldo López Bolaños, recorded by Estrellas de Chocolate in 1958, but which never achieved much popularity. Fania was also a café in Havana that Masucci attended with Larry Harlow. Fania's first recording was *"Cañonazo,"* by Johnny Pacheco, who had gone from his traditional *charanga,* with flute and violins, to a *conjunto* sound with trumpets, which was in keeping with the style of the moment in the 1964 Latin neighborhoods of New York. The creation of Fania had the virtue of unifying immigrant musicians from various countries. Fania then was in competition with other New York record companies, such as Tico, Alegre, Cesta, and the Latin division of United Artists. The company was launched with such a small budget that Pacheco had to do the promotion and deliver his records in his station wagon to Latin music stores in Manhattan.

In order to carry out his plan to conquer the Latino market, Masucci contracted three orchestras at the beginning: those of veteran Ray Barretto, young Larry Harlow, and Bobby Valentín. A bit later, he added a group of musicians that were popular in the Latin community, led by the energetic and creative personality of trombonist Willie Colón. At that time the recording industry was going through a crisis, providing an opening for Fania Records. Competing companies, foreseeing bankruptcy on their horizon, decided to sell their assets to the Fania enterprise. In 1968, Masucci and Pacheco had the brilliant idea to gather the members of their orchestras, who had already made some records together, into a single group under the name Fania

All Stars, with Pacheco as artistic director.

The biggest stars had performed together for the first time at the Red Garter Club, an almost unknown club on the border between the South Bronx and Harlem River Drive. The place was open from six P.M till two A.M., and only occasionally presented popular groups on its stage. Therefore, what in the future would be considered an historical event, that evening went unnoticed, being saved from oblivion only because a diligent sound engineer took the precaution of recording the first public performance of the Fania All Stars. To overcome the fiasco of that first presentation, they brought in impresario Ralph Mercado in order to promote a concert on August 26, 1971, at the Cheetah ballroom, which drew more than four thousand people. Volumes I and II of the Fania All Stars which were recorded that night, have gone on to become two of the highest-grossing bestsellers among *salsa* albums recorded live in the entire history of Caribbean music. The documentary filmed simultaneously and entitled *Our Latin Thing*, which premiered on July 19, 1972, also became famous. The documentary was produced by Masucci and directed by Leon Gast, who would later film a Fania All Stars concert in the stadium of Kinshasa (Zaïre), entitled *Live in Africa,* this time with Celia Cruz.

These albums include classics of the period, such as *"Descarga Fania"* by Ray Barretto, and inspired by the renowned *"Descarga Cachao"* by Israel López (Cachao), which itself was reminiscent of a similar session performed by the Tico All Stars at Carnegie Hall in 1966. In a *descarga* (jam session), a known theme or an improvised one is taken and each instrument plays variations, according to its own technical and musical possibilities. Also included is a free version of *"Anacaona"* by Puerto Rican master

Tite Curet Alonso, "*Ponte duro*" with wonderful solos by Roberto Roena on the bongo drums, "*Macho cimarrón*" with the great Johnny Pacheco on the flute, and the unforgettable improvisations of *soneros* Feliciano, Lavoe, Santos Colón, Ismael Miranda, and Pete (el Conde) Rodríguez in "*Quítate tú.*" It was an initiation full of fireworks for the Caribbean *rumba* that was coming out with favorable omens for an enduring popularity. The success of this project inspired Fania Records to organize another concert at Yankee Stadium in 1973.

After making twelve albums with Tico Records (not counting reissues), Celia asked Morris Levy to release her from her contract, and thus she again became an independent *guarachera* surrounded by uncertain ties, open to any venture that fate had in store for her. This was when Jerry Masucci, enraptured both by Celia's charisma and her indisputable talent, made an insistent phone call to Mexico, where Celia and Pedro lived at the time. He wanted her to perform in a Fania All Stars concert to be recorded live at Yankee Stadium. He was hoping to persuade her to sign a contract with Fania Records. Despite Agustín Lara's promise to organize an orchestra exclusively for her in Mexico City, she finally gave in to Masucci's insistence, and moved to New York. Celia committed herself to the Fania music enterprise in 1973. And this was the beginning of a new phase that initiated the incredible skyrocketing of her musical career. In a group whose members were exclusively male, Celia was the only female vocalist with the Fania All Stars.

The poster for the concert at Yankee Stadium included Mongo Santamaría and Ray Barretto on the congas; Larry Harlow at the piano; the inimitable Johnny Pacheco on flute; Lewis Kahn, trombone, and Nicky Marrero, *tim-*

Copy of Celia Cruz's birth certificate, issued at the municipal district of El Cerro, that gives her birth date as October 21, 1925.

Side view of La Margarita, the tenement where Celia lived during her early years, with her aunt Ana.

A rare studio photo which shows Celia's physical attributes during her early years as a vocalist in Cuba.

*Celia Cruz and her
beloved Pedro Knight.*

**La Sonora Matancera
y Celia Cruz
Artistas de HATUEY
en Radio Progreso.**

*Celia Cruz with the Sonora Matancera as the Hatuey (a well-known Cuban
beer) Stars at Radio Progreso during the fifties.*

An article promoting one of Celia's concerts in a Japanese publication.

Celia singing to a full crowd in La Alameda, a major park in Mexico City, with the Torre Latinoamericana in the background.

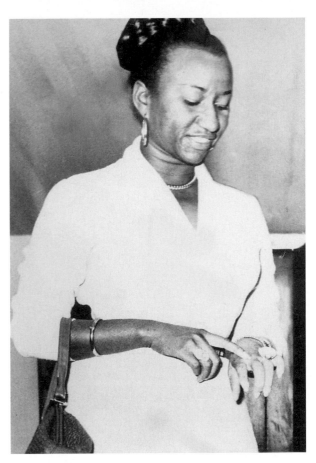

Celia with her usual tight hairdo in Havana, Cuba.

The famous Sans Souci Nightclub, one of the elegant clubs where Celia sang during the decade of the 1950s.

Celia Cruz with a young Tito Puente, the famous timbalero, when she began recording with his orchestra in the 1960s.

Signed promotional photo of young Celia in Cuba during the 1950s.

A collage of photos showing Celia at different points in her career (entitled "Celia, ayer, hoy y siempre: Celia, yesterday, today, and forever"), including the mature Celia as the Queen of Salsa and her husband, Pedro Knight (Cottontop).

Wherever Celia Cruz sang, multitudes gathered. On this occasion, she is performing her usual repertory for the audience at a concert in La Media Torta, Bogotá, Colombia.

Celia, the only female member, with the full cast of the Fania All Stars, at a concert in Nice, France. There, among others, are Pete (el Conde) Rodríguez, Rubén Blades, Héctor Lavoe, Papo Lucca, Ismael Miranda, Johnny Pacheco, and Yomo Toro.

Celia Cruz with Tito Puente at
the Riverside Church during the
Expressions Festival, sponsored by
the Centro Cultural Caribeño de
Nueva York, October 27, 1990.

Celia Cruz with her characteristic
broad smile.

A closer view of Celia during the same
concert at the Riverside Church.

On September 17, 1987, Celia received her own Star on the Hollywood Walk of Fame. Only two other Cubans had received this honor in the movie capital of the world: the television actor and musician Desi (Desiderio) Arnaz and the Mambo King, Dámaso Pérez Prado. Behind Celia is her lifelong friend Tongolele; to her right is her then manager Ralph Mercado; and farther behind, Pedro Knight.

Celia Cruz singing to Pedro Knight, with Tito Puente in the background.

Celia Cruz and Pedro Knight.

Celia with her dear Cuban flag and one of the multiple Gold Records that she received during her long artistic career.

Celia with Linda Caballero, a singer of Puerto Rican ancestry better known as La India, and Pedro Knight.

Celia flanked by Pedro Knight and Cuco Valoy in New York.

Poster announcing "Tribute to Celia Cruz and Her Life in Music, with friends and Celia's colleagues Rogelio Martínez with the Sonora Matancera, Tito Puente, Johnny Pacheco, Willie Colón, and the soneros José (Cheo) Feliciano and Pete (el Conde) Rodríguez, as well as the Conjunto Clásico and the Tropicana Dancers, Saturday, October 23, 1982, at Madison Square Garden.

Ticket in French for a concert with Óscar D'León and Celia Cruz, on Thursday, October 12, 1995, at Arthur's, The King of Your Nights.

Promotion for a Celia Cruz presentation at Symphony Sid, with Joe Cuba, Machito and his Afro-Cubans, and jazz musician Cal Tjader, among other musical attractions.

Interior shot of Celia's old house in Lawton, Havana, where some of her relatives still live, showing some of the photos and awards received during her time in Cuba.

Dolores Ramos Alfonso, Celia's older sister, at the side of the Church of the Miraculous Medal, in the Santos Suárez neighborhood, in January 2004.

A street altar organized spontaneously by Celia's fans in Miami's famous Calle Ocho in the days following her death.

Celia's Star, handprints, and signature at the Plaza de las Estrellas, Mexico City, unveiled in 1996.

An enormous Cuban flag on the facade of the Torre de la Libertad in Miami, where Celia's body lay in state during her funeral, attended by thousands of her fans.

bales; the trumpeters were Ray Maldonado and Víctor Paz; playing the *cuatro* was the famous Yomo Toro; the *bongosero* was Roberto Roena; and Bobby Valentín was on bass; with vocalists Justo Betancourt and Ismael Quintana. Celia Cruz was billed as the guest of honor at the concert. When master of ceremonies Izzy Sanabria announced: "*Dios dio al mundo una bella isla llamada Cuba, en Cuba nació lo que conocemos como la salsa, Cuba dio al mundo la máxima expresión de nuestra música, y para propagar con orgullo lo que es la música de nuestro pueblo, Dios nos trajo a la primera dama de la salsa: la Guarachera del Mundo, ¡Celia Cruz!* (God gave the Earth a beautiful island named Cuba, what we've come to know as *salsa* was born in Cuba, and to show what out music is really all about, He sent us, *La Guarachera* of the world, Celia Cruz!"). She exploded onstage to deafening applause wearing an African costume with a pair of gigantic brass hoops on her ears, and with her customary joy and charisma, she sang her unequaled "*Bemba colorá*": *Pa mí / tú eres ná / tú tiene / la bemba colorá* / by composer Horacio Santos. Bobby Valentín's arrangements for this special occasion were sterling. Celia sang then with a deluxe chorus behind her: Cheo Feliciano, Pete (el Conde) Rodríguez, and Héctor Lavoe.

The event exceeded all expectations with more than 44,000 in attendance who, thrilled to paroxysm, invaded the field, embracing and kissing musicians and vocalists. Because of this, the most emotional Latin fiesta in memory had to be suspended. Amid the initial chaos, a new musical genre was rising on the horizon, one that would produce more records and concerts than any other.

The Yankee Stadium concert was repeated at the Coliseo Roberto Clemente de San Juan, where Celia again sang "*Bemba colorá*," with the same wild reaction, which confirmed her place as the central figure in the Fania All Stars. Later, when the five live albums of the concert were distributed, many fans felt deceived when they found out that the two concerts had been unified under a single title: *The Fania All Stars: Live at Yankee Stadium*. This included the soundtrack from the film *Salsa y Latin Rock*.

After her impressive success with the Fania All Stars at the Yankee Stadium concert, Celia signed a contract with Vaya, a subsidiary of Fania Records, also owned by Masucci and Pacheco. *Esto no se queda así / lo bueno viene, mi hermano, / después conocí a Johnny Pacheco, ese gran dominicano* (This is not all, / the good part, my brother, is still to come; / afterward I met Johnny Pacheco, that great Dominican).

The summer of 1974 brought another album, *Celia y Johnny*, which, with "*Toro mata*" and "*Químbara*," was an immediate success. It was the first recording with the Queen of Cuban rhythms and the ex-king of the *charanga*, Johnny Pacheco, who had now become a full-fledged *salsero* and a legend at that. According to musicologist Héctor Ramírez Bedoya, Pacheco originated the phrase "*matancerización de la salsa*," that is, a musical and thematic format in which Celia was very comfortable since it was similar to the Sonora Matancera arrangement of two trumpets, piano, bass, percussion (*bongó* and *timbal*), *claves*, and for good measure, the *tres*.

This profitable "marriage" of these two central figures in Afro-Caribbean music produced five more records, with hits like "*Cúcala*": *Cúcala, cúcala, cuca, cúcala, que ella sale. / Cúcala, cúcala, cuca, cúcala, qué se hace /* , together with "*Sopa en botella*" in the album *Tremendo caché* (1975); *Recordando el ayer con Celia, Johnny, Justo y*

Johnny Pacheco started his career as a percussionist, but when he got tired of lugging around such heavy instruments, he took up the flute, and soon became a real virtuoso. He was born in Santiago de los Caballeros in the Dominican Republic on March 25, 1935, and came to New York with his parents when he was twelve. His father, leader of a popular orchestra in Santo Domingo, had to leave the island due to dictator Rafael Leónidas Trujillo's daring insistence on having the orchestra named after him. During that time, refusing to follow an order given by the *"Generalísimo"* was to beg for a death sentence. In New York, after high school, Johnny studied music composition and instrumentation at the prestigious Julliard School of Music. After graduation, he joined famous musical groups, such as those of Dámaso Pérez Prado, Tito Puente, Stan Kenton, Tito Rodríguez, and the Catalonian Xavier Cugat.

Pacheco y su Charanga, his first album, achieved tremendous success with his *pachanga* rhythm, solidifying this type of combo in city clubs. After that, Pacheco was an established pillar of the new musical movement taking place in New York, and he has remained so for four decades. His career has been recognized by nine Grammy nominations, ten gold records, and many awards that credit his creative talent as composer, band leader, arranger, and musical producer. He is among the pioneers of the *salsa* movement established during the preeminence of the Fania All Stars, the world in which Celia was the indisputable Empress of Rhythm. In 1980 Celia realized that the time had come to be thankful for all the bounties that life had given her. With this in mind, Johnny Pacheco composed a number mentioned before, *"La dicha mía"* (My Good Fortune), a song that reviewed the full course of her triumphs, through the Sonora Matancera (*Allá en mi Cuba / la más popular /*), Tito Puente, Pacheco himself, and Willie Colón, and even Pete (el Conde) Rodríguez, Papo Lucca and the Sonora Ponceña (*Lo primero que yo hago al despertar / es dar gracias a Dios todos los días / y rezarle a todos los santos / y agradecerles la dicha mía /*) (The first thing I do when I wake up / is to thank God every day / and say my prayers to all the saints / to thank them for my good fortune).

Papo (1976), putting more emphasis on the traditional *son* and the *guaracha*, with innovative tones; *Celia y Johnny eternos* (1978); *Celia, Johnny y Pete* (1980); and *Celia y Johnny de nuevo* (1985), which closed the *salsa* chapter in which Pete (el Conde) Rodríguez, Justo Betancourt, and Papo Lucca had also participated. After this, no one could dispute Celia's well-earned title of "Queen of Salsa."

Among Celia's favorite recordings, she confided that from all the albums she had recorded in her life, she felt most proud of the one called *Reflexiones*, with the Sonora Matancera, which included such classic numbers as *"Marcianita," "No me mires más," "Caramelos," "Mi cocodrilo verde," "Ya te lo dije," "Mágica luna," "Suena el cuero," "Pregones de San Cristóbal,"* and of the one titled *Celia y Johnny*, which she recorded for Vaya Records with the Dominican flutist in 1974, and which included all-time hits like *"Toro mata," "Lo tuyo es mental," "Canto a La Habana," "El pregón del pescador,"* and *"Química,"* among others, "because this was a record from which five or six numbers stuck to me."

"Toro mata" is an Afro-Peruvian rhythm that Celia brought into her repertory after a visit to the South Ameri-

can country. The theme had been taken by Carlos Soto de la Colina, ex member of the Conjunto Perú Negro, from a former version by brother and sister Nicomedes and Victoria Santa Cruz in their work *Cumanana*. The number refers to the difficulties that black slaves faced when attempting bullfighting. *¿Cómo puede usted torear, compadre, / si el toro mata /* was the original version, adding that *la coló no le permite, compadre, hacer el quite /* (How can you do bullfighting, my friend, / when the bull kills. / Your [skin] color does not allow you, my friend, to make the pass). In Soto's new version, and in Celia's voice, we hear: *Toro mataí, / toro mata, toro mata / rumbambero, toro mata. / Apolo no le permite hacé el quite a mi chiche, toro mata. /*

A lot of fun and nonsense has been added to the song.

22

La Lupe

*L*upe *Victoria Yolí (La Lupe),* born December 23, 1936, became a musical phenomenon without precedent on the New York scene in the mid 1960s. She presented a solid rivalry for Celia during this time. However, a series of unforeseen circumstances twisted the brilliant future that La Lupe's talent had in store for her. Despite being under contract with the Tico label, which was acquired by Fania Records in 1975, the Cuban singer did not fit the *salsa* vision that Masucci had in mind for his group, and she was removed from the payroll. A strange case, since at the moment of her greatest glory she had been one of the most popular performers signed with the record company. Masucci was interested in repackaging former hits rather than promoting new music by La Lupe. It was evident that the owner of Fania Records leaned toward the voice and personality of Celia Cruz. He was intent on making her the Queen of Salsa. Around this same time, La Lupe had some troubles that hurt her as a performer.

First, in 1964, there was a freak accident at her home. She had been searching with a candle for a *santería* necklace that had fallen under her bed, and the mattress caught fire. Her whole apartment was gutted. Even though she was unhurt, she lost all her savings, and had to start over. Then her obsession with spiritualism and *santería* (into which she was initiated in 1969 as saint *Ocanto Mi*, crowned *Oshún*, and daughter of *Elegguá*) drove her to spend large sums of money, which, together with poor budgeting skills and numerous expenditures, forced her to file for bankruptcy. She also suffered chronic problems with her vocal cords, not to mention a back injury, caused by another domestic accident, which kept her in constant pain. Besides, her insistence on managing herself had, by 1977, turned her career into shambles.

One of La Lupe's last performances was at the Teatro Puerto Rico in New York. That night she included in her repertory her classic theme "*¿Qué te pedí?*," which she had recorded with Tito Puente; "*Oriente*," her emotional homage to the Cuban province where she was born, as well as hit numbers by Tite Curet Alonso: "*La Tirana*" and "*Puro teatro*." It would be unfair to attribute to Celia the artistic downfall of La Lupe, since while she was at her peak from 1966 to 1972, *La Guarachera* was trying to make inroads into the United States with her first recordings with Tito Puente. At no point did these recordings come close to topping the popularity charts, with the exception of "*Acuario*," which Celia mentions in her song "*La dicha mía*" (My Good Fortune): *Con la Sonora Matancera, "Caramelos," / caramelo', caramelo' a kilo, / y con Tito Puente, "Acu-*

ariooo," / y con Pacheco, "Químbara" / químbara cum químbara;" / con Willie Colón, "Usted abusó," / abusó, abusó. / Esa dicha me la dio el Señor / (With the Sonora Matancera, *"Caramelos,"* / candies, penny-candies, / and with Tito Puente, *"Acuarió,"* / and with Pacheco, *"Quím-bara"* (...) / with Willie Colón, *"Usted abusó,"* (...) / The Lord has granted me this good fortune).

Celia's star was shining brighter with each Fania concert presentation. At the same time, each album that La Lupe recorded with Johnny Pacheco caused her star to grow dimmer. She ended up in the direst poverty. Her last three recordings could not rescue her. *"Un encuentro con La Lupe"* (1974), *"La pareja"* (con Tito Puente, 1978), and *"Algo nuevo"* (1980) went by practically unnoticed and with little commercial promotion from Fania Records. La Lupe died in her sleep from a heart attack on February 29, 1992. She was only fifty-five years old. A crowd of thousands of sad admirers, some in hysterics, gathered at the *Iglesia de Dios* (the Church of God) in the Bronx to bid farewell to the one who had been a Queen of Latin Song. In her honor, La Lupe Way, at the intersection of 140th Street and Saint Ann Avenue in the Bronx, was dedicated on June 13, 2002.

23

Willie Colón, Ray Barretto, and Papo Lucca

Celia's big hits with Fania Records kept coming. She worked especially well with Willie Colón. In 1977, they got together to record *Solo ellos pudieron hacer este álbum* (Only They Could Have Made This Album). With innovative tunes that drew from Brazilian and Mexican music, also including a *merengue* and a *bomba,* "*Usted abusó*" (You Abused Me), became a big success. It was recorded under the direction of Colón, who also did the arrangement. The lyrics of the song say: *Usted abusó, sacó provecho de mí, abusó. / Sacó partido de mí, abusó / de mi cariño, usted abusó. / Y me perdona, por seguir con este tema. / Yo no sé escribir poemas / ni tampoco una canción, / sino un tema de amor. / Cada palabra, cada verso me recuerda / el momento cuando le entregué mi amor. / Usted abusó.* (You abused, took advantage of me, you abused me. / You took advantage of me, you

abused me / you abused my affection, you abused. / And
forgive me for insisting on this theme. / I don't know how
to write poems / or a song either, / but only a theme of love.
/ Each word, each verse reminds me / of the moment when
I gave you my love. / You abused. /) Brazilian singer María
Creuza had popularized the song before as "*Voce abusou*,"
and Celia knew how to interpret it with emotion, always
keeping it in her repertory.

Willie Colón remembers their working together on
those numbers. "I was very apprehensive, because she was
already so famous and I was just beginning. She was very
professional. She always looked for the best way to do the
work because for Celia that was the most important thing.
Her work was above the petty concerns of ego, and that
surprised me. She asked me to direct her. It scared me to
have a star ask that of me. The truth is that I learned a lot
from her. What impressed me most was the high level at
which she dealt with business, how she conducted herself.
She was a great lady in every sense of the word. There were
two Celias: the colleague with whom one shared things
after the show, and the artist who, once up on the boards,
infused everybody with her incredible energy." Celia was
matron of honor when Colón got married.

Colón, born to Puerto Rican parents on April 28, 1950,
in the South Bronx, was only twenty-seven years old when
he and Celia recorded their first album. He was the Fania
All Stars' youngest musician when he joined them. He had
entered the music scene during the *bugalú* (boogaloo) rage,
which was a fusion between Latin music and rhythm and
blues. This singer/trumpet player had begun to carve an
important niche in the *salsa* circuit when he recorded his
first album for Fania Records, *El Malo*, in which Héctor
Lavoe also made his debut.

Héctor Pérez Lavoe was born to a musical family in Ponce, Puerto Rico, in 1946. At seventeen he was already singing with a band and always getting into trouble, when he decided to go to New York in search of fame and fortune, against his father's wishes. He met Johnny Pacheco, recorded a hit with Willie Colón, and sang in his band at El Tropicoro Club, but he could not handle sudden success and developed a drug problem. His first solo album, *La Voz* (The Voice), was also a hit. His first collaboration with Fania was *"Mi gente,"* also a hit. This very much loved *"jibarito"* had a gift for improvisation and developed a coarse street style. His successful numbers were *"Calle Luna, calle Sol," "La murga de Panamá," "Periódico de ayer"* (by prolific composer Catalino [Tite] Curet Alonso), *"Rompe saragüey,"* and *"Quítate tú."* He became known as The Voice and was compared to Frank Sinatra. After many personal tragedies and a failed suicide attempt, he died in total poverty in New York in 1993.

Colón cultivated a tough guy image, which he maintained well into the seventies, following a lifestyle similar to that portrayed in his compositions after *"El Malo"* (The Bad One). Lacking the academic foundation of Johnny Pacheco or Eddie Palmieri, self-taught Willie Colón introduced two trombones with an urban sound of social sensibility that was well received by the Hispanic community, particularly when he extracted an aggressive tone from his instruments and gave his lyrics a dramatic charge underscored by the charismatic presence of his vocalist Héctor Lavoe. In the twelve albums they did together between 1967 and 1975, Colón included in his compositions violent elements from daily life, personal disappointments, sometimes with tragic connotations, and stories about his neighborhood that deeply touched the popular tastes.

Willie Colón also recorded hit songs as a soloist, and together with other famous singers like Rubén Blades (born in Panama to Cuban parents), with whom he shared musical affinities and a political identification that would later lead him to run for public office and to become a human rights activist.

After Willie and Celia's success with *Sólo ellos pudieron hacer este álbum*, they combined forces again to do *Celia y Willie* in 1981 and *The Winners* in 1987. By then, Celia had achieved what she had always dreamed of: the general acceptance of music lovers and *salsa* fans, which numbered in the millions around the world.

During her long career, the Guarachera of the World accumulated many honors and national and international prizes, among them the Grammy in 1990 for best Latin album, *Ritmo en el corazón*, which she recorded in 1988 with Ray Barretto. Barretto is one of the big *salsa* stars who had the opportunity to accompany Celia in many concerts and recordings. Ray Barretto, the conga percussionist, was born in Brooklyn April 29, 1929, to a family that had immigrated from Puerto Rico. After serving in the army, he returned to Harlem, and listening to Duke Ellington and Count Bassie, he was seduced by jazz. He began his career by participating in jam-sessions with famous jazz musicians, such as Charlie Parker, Max Roach, Cal Tjader, and Dizzy Gillespie, and then joined José Curbelo's orchestra and worked for the first time with Afro-Cuban music. In 1957, he replaced Mongo Santamaría playing the conga in Tito Puente's band, where he took part in the hit album *Dance Mania*. His debut as bandleader and composer was in 1961, when he organized a *charanga* (with flute and violins), which was beginning to popularize the rhythm that gave name to his production *Pachanga with Barretto*. It was followed by *Latino*, in which he introduced a tenor sax, and then by *Charanga moderna*, which included his big hit "*El Watusi*," one of the twenty bestselling records of 1963.

Barretto signed with Fania Records in 1967, taking a decisive step toward stardom. He transformed his orchestra in order to record "Acid," an R & B number with a jazz feeling that made his name known in the Latin community, and he became even more popular when he joined the Fania All Stars in 1968. Barretto recorded, with vocalists Rubén Blades and Tito Gómez, another chart-topper in 1975. With various hits and misses, the *conguero* joined Celia Cruz and Adalberto Santiago in 1983 to record *Tremendo trío*. It was immediately embraced by *salsa* fans, and also won the Asociación de Críticos de Espectáculos (ACE) Award as best *salsa* album of the year. With their second production, *Ritmo en el corazón*, they saw their efforts again rewarded, obtaining the Grammy in 1990.

Another singer closely associated with the names of Ray Barretto and Celia Cruz is Adalberto Santiago, a *sonero* who managed to join the Fania All Stars after being a member of Barretto's orchestra since 1966. In his native Ciales, Puerto Rico, he became a fan of the Cuban *soneros* Benny Moré and Félix Chappotín. He began his musical career singing in trios, and accompanying himself on the guitar or the bass, but in New York during the *salsa* fever, he was one of the most sought-after backups among all the musical groups. In 1973, he abandoned Barretto to form Típica '73, an orchestra with four other members, which was the featured group in some of the Fania All Stars concerts. Later he joined the group Los Kimbos, before he came back to Barretto's fold to record with Celia Cruz *Tremendo trío,* which received international recognition. As a composer, he has distinguished himself in themes that delve deeply into his ancestral roots, like *"Aprende,"* with Típica '73, and *"Enamorado,"* with Los Kimbos, besides some *bombas* and *merengues.*

One of the pianists Celia Cruz preferred was Papo Lucca, an arranger, producer, composer, and musical director of the Sonora Ponceña. The friendship between Celia and Papo Lucca started in 1974 when the musician was invited to join the sessions that led to the recording of the album *Celia & Johnny.* Lucca, a child prodigy, had already recorded at twelve a master piano solo in "Smoke Mambo." Born in Ponce, Puerto Rico, in 1946, Enrique Arsenio Lucca inherited his vocation for music from his father. Don Enrique (Quique) Lucca, a guitarist, had founded the Orquesta Internacional in 1944, but in 1954 he renamed it the Sonora Ponceña in honor of the Sonora Matancera because he specialized in playing the *son.* Papo Lucca made his orchestra debut at eight, after which he became an irreplaceable member of that musical family. His first arrangement was for *"Caramelos,"* included in Tito Puente's record *Pachanga con Puente.*

The Sonora Ponceña rose to greater popularity when, under contract with Inca Records, it was acquired by Jerry Masucci and became part of Fania Records. In 1976, Lucca replaced Larry Harlow as pianist in the Fania All Stars, playing the accompaniment for Celia in numerous concerts until Masucci decided to group some of Celia's classic numbers together with Johnny Pacheco, Justo Betancourt, and Papo Lucca in the production *Recordando el ayer.* This album included such titles as *"Besito de coco," "Ritmo, tambor y flores," "Reina Rumba," "Vamos a guarachar,"* and *"El yerbero moderno."*

This album also featured Justo Betancourt, a Matanzas native and a traditional *sonero* who was able to widen the scope of the *guaracha* with innovative colorations that earned him fans and recognition from the seventies on. When he arrived in New York, Papo worked with the orchestra led by Orlando Marín and Johnny Pacheco, before joining the Sonora Matancera as a vocalist and touring the United States and Latin America with it for five years. Later he sang with big names like Eddie Palmieri, Ray Barretto, and Mongo Santamaría.

His popularity as a *salsa* singer began to take root when he recorded *Los dinámicos*, with Pacheco's collaboration, and his *salsa* classic of all time "*Pa' bravo yo.*" Justo Betancourt was one of the first soloists that Fania Records had under contract in 1972, and it was with this record company that he had the opportunity to accompany *La Guarachera del Mundo*. In 1976, he settled in Puerto Rico, where he organized the Borincuba orchestra of which Tito Rojas was a member. Sometime later he would excel as a soloist leading his own group. Betancourt returned to New York in 1985 to record a song for the album *Homenaje a Benny Moré, Vol. 3*, with Celia Cruz and Tito Puente's orchestra.

One of the most loved *salsa* musicians, the prolific Pete (el Conde) Rodríguez, had also participated in volume 2 of the trilogy in honor of Benny Moré, singing the famous songs of the *Bárbaro del Ritmo*. *El Conde* (the Count) had been given this nickname for his distinguished bearing, his affability, and his unfailing readiness to be helpful. He was a talented *sonero,* at the right moment bringing out his warm, harmonious voice. He also had a talent for playing the *maracas*, singing backup, and dancing onstage. Rodríguez was an artist whom Celia very much admired, musically and personally.

Pedro Juan Rodríguez was el Condé's real name. Born in Ponce, Puerto Rico, he made New York his home. In 1963, he was playing the *conga* and singing at a bar in the Bronx when Johnny Pacheco invited him to participate in Barretto's recording *"Suavito."* He then became the vocalist for the album *Cañonazo*, with Pacheco's reorganized orchestra, inaugurating the golden age of Fania Records in 1964. From a historic point of view, this is a fundamental album, because it signals the beginning of the end of the *charanga* craze and starts the transition to the sound of *conjuntos* with vocalists, trumpets, percussion (*timbales, conga, bongó*), double bass, and piano as the basic structure of the *salsa* orchestra.

El Conde was identified with the *sonero* and *charanguero* traditions, and from this time on he participated in numerous recording projects, including his popular album *Este negro sí es sabroso*, which included his hits *"Pueblo latino"* by Catalino (Tite) Curet Alonso, and his well-known *"Catalina la O"* by composer Johnny Ortiz, also included in the documentary *Our Latin Thing*. In 1980, he joined Celia and Johnny to form their famous trio, considered by critics to be one of the most important contributions of Caribbean music. Such numbers as *"Me voy contigo"* and *"La madre rumba"* had a permanent impact.

To be enjoyed also in this record is the original version of *"La dicha mía,"* in which the Queen of Salsa, as mentioned before, gives thanks for her good fortune in life, and recounts her professional career, rendering a moving homage to the musicians that have accompanied her.

24

More Musical Friends

Right after the success of the first experiment joining Celia with other musicians and singers working in the same style, the next step was to put together the talents of Celia and Papo Lucca. This resulted in *La Ceiba* in 1979, which Lucca produced, including *"Soy antillana," "Fina estampa," "Ábreme la puerta,"* and *"La ceiba y la siguaraya,"* a number in which Celia rendered an affectionate tribute to the giant ceiba tree, one hundred years old, that she remembered seeing when she was a child living with her aunt Anacleta in the *solar* La Margarita, in the Havana neighborhood of Santos Suárez.

Papo Lucca arranged one of Celia's biggest hits, *"La negra tiene tumbao,"* with Sergio George and Isidro Infante. Also taking part in the recording, watching over the tones, was its producer, Johnny Pacheco, intimately associated with many of the recordings made by the Queen of Salsa during the preceding three decades: *Esa negrita que va caminando / esa negrita tiene su tumbao. / Y cuando la gente la va mirando, / ella baila de lao, / también apretao, apretao, apretao /* (That "*negrita*" that goes by, / that "*negrita*" has her beat. / And when people look at her, /she dances sideways, / and also very tight). Unlike all the further compilations, reissues of classic collections, and re-recordings ad infinitum, the album *La negra tiene tumbao* offers, with sugar, ten brand-new numbers. It is overflowing with tropical rhythms, with fusions, as with rap, providing a combination of trumpets and trombones that Celia insisted was necessary in order to "renew ourselves, not to go on doing the same *salsa*, the same *merengue*. I agree with mixing things up, and though it is not the first time I work with Johnny Pacheco, Sergio George, and Isidro Infante, it is always a very special opportunity to relive beautiful musical experiences with these three geniuses. It is a blessing to have them by my side."

For this second production with Sony Music, Celia invited Puerto Rican musician Mikey Perfecto to add the rap segments. And as usual, there was an invitation to dance with "*Tararea Kumbayea,*" a fusion of very catchy tunes that make the most circumspect of mortals dance with abandon. Her life is summarized in the autobiographical number "*Corazón de rumba,*" in which she says, *Mi bandera es la alegría / y mi causa es cantar* (Joy is my flag, / and my cause is to sing). Her *tumbao* seduced the jury for the Grammy Awards, and they decided to grant the seventy-seven-year-old Celia Cruz the award for best *salsa* recording of the year 2002. *Si quieres llegar primero, / mejor se corre despacio. / Disfruta bien de la vida, cariño, / aunque tomando medidas. ¡Azúcar! /* (If you want to get there first,

/ better run slowly. / Enjoy your life fully, my love, / though taking care. / *Azúcar!*).

Celia had achieved one of her countless big hits with *Tributo a Ismael Rivera* in 1993. She had met Ismael in that necessary transit for musical performers between New York and San Juan. He was one of her favorite vocalists. Of humble origins and gifted with a wondrous voice, Ismael Rivera (Maelo) was a star of Afro-Caribbean music ever since his debut as a *sonero* in his native San Juan during the early fifties. Benny Moré, who was one of his admirers, gave him the moniker of *El Sonero Mayor* (the Greatest Vocalist-Improviser), and he reached international fame when he joined the combo of his childhood friend Rafael Cortijo. From 1953 to 1962 the *Combo de Cortijo* was a star orchestra in Caribbean music, making innovative experiments with Rivera's folk airs in the performance of *bomba* and *plena*, the typical genres of Puerto Rico. As he used to say, his singing reflected the story that the chorus of his people dictated to him, and he assimilated their experiences with the words heard on the corners of his neighborhood.

This music reached so deeply into the New York Latin community that in 1958 the combo was engaged to perform in the legendary Palladium Ballroom, where they played with other orchestras led by Machito, Tito Puente, and Tito Rodríguez. After serving a sentence of a few years for cocaine possession, Rivera organized his own band in 1967. With *Los Cachimbos* and a renewed Christian faith following a visit to the Cristo Negro de Portobello (Panama), his troubled musical career continued.

One of Maelo's best-remembered performances was a duet with Celia Cruz and the Fania All Stars, "*Cúcala*," recorded live in 1978. He had already sung that number in 1959 with Cortijo, and Johnny Pacheco included it in *Tremendo caché,* which he did for the Queen of Salsa in 1975. Like his compatriot Pete (el Conde) Rodríguez, Maelo (*El Sonero Mayor*) died at home of a heart ailment. The album Celia recorded in honor of her old friend and colleague included his most memorable hits, such as "*Las caras lindas*" (by his friend Curet Alonso), "*Quítate de la vía, Perico,*" "*Perfume de rosas,*" "*Maquinalandera,*" "*Yo no quiero piedras en mi camino,*" "*El negro bembón,*" and "*El Nazareno.*"

For a time it was often said that the best way to give a new musician a career boost was to pair him with Celia in a recording. But in reality Celia was able to recognize talent and chose very carefully who worked with her.

25

New York, Wednesday, July 23, 2003

Talula Medina and Carlos García were pursuing the difficult mission of finding the last resting place for Celia Cruz at Woodlawn cemetery, the day after she was buried, in order to render a personal tribute to the deceased Guarachera. Talula and Carlos tried to find their way through the labyrinthine burial grounds, consulting maps, references to maps, and photos in hopes of locating their objective. The peaceful surroundings of the beautiful hundred-and-forty-year-old cemetery, at the north end of the *"Condado de la Salsa,"* was in obvious contrast to the energy and eagerness of the couple.

Celia was granted a funeral that rivaled that of a president or great historic personality. The vigil for her in New York was held in the same chapel that had held the remains of luminaries like Judy Garland, Jacqueline Kennedy and her brother-in-law Robert Kennedy, as well as Tito Rodríguez and Jerry Masucci, who brought Celia to the heights of her success. At Woodlawn Cemetery, Celia's last resting place, other famous musical stars have been buried: Louis Armstrong, Duke Ellington, Billie Holiday, and Miles Davis. It is also the resting place of other important figures in the world of *salsa*, such as Frank Grillo (Machito), Héctor Lavoe, Charlie Palmieri, and La Lupe, Celia's rival in New York.

Instead of her beloved Cuba, to which the performer could never return, Celia and Pedro Knight had chosen a plot in that cemetery for their family pantheon. Every two or three blocks, the followers of the Diva would ask a member of the army of gardeners that were taking care of the place, but all had the same answer. Stopping the motor of his mowing machine, one of the gardeners told them, "We don't know where she is. In the case of celebrities, there is a lot of secrecy, because there are people who might try to desecrate their tombs." García turned to Talula, "Just imagine, with all those jewels and other belongings," he said. "I'm sorry, but you are not going to be able to find her," the worker said politely. "God bless her, wherever she is!" Talula Medina said. And after a pause, she wondered, "And what about her sister, the one who came from Cuba? Is she going to stay?" To which García riposted, "What is she going to go back for? Someone has to take care of Pedro now, and she will be fine here."

Celia must be resting in peace.

26

The Eighties, Nineties, and the New Millennium

To honor her long association with the Sonora Matancera, in 1982 Celia Cruz rejoined her old friends from the Sonora to record *Feliz encuentro.* Celia wanted to do this grateful recognition with brand-new numbers like the one that gives title to the album, "*Feliz encuentro,*" and songs like "*Quinto mayor,*" "*El becerrito,*" "*Tierra prometida,*" "*Herencia africana,*" and "*Lamento de amor,*" and then to end with "*Celia y la Matancera.*"

She reunited with the band yet again, seven years later, when actress and announcer Gilda Mirós organized the "most extraordinary historical and cultural event of the Hispanic world," to celebrate sixty-five years of the Sonora Matancera.

From Thursday, June 1, 1989 at Carnegie Hall, to Saturday, June 3 at the Acoustic Band Shell in Central Park, there was a series of concerts that gathered a multitude of nostalgic fans and young admirers who for the first time saw together under the same roof such old glories of Caribbean music. Producer Mirós achieved the feat of reuniting the surviving members of the *conjunto*: Javier Vázquez at the piano; Félix Vega Junior, first trumpet; Calixto Leicea, second trumpet; Ken Fradley, third trumpet; Elpidio Vázquez on bass; Mario Muñoz (Papaíto) on *timbales* and *paila*; Alberto Valdés, *conga* and backup; Carlos Manuel Díaz (Caíto), *maracas*, backup, and *tambora*; and Eladio Peguero, known in the music world as "*Yayo el Indio*," vocalist, chorus, and also on the *güiro*.

In New York, Gilda Mirós gathered under the baton of Rogelio Martínez and his guitar: from Argentina, the *ex-pachanguero* Carlos Argentino and Leo Marini (*La Voz que Acaricia*); from Puerto Rico, singer-composer Bobby Capó; Daniel Santos (*el Inquieto Anacobero*), from his quiet retirement in Ocala, Florida; from Barranquilla, Colombia (though he lives in Caracas, Venezuela), Nelson Pinedo; from Miami, Roberto Torres (*el Caballo Viejo*); from the Dominican Repúblic, "*El Negrito del Batey*" (Alberto Beltrán); from Cuba (exiled in Mexico), Celio González, known as "*El Flaco de Oro*"; as well as Vicentico Valdés (*la Voz Elástica*); the singer who arrived in Mexico with the Sonora in 1960, Alberto Pérez Sierra; and of course, the star of stars, ladies and gentlemen, dear fans, *La Inigualable* (the Unmatchable), *La Guarachera del Mundo* is here with us (anticipated ovation), the Queen of Salsa...CELIA CRUZ!!

The audience gave her a long and raucous standing ovation until Celia gestured, with a pleased smile, looking splendid in her red *rumbera* costume with flounces, and a curly wig. She shouts in her clarion voice into the microphone: "*Azúuuucar!*" And now the whole place is shaking, the window panes in legendary Carnegie Hall are vibrating, the nervous ushers look quizzically at each other; it seems that the balconies are coming down, until there is a hush and her fascinating voice is heard, and with the sounds of trumpets and percussion, she intones: *Songo le dio a Borondongo, / Borondongo le dio a Bernabé / Bernabé le pegó a Mochilanga / porque le echó burundanga, / le jincha los pies, Monina* (Songo hit Borondongo, / Borondongo hit Bernabé / Bernabé hit Mochilanga / 'cause he threw a lot of garbage at him, / which makes his feet swell, Monina). And then, with a wink of her smiling eyes, she asks: "Why did Songo hit Borondongo?" and the audience chorus responds, "Because Borondongo hit Bernabé." "Why did Bernabé hit Mochilanga?" "Because Mochilanga threw burundanga at him…" Because of its humor, this is the most famous tongue-twister in Latin music.

For that unforgettable birthday party, vocalists Jorge Maldonado and Welfo Gutiérrez (under the artistic direction of Joe Quijano) were also invited. A few could not attend for various reasons: singer Carmen Delia Dipiní, the duo of Olga and Tony, Gloria Díaz, Willie (el Baby) Rodríguez, and Justo Betancourt.

The Sonora Matancera has been included in the *Guinness Book of World Records* as the musical group with most radio programs in the world, the largest number of recordings issued, reissued, compiled with old or new covers, and it holds the record for having singers of the most nationalities, not to mention a long list of hits that continue to be close to the hearts of its faithful followers, record collectors, and tropical music historians.

During the eighties, the *salsa* boom began to wane. It had started in the late sixties, propelled by Fania Records, the Fania All Stars, and the handful of impresarios who had become rich with the singular bonanza. A series of circumstances combined to produce this crisis, and a very important one was the exodus of musicians and vocalists in search of independent outlets, mostly motivated by economic reasons, causing a diaspora.

Rubén Blades and Willie Colón joined forces to sue Fania Records for a supposed nonfulfillment of their royalty payments according to contract. In fact, they engaged a lawyer who specialized in the entertainment business, in order to demand the cancellation of overdue quotas that both artists had accumulated. Besides, in its eagerness to expand, Fania Records had bought the licenses of all the *salsa* record labels, becoming an unmanageable monopoly for Jerry Masucci and Johnny Pacheco, who was more interested in concentrating his energies on his musical vocation.

During this time, some new musical groups managed to bring a wave of fresh air to the production of well-known stars, like Bobby Rodríguez and his La Compañía; Típica '73, with Sonny Bravo and Alfredo de la Fe; La Flamboyán, led by Frankie Dante; Ángel Canales and the pianist Marcolino Diamond with the Conjunto Sabor; and Los Hermanos Lebrón, with a style halfway between that of New York *salsa* and the special flavor of Cortijo and his Combo. However, none of them, not even the duo of Richie Ray and Bobby Cruz, who were a musical wonder, ever managed to equal the popularity of the Fania All Stars with the charismatic and unexcelled voice of Celia Cruz.

Also contributing to this decadence was the slow but incisive incursion into the popular taste of the Dominican *merengue*, Juan Luis Guerra's poetic *bachata*, and the romantic ballad style of Julio Iglesias. Latin Americans in the United

States were going through a transformation. One must keep in mind the sociopolitical changes occurring on the rest of the continent which gave rise to a renaissance of native musical genres and to the fusions between popular music and the folk music of various regions, as well as the so-called erotic or romantic *salsa*, which the extreme moralists called *pornosalsa*. This music abandoned the Latino neighborhood clubs and moved to the suburban hotels in the voices of Frankie Ruiz, Gilberto Santa Rosa, and Tony Vega. And because of a decrease in the demand for *salsa* albums, distributors like Columbia and Atlantic Records renegotiated contracts with terms that were less favorable to the Fania company. Also contributing to their decline was the failure of the film *The Last Fight*, which featured Willie Colón and Rubén Blades. Masucci had laid his best hopes for recovery in this project. With all these difficulties, the moving force that Masucci represented was exhausted after fifteen years of hard work, and he announced his retirement.

By the late eighties, only a few albums were recorded, and they never achieved the popularity of *salsa* in its golden era. In 1979, the Fania All Stars (without Celia) traveled for the first time to the Festival de Varadero (Cuba), where they recorded *Havana Jam*, which had only versions of old numbers and was a disappointment.

Then came *Spanish Fever*, which passed without glory despite having excellent jazz musicians and a good cut, "*Sin tu cariño*," by Rubén Blades. At the end of 1979, *Cross Over* included the much-admired "*Isadora*" by Maestro Tite Curet Alonso, which Celia sang, saving the album from oblivion. Experiments with Latin jazz followed, trying to break into the Anglo market with *California Jam* and *Social Change*, which included as guest artist a saxophonist from Argentina, Leandro (Gato) Barbieri in a pleasant rendering of *"Samba pa' ti"* by Santana. In the same way, the Gypsy Kings' greatest hits were assimilated into a *salsa* rhythm, and there was a failed return to the *charanga*, to cite just a few.

To celebrate Fania's twentieth anniversary in 1986, the live concerts in Africa and Japan were reissued, and in 1996, to commemorate the thirtieth anniversary there was a tour with the same old stars, though some important ones were missing and the aura of their glorious past was gone. The Fania All Stars ended its production of new material with the album *Lo que pide la gente* (What the People Want), which included an energetic Latin jam session and the numbers *"Por eso yo canto salsa"* and *"Usando el coco,"* two masterly renditions by Celia and Héctor Lavoe.

It is nonetheless important to remember that the art of Celia Cruz was enhanced by the Fania All Stars, which established her as the Queen of Salsa, making her a revered icon in all of Latin America and an ambassador for Caribbean music the world over. Celia knew how to take advantage of the historic moment in her career to make herself a star above all stars, gaining immense popularity until she became a magnet for the multitudes and a wondrous seller of records. Her participation in the Fania All Stars, moreover, guaranteed her a privileged place as a concertist in all kinds of musical activities. Toward the end of her career, the greatest *salsera* kept a schedule of about seventy concerts annually at an age when many of her colleagues were enjoying peaceful retirement. Her appearances were always more profitable than the income received by any of her colleagues, but she stayed with the Fania All Stars until her last tour, in March 2001.

Throughout her life, Celia's participation in charitable endeavors was outstanding. After attaining both fame and fortune, she established the Celia Cruz Non-Profit Foundation in 2002. The foundation offers scholarships for young musicians, thus fulfilling one of her most cherished dreams. About this she said, "I had been dreaming for a long time of creating such a foundation, but with the heavy schedule of performances and constant traveling, I didn't have the opportunity. This new step renews my interest and my desire to continue contributing to our society." One mission of the foundation is to provide Hispanic children of little or no means with scholarships, so that their dreams may come true in the music world; it also provides help for cancer victims. Besides Celia's own resources—there are some indications that at the end of her career she was making more than four million dollars a year—the foundation has received donations from individuals, government institutions, and private businesses.

A good portion of her income throughout her career was anonymously donated to charitable endeavors. Omer Pardillo-Cid, president of her foundation and her professional representative, has emphasized the fact that Celia Cruz was a genuinely caring human being who always collaborated anonymously with noble causes. Her widower, Pedro Knight, explained that "she did not like her left hand to know what her right hand was doing, that she was a giving, generous person. She was not like many other artists who do something and then reveal it to all the media. Celia has done hundreds of good things around the world, and she never spoke about them; this was not even known in New York. In Perú, for instance, she has built homes for poor children, as well as in Nicaragua, Venezuela, Honduras, and Costa Rica. She has devoted her time and talent to good causes, and we want to keep alive her image and her real personal character."

On October 21, 2003, in commemoration of Celia's birth in 1925, the Celia Cruz Foundation granted its first scholarships to five young Latinos with scant economic resources, so that they could study music at the school of their choice. Since her death, the foundation continues to operate, allowing the Queen of Salsa to keep giving out her "sugar" to the neediest within the Latin community. Celia requested that all box office receipts from the concert given in her honor on March 13, 2003, be donated to her foundation. During her wake, her family asked people to send donations to the Celia Cruz Foundation instead of flowers. For her part, Sofía Ayllon, the promoter for Sony Records, confirmed that a portion of the revenue accrued from the sale of the single *"Diagnóstico"* be sent to the Celia Cruz Foundation for the scholarships and the fight against cancer.

27

Celia and Commercialism

I t is at this point in her career that Celia decided to pluralize her many musical interests, venturing into other genres and creating fusions with rhythms alien to the *salsa* that fit her wondrous voice, and she did this without rejecting her musical past. "*El que no cambia se estanca*" (He who does not change, stagnates) was the Spanish proverb she always repeated when she talked about her incursions into various genres. Therefore, to pigeonhole her with the familiar labels of "*Guarachera*" or "Queen of Salsa" would be to limit her reach without really defining her. Above all, it would be fitting to call her Queen of Popular Music because her songs are joyous hymns for any public, and the language does not matter. Celia started to develop projects together with various musicians who broadened her artistic spectrum and took her voice to other audiences without any need to pursue the longed-for crossover that was the ambition of other vocalists.

The Rumba Queen, as Colombian writer Umberto Valverde called her, even participated in the album *Tropical Tribute to The Beatles* in 1996, in which she sang "*Obladí, obladá,*" a theme that denotes the influence of Latin music in the use of *clave* that the Liverpool group had assimilated, but adds the element of joyous *salsa* that seasons this number. The song, originally written by Paul McCartney, was included in the double album *The Beatles*. The adaptation to Spanish was done by J. Córcega, who combined elements from the life of Celia and Pedro Knight: *Pocos años después / un hogar, tranquilo hogar, / un nidito de amor / para disfrutar / del cariño de los dos. / Pedro dirigiendo, hace su labor / y sus chicos le van al compás. / Celia, en casa, colorea su rubor / y por la noche con la orquesta va a cantar / Obladí Obladá, vamos pa'llá / que la fiesta va a empezar. / Obladí Obladá, vamos pa'llá / mira que sabrosa está.* (A few years later / a home, a peaceful home, / a little love nest / to enjoy / the love they have for each other. / Pedro does his job leading [the orchestra] / and his boys follow his rhythm. / Celia, at home, allows her blush to color her cheeks / and in the evening she sings with the orchestra / Obladí Obladá, let's go, / the party is beginning. / Obladí Obladá, let's go, / see how good it is.)

On a London BBC program hosted by Lina María Holguín, Celia explained her participation in this project, remembering that when it was presented to her, Ralph Mercado and Óscar Gómez had already selected the songs. She would have preferred the song "Yesterday" (which was sung in this compilation by José Feliciano) because at the height of the British group's popularity she was working seasonally in Acapulco and on many occasions she had to sing "Yesterday," in her bad English, to the American tourists. "I don't believe Ralph Mercado has committed sacrilege," she added about the controversial recording, "since this music can be done in any rhythm, even as a *merengue*. And young people identify with these melodies; besides, The Beatles are a phenomenon of this century," she concluded.

To take advantage of her moment of glory, there were also some opportunistic projects based solely on the pretext of her popularity, with the lone goal of making money. Her hair stylist, makeup artist, and wardrobe mistress, Ruth Sánchez, let her imagination run free with a proposal to make a doll in Celia's image, a kind of Black Barbie that would be a sensation among her fans. The doll would sing "*Guantanamera*" and cry "*Azúcar!*" The basic design was presented and approved by a group of investors who decided to support it. Celia and her manager then, Ralph Mercado, would receive a percentage of the profits. But Celia explained that she had joined this project because Mrs. Sánchez needed a sizable amount of money for her sick son, who required special care and treatment.

Before the doll debuted in 1998, Celia stated that if the expected profits were obtained from this initiative, she would be proud of having helped one of her most faithful assistants. She was not going to receive even one doll, but she was going to buy one, hoping for the success of the project. One of her requirements was that the dolls have a wig like hers, the same makeup with thick eyelashes like her fake ones, and a costume like hers, with flounces, and hoops like those of a *rumbera*. The doll was manufactured, and Celia was happy to know that by using her image, she was helping a friend. She even promoted the doll wherever she performed. Since Celia had no children, she occasionally played with her doll (which seemed to be lighter skinned), changing its clothes, combing its hair, and saying funny things to it.

One of the projects that was harshly criticized (a news outlet even characterized it as "diabolic") was her "psychic line." Celia defended herself, explaining that Michael Jackson's sister, Sylvester Stallone's mother, singer Dionne Warwick, and many other famous people had psychic lines in their names. Moreover, Celia added that all this criticism had had a positive aspect: it had benefited the sales of her last album. According to her, the same Miami lawyer (she did not mention his name) who had started Dionne Warwick's line had offered to back hers. The idea was better than having a psychic television program. The famous singer could be heard claiming that the line had good psychics, whom she herself had certified through testing and personal interviews; but in reality she was no psychic, she was just endorsing the line. Her role was limited to a recorded greeting: "You have reached Celia Cruz's psychic line; I am going to transfer you to one of my best psychics." As she explained, "I do my job, and the psychics do theirs with the clients. The line has been quite a success, people call at all hours, and I am not sorry to have started it; on the contrary, I think I have done a good deed and if I had to do it again, I would not hesitate for a second." She added that Enrique Rudulfo, the Venezuelan in charge of the program, had suggested to her that she explain her real motives on a visit to Cristina Saralegui's program, but she never did.

Celia was convinced that many famous people were disposed to endorse such services, including people wealthier than she was, and that negative criticism had never intimidated her to stop carrying out her objectives. Instead, it was a great stimulus to venture into the riskiest projects, no matter how wild they seemed. "I should have retired already," she explained, "but it is now that I am receiving the best and most challenging job offers: films, soap operas, and recordings. These are the things that encourage me to go on living; no matter how much this enrages my enemies, I continue to share my life with all the needy persons I can reach."

On that same occasion she commented on the negative criticism she was receiving for the role of santera that she was playing in a soap opera: "I am not an actress, but I play my part as best I can, and many people liked it. All of this is reflected in the good publicity that I am enjoying. Some people are determined to criticize me, but the more they try to do me harm, the more popularity I gain. So, if I am called for another soap opera, I would gladly say yes."

28

Duets and Boleros by Celia Cruz

Rogelio Martínez, during his time with the Sonora Matancera, did not usually encourage duets, so only rarely is a second voice heard in his recordings, except for the backup by Laíto and Caíto, who sometimes added a bit of dialogue. In the 1954 *guajira "En el bajío"* (In the Lowlands) by composer J. C. Fumero-Castro, Celia sings in with Laíto: *El domingo próximo / espérame allá en el bajío / y verás el gran palmar / que tengo juntito a mi bohío. / Linda guajira, cómo te quiero. / Y al despuntar el día, / qué alegre canta el gallo. / Divisarás desde allí mi sitial / y mi caballo, / que será nuestra felicidad.* (Next Sunday / wait for me in the lowlands / and you will see the great royal palms / I have next to my *bohío* (thatched-roof hut). / My pretty *guajira* (girl from the countryside), how much I love you. / And with the new daybreak, / how happy the rooster sings. / From there you will see my place, / and also my horse, / and we'll be happy). In the 1978 album *Eternos*, with Johnny Pacheco, a fine Dominican voice replaces Laíto's and a melodious flute is added.

In 1955, Celia sang a *bolero* with Alberto Beltrán (*el Negrito del Batey*), "*Contestación a Aunque me cueste la vida*" by Luis Kalaff and Laíto. A year later, with Celio González, she sang "*Madre rumba,*" a *guaracha* by Humberto Jauma. And in 1961 she sang with Carlos Argentino the *bolero* "*Mi amor, buenas noches*" by Roberto Puente. One can also hear, in a live recording at the Havana radio station CMQ, a duet with Bienvenido Granda, "*el Bigote que canta*" (The mustache that sings) in the *guaracha* "*El de la rumba soy yo*" and in "*El pai y la mai,*" *seis chorreado* by Daniel Santos. When Haitian singer Martha Jean Claude went to Havana invited by Celia Cruz, she got herself a contract to sing at the Tropicana. She recorded only one song with the Matancera, the *congo* "*Choucoune*" (Yellow Bird), a Haitian folkloric rhythm that she sings in a duet with Celia. *La Guarachera* had invited Claude to Cuba during one of the many visits Celia made to Haiti. Celia was a Black Goddess in Haiti, and at the airport she got a reception fit for a head of state, with the Municipal Band playing themes from the Sonora Matancera, fireworks, and an overly excited, admiring multitude.

Celia performed her first duet in 1949 while touring in Venezuela with Las Mulatas de Fuego. In the seventies, as Celia's fame expanded all over the world, many vocalists climbed on the bandwagon of her popularity to share it or to advance their own careers. Her generous spirit kept her always open to any sensible suggestion, but she also took care not to enter into opportunistic alliances that would damage the image that she had forged through several decades of hard work. She often donated her participation in benefit concerts for other needy musical stars, or in tributes to those deserving the honor of her presence.

In 1978, Fania Records issued a live disk, recorded in various locales, of fresh, enjoyable *salsa*, which includes a version of an old tune by Rafael Cortijo, "*Cúcala*," sung by Celia in a duet with Ismael (Maelo) Rivera. And in *Commitment*, a 1979 album, one can listen to a marvelous duet by Celia and Pete (el Conde) Rodríguez, titled "*Encántigo*."

During the eighties and nineties, Celia's recordings were a teaching model, a mix of both eclecticism and risk-taking. Though not everything met with the same success, her interpretations of genres other than salsa were well received by her admirers. David Byrne, ex member of The Talking Heads, recorded a bilingual duet with Celia, "Crazy for Love."

In 1993 Celia appeared in the Mexican soap operas *Valentina* and *El alma no tiene color* (The Soul Has No Color). Since she was not recording, Ralph Mercado, her manager then, developed the idea of compiling her popular duos with other artists, in *Celia's Duets*. Some of the songs had been recorded long before, like her classic "*Usted abusó*" with Willie Colón and "*La candela*" with Ángela Carrasco. Among the more recent ones were "*Cuestión de época*" with José Alberto (el Canario), whose orchestra had accompanied her on many occasions, and "*La voz de la experiencia*" with La India.

The old duet of Celia's voice in dialogue with Tito Puente's *timbales* was not overlooked; and neither were "*Caballero y Dama*" with Willy Chirino; "*Las pilanderas*," a Colombian theme sung with her dear friend Matilde Díaz, ex-vocalist with the orchestra of Lucho Bermúdez; "*La carimba"* with the Dominican *merenguero* Johnny Ventura; *"Encantado de la vida"* with Puerto Rican José (Cheo) Feliciano; and *"Soy loco por ti, América"* with Brazilian Caetano Veloso.

Though on Celia's visit to Argentina in 1988 she cut four records with Los Fabulosos Cadillacs, only *"Vasos vacíos"* (a tremendous hit in the country of the *gaucho*) was selected for this CD and, as Celia told it, she very much enjoyed the studio session with the ska group, more than when she worked with David Sanborn, because with him she had to record in English, but with these rockers, the Cadillacs, they all worked perfectly in Spanish.

As a special attraction for her album *Mi vida es cantar* (1998) with musical production by Isidro Infante, there is a *merengue* duet with Kinito Méndez titled *"Me están hablando del cielo,"* a catchy tune by William Liriano and Méndez. In a similar vein, there is harmonious coupling with Óscar D'León, the very festive and flavorful *"El son de Celia y Óscar,"* a self-proclaimed mutual admiration society, as well as a splendid fusion, *"La guarapachanga,"* arranged by Omar Hernández, and with a trumpet backup by Cuban exile Arturo Sandoval, which was included in the CD *El tren latino*. La India, in her 1997 album *Sobre fuego* included the duet *"La voz de la experiencia"* with Celia Cruz, in honor of her idol and teacher.

Celia's incursion into rock and pop brought her to record with a group from Spain, *Jarabe de Palo*, and with Lolita she cut a duet, *"Ay, pena, penita,"* a song made popular by Lola Flores (La Faraona), Lolita's mother and a very good friend of Celia. Among Celia's first interpretations, *"Tu voz"* was the *bolero* that she chose to sing in 2000 with the wonderful Mexican singer Vicente Fernández for the album *Siempre viviré*. She had already received in 1998 a

Grammy nomination in the category of best rap interpretation by a duo or group for her version of "*Guantanamera*" with Haitian rap singer Wyclef Jean, with The Fugees.

The list of names that joined the diva to sing duets or in alternating voices is as ample as it is diverse, and in it we find Dionne Warwick, Patti LaBelle, Diango, Azuquita in Spain, and Luciano Pavarotti, with whom she sang "*Guantanamera*" in a benefit concert for victims of AIDS that the distinguished tenor does every year in Italy. She also has a duet with Gloria Estefan in the song "*Tres gotas de agua bendita.*"

In another rap theme, "*Ella tiene fuego,*" Celia sang with the Panamanian rap singer El General. This is the first number in her last album, *Regalo del alma*, recorded when she was seventy-seven years old, and which won yet another Grammy, posthumously, in 2003.

29

The Majesty of the Bolero

During the time she performed with the Sonora Matancera, Celia recorded the wide range of Cuban dance music in her inimitable style, but the Sonora had its special *boleristas*, such as Bienvenido Granda and Celio González, who also attempted other genres, and even Daniel Santos, who included in his repertory some romantic titles. Despite this limitation, Celia recorded a series of beautiful *boleros* with the Sonora, among them *"Desvelo de amor," "Aunque me cueste la vida," "Palmeras tropicales," "Tuya más que tuya," "Nostalgia habanera," "Ven que te voy a buscar,"* and her most popular, *"Tu voz,"* by composer Ramón Cabrera.

Celia insisted that without *guaguancó* and without *bolero, salsa* would never have come to be, and therefore she felt a special affection for these genres which acted like magnets for her sensibility as a singer. On various occasions she expressed her regret at not having recorded a full album of *boleros*, convinced as she was that it would have been a success. "Just consider how well received are the *boleros* by Luis Miguel and Gloria Estefan," she lamented in an interview, "but I cannot do that because, later, people are going to say that I copied them, and I am, above all, a creator." She relented in 1993, and her old record company, Seeco, released the album *Celia Cruz: Boleros*, including her classic ones *"Tu voz," "Espérame en el cielo," "Cuando tú me quieras," "Mi amor, buenas noches,"* and *"Quizás, quizás, quizás."*

Even though the twenty-first century greeted Celia with an unexpected commercial exuberance, largely because of her new contract with Sony Records, she recognized that though she dreamed of doing an album of *boleros*, she had been contracted to sing only *salsa*. However, in March 2002, Celia got the green light from Sony Records to do an album of *boleros*. She planned to start the selection and have everything ready by November. A record company had already released a compilation in Colombia, *Celia Cruz: Mis mejores boleros*. As she told the story, she would put into a little box the titles of the *boleros* she wanted to perform and among them there were those by Concha Valdés Miranda, the sisters María Luisa and Teresa Diego, and some by other composers who had given her their music.

In 2002, Sum Records released a splendid compilation for those who admire Celia's romantic side. It included numbers such as *"Te busco," "Esperaré," "Bravo,"* and *"Preferí perderte."* Celia was part of the *bolero* bonanza with the 2003 compilation *Son boleros, boleros son*, which includes *"Perdón"* and *"Plazos traicioneros,"* as well as the definitive album *Siempre Celia Cruz: Boleros eternos*, released by EMI Latin, with sixteen songs, and among them, *"Siento la nostalgia de palmeras," "Bolero, Bolero," "Piel canela," "¿Quién será?," "Luna sobre Matanzas," "Palmeras tropicales,"* and *"Espérame en el cielo."*

30

My Life Is Singing

The magic of Celia's voice is crystal clear in the *bolero-mambo* entitled *"Tu voz"* (Your Voice) by composer Ramón Cabrera and first recorded by the Sonora Matancera in 1952: *No sé qué tiene tu voz que fascina. / No sé que tiene tu voz tan divina, / que en mágico vuelo / le trae consuelo a mi corazón. / No sé qué tiene tu voz tan divina. / Tu voz se adentró en mi ser y la tengo presa. / Tu voz, que es tañer de campanas al morir la tarde. / Tu voz, que es gemir de violines en la madrugada.* (I don't know what your voice has that fascinates me. / I don't know what your divine voice has / that in a magical flight / brings consolation to my heart. / I don't know what it is your divine voice has. / Your voice has entered deep into my being and I have imprisoned it. / Your voice, which rings like bells when the day dies. / Your voice, like plaintive violins very late at night.) This song is included also in the album *Siempre viviré,* as a *bolero-ranchero,* in a duet with Vicente Fernández, as previously mentioned. For its grace and unique individual style, tropical and sweet, the voice of Celia Cruz has been compared to that of another legend of Afro-Cuban music, Benny Moré. But the Diva's voice was considered as classic as that of Ella Fitzgerald, Sarah Vaughn, Edith Piaf, Maria Callas, or Billie Holiday.

For more than half a century her voice sweetened the *guaracha,* the *guaguancó,* the *bolero,* the *son montuno,* and *salsa* with her joyous trademark, *Azúcar!,* injecting her energy into a public always thirsty for her melodies. From the moment that the leader of the Sonora Matancera heard her, back in 1950, he was impressed with the peculiar register of her voice. Her classics belong to that period: *"Cao cao maní picao," "Burundanga," "Tu voz," "Dile que por mí no tema,"* and *"Sopa en botella."* Her voice was unique in that she could endow any genre, be it *guaracha, bolero, mambo, chachachá,* and even *ranchera* or rap, with such a level of virtuosity and developed sense of rhythm, that even from the most inane lyrics she was able to extract some poetry and the warm cadences that recall the movement of the sea and the swaying of palm trees of her tropical Caribbean. In fact, for her ability to improvise as well as the powerful, pure, and clear timbre of her voice, she became the symbol of Caribbean music. Her ability to stay on top for five decades, although with the normal ups and downs of any career, was based fundamentally on her ability to sing the whole musical scale accurately, without marring even a single note.

In this sense, she was an authentic artist springing from the humble strata of society, who carved her popularity thanks only to her voice and her talent, without any need to make use of the recording studio miracles that actually manufacture personalities of pop music like on an assembly line, utilizing advanced technology, plus the promotional machine that only cares to accrue fame and fortune with ephemeral successes. Celia's solid artistic reputation resulted not only from her voice and stage presence, but from her careful selection of the numbers she sang, as well as her active participation in all the artistic decisions inherent to the production of her recordings, circumstances that brought her into the position of intellectual creator of her success and of the impact of her music around the world.

Celia would meticulously analyze the lyrics of her songs before deciding which ones to sing, taking an active interest in figuring out the musical development of the song so that she would not sound repetitive. In order to achieve this, she would use different musical arrangers, without limiting herself to using the services of Severino Ramos while she was with the Sonora. She also used Nino Rivera and Roberto Puente (the composer of *"Caramelos"*). On certain occasions she even had four arrangers working at the same time on her songs, one reason that her numbers never sounded monotonous. Her success and her popularity at the international level had many personal elements of her natural talent, such as her decisive intervention during the different stages of her record production.

The enormous collection of Celia's wigs (her stylist has said that she had more than a hundred and fifty) and colorful costumes (all designed under her strict supervision) were her stage props, while the sound of musical instruments was always the backup for her resounding voice, her perfect vocalizing, her indispensably Cuban, percussion-like rhythm. Her voice became the heritage of all Latin Americans, of all peoples in a wide geographical extension, of the whole world. With eyes closed, one can listen to

many female vocalists, but one would always be able to
identify Celia's voice, no matter who accompanied her, be
it the Sonora Matancera or the Sonora Ponceña, Tito Puente or Johnny Pacheco, or any of her other accompanists.
She cured all sorrows, lifted spirits. Anyone who attended
one of her concerts and did not dance, in the theater seat
or in the aisles, would surely be gravelly ill, because her
energy and vibrant smile were totally contagious.

Celia left a record of her artistic vocation in her song
"Mi vida es cantar" (My Life Is to Sing) by composer Ara-
bella, arranged by her bandleader, Isidro Infante: *Azúcar!*,
the *bongó* is heard first, and then the piano: *Cantar para
mí / es como ser / dueña del universo, / poder expresar
con mi voz / lo que llevo por dentro, / hacerles a ustedes
sentir / sensaciones grandiosas, / y en cada nota conjugar,
/ cantando muchas cosas. / Y cuando la magia de algún
son / invade poco a poco el corazón, / vuelvo con su ritmo
sabrosón y el sentimiento. / Siento los cueros repicar y mi
cuerpo no cesa de bailar, / dejándome llevar por el compás,
/ qué bien me siento. / Y es que el canto, yo lo llevo por
dentro. / Cantando yo viajo el mundo, / brindándoles sentimiento, / tres amores tengo dentro / que me alegran el
corazón: / Cuba bella, el son y la rumba, y mi "Cabecita de
Algodón." / Lo que soy, es la gracia de Dios. / Su amor me
dio este talento / que les brindo con mi voz, con mi voz. /
¡Azúuucar! / Yo nací cantante… / Les dejo mi vida, mi voz.
/ Muchas gracias por tanto amor.* (For me, to sing / is like
owning / the universe, / to be able to express with my voice
/ what I have inside of me, / to make you feel / great sensa-
tions, / and for every note to include / many things in my
song. / And when the magic of a *son* / slowly invades my
heart, / I come back with its irrepressible rhythm and its
feeling. / I feel the drums playing and my body can't stop

dancing, / I let the rhythm take me, / how good I feel. / And it's that singing is inside me. / Singing I travel the world, / offering my feelings, / three loves I carry with me / that make my heart happy: / beautiful Cuba, the *son* and the *rumba*, and my "Cottontop." / What I am, is by the grace of God. / His love gave me this talent / that I bring you with my voice, with my voice. / *Azúuucar!* / I was born to sing . . . / I give you my life, my voice. / Many thanks for so much love.)

When an inquisitive interviewer asked her how she could explain having stayed on top as the Queen for so many years, she answered: "No one can equal the timbre of my voice, which was a gift from God. It is not easy to imitate something that comes naturally. I vary my singing and I love my work. However, there have been a few girls—I do not think that they wanted to imitate me or be like me, even out of admiration—who, to start their singing careers, instead of looking for music that I did not sing, wrongly choose something that I have already done. Second parts are no good." Sometime later she explained, "The secret [to keeping myself on top] lies, I believe, in perseverance, dedication, seriousness, and responsibility. Music for me is like an altar, it is everything; that is why I respect it. If one day my voice should falter, I would not know what to do; I know nothing else. That is why I always fulfill my obligations, and try to behave in the proper manner, with discipline."

That was the secret of her success. All those who knew her coincide in remembering her sense of duty, and her careful attention to preserving her health so as not to miss any professional commitment ever. "In fact, I take very good care of myself. I am always busy with something. I only sleep at night." She went to bed early or sought refuge in her hotel room to write letters and cards to her friends and acquaintances. On one occasion some local friends popped in at her hotel in Cali, Colombia, wanting to celebrate the success of one of her concerts. When they phoned from the lobby at ten o'clock, Pedro answered and informed them that she was already asleep.

In spite of her star status, she did not have the vices often associated with the dissipated life of some musicians. She didn't drink, except on a few occasions of celebration, she didn't do drugs or smoke any kind of weed or tobacco. She led a typically domestic existence but transformed herself into an explosion of joy the moment she stepped on a stage. According to a journalist from Barranquilla, Markoté Barros, who interviewed her on many occasions, "As soon as she arrived at a hotel, the first thing she asked for was stationery and a pen to write to her friends to thank them for some favor, a well-made interview, or to wish them a happy birthday or happy anniversary. I have more than a hundred letters and postcards that she sent me from any place in the world after I interviewed her in 1955 during her first visit to this city. I always knew when she was coming to Colombia because she would let me know beforehand. But I always respected her privacy, and would not reveal anything she told me, because she was my friend."

Markoté Barros reports that one of "her most endearing gestures was on September 19, 1991, when she was performing in the Roberto Meléndez Metropolitan Stadium, in Barranquilla. She remembered my birthday, and she congratulated me from the stage, "Happy birthday, Markoté! Where are you?" and she asked the audience to congratulate me too. That was a big day. Tito Puente was there to promote his one-hundredth LP, with the Japanese orchestra La Luz and Óscar D'León. I was very much surprised, *caramba!*, that she remembered me in front of forty thousand spectators. The next day I went to her hotel to thank her. All the orchestras that had come were there, and I remember that she told me, "Ay, Markoté! I heard you wrote that I am going to retire. No, I intend to retire the way Miguelito Valdés retired, right on the stage." The journalist explained he had not written that she was retiring, but that there was a rumor going around that Celia Cruz was going to retire from the musical stage the following year.

The following is a transcription, as an example, of one of those letters, written on yellow legal paper, in large handwriting and double-spaced, kindly provided by Markoté Barros:

New York, March 18, 1991

Dear Marco T:

Don't think that I have forgotten you. And if, I don't know how, you did not get your Christmas card, I did send it to you, and I have a record that I did.

I am really very busy, flying from one place to the other, and sometimes I have no time to pick up my mail, and not all hotels sell postage stamps, but Pedro and I truly don't forget you.

I received your letter on my way back from California, because I don't know whether you are aware that I am going to take part in a movie called The Mambo Kings Play Songs of Love, and I was there for rehearsals. Filming begins in April, here I'm sending you something Alberto Minero wrote in Diario-La Prensa.

Here are some clippings. Thanks for the ones you sent me.

I am very sorry about your daughter, R.I.P.

Well, Marco, Pedro joins me in sending you a greeting
and wishing you the best.
Hugs, your friend,
Celia Cruz

Hers was an expressive signature, with the C's forming
two ovals that enclosed her first and last names. The en-
velope of one of these letters, dated April 19, 1994, with
her peculiar handwriting, has the logo of the Bauen Hotel,
Avenida Corrientes, Buenos Aires, Argentina, and the return address is P.O. Box 110107, Cambria Heights, NY
11411, U.S.A.

There are numerous testimonies about her thoughtfulness in remembering her friends on their special days, or
simply to say hello. It was also a way to make use of her
time while she waited for her presentations and a chance
to have quiet time.

Because of her discipline, professionalism, and a profound
respect for her public, when she arrived at a city to fulfill a
contract, she preferred to do a press and media conference
before conceding private interviews. "I do not like to sacrifice my voice," she admitted. "In general, when I have an
engagement, I avoid talking much in order not to abuse my
throat. Moreover, the day I have to sing I practically do not
speak, only what is strictly necessary. I read, answer mail,
watch television—and Pedro helps me a lot with this."

Yomo Toro, the veteran *cuatro* player from the Fania
All Stars, recalls: "She always sent me postcards from her
trips, and brought perfume for my wife." Joe Cuba, leader
of the sextet named after him, who enjoyed a long friendship with Celia, has this to say about her personality: "She
was a real lady who commanded respect not only for her
manner and her professionalism but also for her incredible

talent. However, her simplicity and lack of airs were even more impressive than her talent."

Ray Barretto, distinguished New York percussionist, was always aware that "Celia Cruz was a star, but she was a very humble woman, never playing the role of diva or central figure; she was one of the boys in the group, and was always the first or second to arrive at the recording studio. She was never late, the perfect model of professionalism. She was always ready to do her job, she was impeccable."

Panamanian singer-composer Rubén Blades considers Celia Cruz a classic icon whose dynamic presentations have become a hallmark of our Hispanic-Caribbean culture. "Celia Cruz could take any song and make it unforgettable. She transcended matter. With Celia, even the simplest of songs got infused with her vigor and personality. I don't think one can listen to anything she did and be indifferent. With her powerful voice and her spectacular presentations, she helped take the world of *salsa* to an international level, and her legacy will live forever. Real death occurs when one forgets, but we are not going to forget Celia ever."

Izzy Sanabria, who traveled with the Queen of Salsa around the world as master of ceremonies for the Fania All Stars, comments: "Celia led an extremely joyous life, she never needed alcohol or drugs, her life was her music, her public, and, of course, Pedro. She was a person of unequaled talent, but where she shined the most was in her character. She was an extraordinary human being, with incredible traits. When my baby girl was born, she sent us a card, and from then on, every year she sent a birthday card. That is just an example of how Celia Cruz was, her unbelievable thoughtfulness. She never forgot a birthday, baptism, wedding, or Christmas card, no matter where she was. She was always very thoughtful with her friends, and she always wrote personally, by hand."

Sanabria (Señor Salsa), now retired under the warm Florida skies, believes that "Celia achieved 99 percent of what she intended in life, based on her talent and disposition. The only thing missing was her return to Cuba, but her death has also been lamented by the Cubans on the island, who continued to follow her career even though her music was forbidden there for some time. I think that though her life has been full of successes and satisfactions, now is when her true influence is going to be felt, because Celia Cruz opened doors for many women to enter the world of entertainment. When she began performing, she was a pioneer, and there were few really successful women in the world of entertainment. Her manner and her merriment were contagious, and she knew how to take that joy to her public, never compromising her principles. She was truly an incredible woman, and her legacy will never be forgotten."

Celia never forgot the woman who was her matron of honor when she married Pedro Knight. Tita Borggiano, widow of the great singer Rolando Laserie, gets sad and her tired eyes fill with tears when she remembers her good friend and companion in many ventures while Tita toured with her husband. "Celia gave a lot of attention to detail, she once gave me a doll that I always wanted and that I still have. She had a prodigious memory, she never forgot anything or anybody. On my birthday she was the first one to call or send a card, and unfortunately she died the day before my birthday, on the sixteenth, and my birthday is the seventeenth, so I had to resign myself to spending my day without her, and remembering her with the affection she deserved."

Miguel Pérez, a New Jersey journalist who had the opportunity to interview her several times, evokes the happy times when every time he wanted to impress his visitors, he had a secret weapon: he showed them the birthday cards he had received from Celia in the last twenty years. They were not just ordinary cards. They showed the address and the names of the senders printed, "Los Knights" (the Knights) and were from both Celia and Pedro, her beloved husband. "Twenty years ago, when I interviewed her for the first time, I told her that it would be published on August 6, 1983, which happened to be my birthday. Celia never forgot that, and from then on until her last moments, no matter where she was—always traveling as chief ambassador of our Latin music—she would send me a greeting. She always made me feel she had adopted me, as if I were the son she never had. Anywhere, even in the midst of a big crowd, she always recognized me. But I am sure I am not alone in this. The Knights felt that much affection for a lot of people, and that is the true testament of Celia's success."

Celia's personality always drew praise among her friends and colleagues; she was a woman who won anybody's heart for her great humility and lack of pretense. She was an endless source of energy that she generously spread around to everybody with the overflowing enthusiasm that was her trademark, and of a professionalism reinforced by discipline. Never forgetting the humor of popular sayings and the funny anecdotes from her life, she made everybody around her feel relaxed. She always fulfilled her responsibilities with a great devotion to her work, carried with the zeal of a vital mission, and completely in tune with her public, who returned her love and idolized her.

31

Celia Cruz in Film and Television

From the beginning of her singing career, Celia Cruz was a permanent guest at Cuban radio stations. In the times before television, radio programs enjoyed large audiences, not only on the island but in the whole Caribbean area, where radio waves carried without difficulty. In Cuba, as well as in Latin America, musical programs and soap operas were tremendously popular. Radio provided practically the only entertainment besides movies, which also attracted large audiences.

In fact, Celia started her artistic career by winning radio contests in Havana. That was the first step for many aspiring artists who wanted to join the entertainment world at a time that was marked by the incipient technology and the economic limitations of a large sector of the population. Once Celia joined the Sonora Matancera, her radio presence increased, and when television started in 1950, musical groups and their vocalists appeared regularly on the small screen. The Sonora was often the guest of honor with its female star, the restless *Guarachera*.

In order to help the precarious family budget, Celia's melodious voice was often given contracts to sing jingles for radio and television commercials. Among the more memorable was the one for Hatuey beer, which she sang at her highest register: *Hatueeeyyy, la gran cerveza cubana, pedacito de domingo que usted se merece...* / She also sang *Café Pilón, sabroso hasta el último buchito*; Candado soap; Colonia 1800; Nela cheese and butter; and Partagás cigars and cigarettes: *Dále más gusto a tu gusto / con Partagás, / que es todo gusto, / es un Partagás.*

In the United States Celia was the publicity spokesperson for Eastern Airlines and Wesson peanut oil. The first time she endorsed a publicity campaign on television was *Volar en Eastern / eso sí es volar*. She participated in three commercials; in the first one, she was alone; for the other two Pedro Knight joined her, which was a total success. They both worked in commercials for six years. In fact, it was during the filming of one of those television ads that she affectionately referred to Pedro as her Cottontop in public for the first time. The director of the commercial thought it was funny, and he asked her to include it.

Celia's first experience as an actress came to her through her friendship with María Teresa Coalla, who created a character especially for Celia in a soap opera broadcast by Radio Progreso in the fifties. Her director was Bernardo Pascual, who was then married to Delia Fiallo, later famous in Miami as a soap opera scriptwriter. Celia was afraid of ridicule, but her friends and colleagues at the radio station encouraged her with only one advice: to be herself, without imitating any other actress. Her success was overwhelming. The rival station also had a soap, *Divorciadas*, with the highest rating, but after Celia joined the Radio Progreso soap opera, its ratings improved until it bypassed the competition. The best actress award that year went to Celia.

Something similar happened when film producers discovered the possibilities of the popularity that Celia, the Sonora, and its principal interpreters enjoyed. Films produced in Mexico and Cuba in those times usually included a scene in a cabaret with a variety show, with famous performers singing the songs popular at the moment. In the fifties the Sonora took part in Mexican and Cuban movies, such as *El ángel caído*, with Daniel Santos and Rosita Quintana; *Ritmos del Caribe*, also with El Inquieto Anacobero (Daniel Santos) and Amalia Aguilar; *La mentira*, with Bienvenido Granda; and *A romper el coco*, with Amalia Aguilar. First the radio, then the television programs, and particularly the movies helped popularize Cuban music, and of course the Sonora Matancera, in the countries where these movies were shown.

Some of these movies featured Celia Cruz with the Sonora. The film *Una gallega en La Habana* (1955), starring the actress Niní Marshall, is the funny story of a woman from Galicia (Spain) who comes to the the port of Havana and is wrongly identified as a smuggler of jewels. The mistaken identity provides occasion for a series of comical incidents, interspersed with performances by the Sonora Matancera and the voices of Celia Cruz and Nelson Pinedo.

Olé Cuba is another comedy filmed in Cuba, with Leopoldo Fernández and Aníbal de Mar in the roles of Pototo and Filomeno, two popular Cuban characters of the time, who in their attempt to help a stowaway from Spain (flamenco dancer Miguel Herrero) stay in Cuba, get into a lot of trouble. Here Celia and the Sonora share the spotlight with Xiomara Alfaro and the Orquesta Riverside.

Amorcito corazón (1961) is a Mexican comedy about a married couple who decide to rent a baby, but things get complicated. Directed by Rogelio A. González, and starring the most popular actress then, Rosita Quintana, and the actors Mauricio Garcés and Fernando Casanova, it makes a special presentation of Las Mulatas de Fuego. With the initial credits, the trumpets from the Sonora Matancera are heard, with Celia singing "*Tu voz,*" and then Willy (el Baby) Rodríguez in "*La pachanga,*" with Albertico Pérez Sierra and Rogelio Martínez doing the backup. At the end of the film, they all sing together "*Amorcito corazón*" by Urdimale-Esperón.

In the film *Piel canela,* of which the theme song made Puerto Rican singer Bobby Capó famous, Celia was also invited to sing with the Sonora Matancera, and she later had small musical interludes in such Mexican films as *La venganza de la momia* and *Juegos de sociedad.*

By the end of the eighties Celia was invited, as one of the best representatives of Caribbean rhythms, to participate in several documentaries about music, such as *Pequeña Habana, Guantanamera, La bamba*, and *Yo soy: Del son a la salsa.* This last documentary, by Rigoberto López, caused a stir when shown in the 19th Film Festival of New Latin American Cinema, held in Havana in 1996. Cubans on the island were able to see a fleeting image of Celia Cruz, thirty-six years later, for the first time since her exile in 1960 with the Sonora Matancera. People could not believe their eyes, there she was, the forbidden *Guarachera del Mundo*, in a dialogue with Tito Puente and singing fragments of "*Burundanga.*" Some in the audience reacted with shouts of joy, excited applause, and manifestations of gratitude. The pandemonium was such that the showing of the documentary was about to be suspended. After this, the heavy curtain of censorship in Cuba descended again over Celia Cruz, until the news of her death spread like wildfire, burning particularly in the memory of those who a long time ago had known her and seen her perform.

The first American film in which Celia sang was *Affair in Havana* (1957), directed by Lázlo Benedek (who had filmed *The Wild One* in 1954 with Marlon Brando). The main actors were John Cassavetes and Raymond Burr. Filmed in Havana, the story is about a composer who falls in love with a woman married to a man in a wheelchair.

The pairing of her voice with David Byrne's in "Crazy for Love" in the film *Something Wild* in 1986 contributed to the critical success of the film as well as of its soundtrack, an eclectic mix of ten songs by various bands and artists. This Scottish singer declared afterward that he still remembered the impact Celia Cruz had on him. "She sang over a yard away from the microphone, and even so, she covered my voice." It has been said that this is the best film of director Jonathan Demme before he joined the Hollywood commercial circuit. It was filmed in New York City with actors Jeff Daniels and Melanie Griffith. The story is about a wild girl who drags someone she meets into dangerous adventures, which nonetheless help liberate him from domestic doldrums and an asphyxiating daily routine.

Up to this point Celia's contribution to films had been limited to singing. In 1991 director Arne Glimcher called her for a speaking part in *The Mambo Kings*. The dialogue was in English, a language that Celia never really mastered. She had insisted on keeping her native Spanish even after forty years of living in the United States and acquiring international fame. She rejected those who insisted that she venture into a "crossover," by singing in English. This can be seen as nationalistic, or as a symbol of her Latin spirit, and it never limited her access to the global markets that have a larger distribution in English. In fact, this may have contributed to the increasing awareness of the Spanish language in the United States.

In her concerts with multilingual audiences, Celia always apologized: "My English is not very good looking," she said jokingly, a literal translation of the Spanish for "My English is not very pretty." For the movie she had a tutor who taught her to pronounce the words but, of course, keeping her Spanish accent. The film is based on the famous Pulitzer Prize-winning novel by Cuban-American writer Oscar Hijuelos. Armand Assante and Antonio Banderas (in his first English role) play two brothers, one of whom has fallen in love with a gangster's moll, and they leave Cuba for New York, where they hope to conquer the world with their music. Though the film in general received negative criticism, especially compared to the novel, the music rescues it, the *mambo, rumba,* and *chachachá* that energized dancing at the Palladium Ballroom in New York during the fifties, and which served as a prologue to the *salsa* fever that swept the country in the sixties. The film soundtrack is an anthology of Afro-Caribbean music, and it includes versions of the boleros *"Quiéreme mucho"* and *"Perfidia,"* sung by Linda Ronstadt; "El Bárbaro del Ritmo" (Benny Moré), captivates with his classic *"Cómo fue"*; the resounding trumpet of *"Mambo caliente"* is Arturo Sandoval's; Antonio Banderas debuts as a singer in *"Bella María de mi alma,"* and Los Lobos sing it in English. In a special cameo, Tito Puente is on the *timbales* for *"Ran Kan Kan," "Cuban Pete,"* and *"Para los rumberos."* And in her most significant role in her sporadic film career,

Celia Cruz plays Evalina Montoya, the rich owner of Club Babalú.

In 1995 Celia made her final appearance in an American movie, *The Pérez Family* (in Spanish, *Cuando salí de Cuba*), with Marisa Tomei, Alfred Molina, and Anjelica Huston; and directed by Mira Nair. Celia plays the role of a *santera*. The story is about Cuban immigration. While on the way to reunite with his wife, after twenty years in a Cuban prison, a man gets to know an ex-prostitute during the Mariel exodus of 1980. She is dreaming of rock and roll and John Wayne movies. Because they have the same surname, they are listed as husband and wife, which gives them priority as a family. Then she visits the *santera* to ask for advice.

Celia's participation in a documentary distributed by Columbia Pictures put Caribbean music on the world map, interpreted by the best *salsa* vocalists at that historical moment, such as Héctor Lavoe, Cheo Feliciano, Ismael Miranda, Justo Betancourt, Ismael Quintana, Pete (el Conde) Rodríguez, Bobby Cruz, and Santos Colón. The 1976 film *Salsa*, co-directed by Masucci and Leon Gast, fused original fragments from the concert at Yankee Stadium, August 24, 1973, and the 1975 concert, with some numbers filmed in San Juan, Puerto Rico, when the group opened there in 1976 in the brand-new Coliseo Roberto Clemente, where Celia made her official debut with the Fania All Stars in a masterly, definitive rendition of *"Bemba colorá,"* her all-time hit, with multitudes singing in chorus.

It has been said that there is a substantial difference between the focus of the film *Our Latin Thing* and the final version of the film, *Salsa*. For *salsa* to break into larger audiences in the United States and Europe, with millions in profits, it was necessary to make some cosmetic fixes for the second production. If *Our Latin Thing* was about *salsa*'s urban roots in the marginal poverty of the Latin ghetto, *Salsa* highlights the phenomenon of this music as a fundamental element of popular culture to be enjoyed by the large majority, unrelated to minority groups or ugly poverty. That was the main premise that encouraged the *salsa* bonanza and generated the mass consumption of its products, but which, at the same time, would weaken the essence of this musical genre and drive it to its final demise. Through these documentaries, the acceptance of *salsa* as a generic term comprising various rhythms was consciously made universal and popularized successfully by Masucci, Gast, and their work team.

Celia was also invited to form the staff of actors, vocalists, and musicians who participated in the adaptation as a musical of *Salsa*, which had a romantic character, and opened March 19, 1988 under the same title. It was performed by Puerto Rican singer Robi Draco Rosa, with Rodney Harvey, Magali Alvarado, Miranda Garrison, Moon Orona, and Loyda Ramos; and accompanied by Mongo Santamaría, Tito Puente, Willie Colón, and a long list of musicians, under the direction of Boaz Davidson. It was a film that did not make big waves, and was limited to being an example of commercial exploitation at an important juncture in the development of *salsa*.

In 2003, Celia acted as host in the didactic documentary *La Cuba mía*, which follows the course of Cuban music in the fifties, with the famous figures of the Trío Matamoros, Rita Montaner, and Rolando Laserie. Under the direction of Óscar Gómez for Spanish television, it was filmed in New York and Miami. Using archival material, the film recreates the period just before *salsa*, focusing on the cultural and musical heritage of the island through interviews with personalities who are exiles, like sax player Paquito D'Rivera and trumpet player Arturo Sandoval. A jam session is also included with the participation of distinguished musicians such as Juanito Márquez, Albita, Willy Chirino, Donato, and Miliki. And Celia Cruz, naturally, sings two numbers, *"El son sigue ahí"* and *"La Cuba mía."*

Celia's first role in a television soap opera was in 1993 in *Valentina*, a Mexican production with the famous actress Verónica Castro and actors Hugo Acosta and Juan Ferrara, under the direction of Luis Vélez. As Celia recounted later, it was Verónica who asked her to consider accepting this project. As Celia was hesitant, she asked Verónica to discuss it with her representative, but she refused, saying, "I want to hear when you say that you accept." This encouraged Celia to accept immediately. She played Lecumé, a soothsayer who could tell the future by reading seashells.

Celia's role did not last long, because the soap opera did not get high enough ratings and the executives of Canal Televisa ordered makeshift, radical changes in an effort to try to rescue it from disaster. Celia had played Lecumé with her characteristic humor and dignity, but with the new locale and new characters, Lecumé disappeared. It was all to no avail, the soap did not succeed like the others Verónica Castro had starred in, and she was then the queen in this type of entertainment. Television critics considered that though Celia was a marvelous interpreter of Caribbean music, her performance as an actress was less than spectacular.

The story of another soap, *El alma no tiene color* (1997), with Laura Flores, Arturo Peniche, and Rafael Rojas, was different. It was well received, and Celia had a better role. The plot was, as usual in these Mexican melodramas, a hackneyed and repeated story of hidden or overt racism in

Latin America. Blond Guadalupe is forced to abandon her poor, schoolteacher boyfriend, and marry wealthy Lisandro to save her father from economic ruin. When she gets pregnant, Lisandro is very happy, but when the child is born with dark skin, he is furious and abandons her, believing she has committed adultery. Guadalupe's father presses her black wet-nurse (Celia) not to reveal the secret of her real identity. Of course, the secret is that the black nurse is really blond Guadalupe's mother. As Juan Osorio tells it, and he was the director of the soap opera, Celia was a respectful actress who memorized her lines and methodically followed the plot. One day he authorized her to improvise, but Celia answered, "No, this is a discipline, and I have respect for the script." On a personal note, the Mexican director was very grateful to Celia and Pedro. Their advice and moral support were important factors in his overcoming drug addiction.

As Celia's fame increased, some people began insisting on the need for an autobiography, but she always refused, saying, "For that kind of book to sell, it must talk about childhood misfortunes, scandals, tragedies, and things that never happened to me." With the same skepticism and wit, she spoke about finally making a movie of her life. "In the movies you need drama; for instance, Al Capone died at home, but to make him more attractive for the movies, he always dies in a gun battle with the police," she answered to those who insisted. However, she agreed to have television personality Cristina Saralegui and her husband, Marcos Ávila, go ahead with a project of a full feature movie of her life, with Whoopi Goldberg as Celia. "That was, I think in 1992, when Whoopi came to Miami for the concert organized by Emilio and Gloria Estefan to benefit the victims of hurricane Andrew," Celia explained.

Whoopi received the Oscar in 1991 for best supporting

actress for her portrayal of a medium in the film *Ghost*, with Patrick Swayze and Demi More. Celia Cruz wanted a film that reflected her life's reality, her career, and her love story with Pedro. However, one of the principal obstacles to getting the "biotainment" going was Whoopi's tight schedule, but she was determined to go ahead with this filming project and follow it to its conclusion because, as she confessed, "I have always dreamed of participating in a production that portrays the life of this singer I admire deeply."

Although the popular actress does not speak Spanish, Celia taught her to yell *Azúcar*, and Whoopi was interested in the project. As the news spread, opinions were varied. A large number of Celia's fans were opposed to having an American, who "did not sing, dance, or know how to cry out '*Azúcar!*'" portray their beloved Guarachera. She could never have Celia's happy *tumbao* (rhythm). However, Pedro Knight confirmed that Celia had agreed to, and signed, the contract. "Celia loved Whoopi and, besides, this was an American idea," Pedro Knight added. On her part, Whoopi said that "to see a woman with skin the color of a chocolate bar completely win over thousands of people with her voice and her energy helped me to believe that everything is possible in life."

32

Ruth *Sánchez, Celia's makeup artist* and stylist who for more than two decades would shape Celia's onstage image, fulfilled her final commitment to Celia just as she had done many times before the Diva's big concerts. After she finished the job, Ruth confessed that she had to summon all her courage to do it. To comply with Celia's wish to look impeccable even after death, on the day of the vigil Sánchez went to the funeral home to give the performer the finished image with which she usually had presented herself in public.

This time it would not be for her next concert, or her next tour, but for the farewell ceremony, which many would have preferred not to have happen. "As I was combing her hair, I saw the transformation: she did not seem dead," Mrs. Sánchez said. She detailed her experience when she first approached Celia's body. "First I looked at her from a distance, then I got close little by little, kissed her on the forehead, and asked for strength. As if she were getting ready for a concert, that is the way I wanted Celia to start her long journey," her stylist added.

She admitted that before starting her assignment, she had prayed for strength to accomplish the task at hand. She said, "Celia Cruz, you have to give me the courage I need to do this; you know that the dead frighten me." But she finally completed her task with the same professionalism she had exercised during all the time she worked for the Diva. "When I was through, she appeared ready for a concert. God, and perhaps Celia, answered my prayers and gave me strength."

"She was always very kind and generous. I would venture to say she died without knowing how great she was. I told her that once, and Celia replied, 'Oh, Ruth, you say that because you love me so much.' She was a humble woman, genuine, a real friend, a mother, an aunt. Celia had her feet on the ground."

Ruth also recalls that Celia never complained. "She would only ask for a few things; she never made anyone feel bad. In the more than twenty years I worked for her, she was always nice to me. I was not a cosmetician by profession, but I must say I learned a lot from her, she was a teacher." Celia had given her the opportunity to be part of her world, Sánchez added nostalgically. The same stylist was also in Miami ready to take care of Celia's hairdo and makeup before her body was placed on public view. In the capital of the Cuban exile community there were two wigs and two different gowns waiting, for the two days the performer was going to be laid out in New York. The woman who not only managed to make her look splendid for the stage, but who also was her friend and confidant, commented, "She looked as she deserved to look, like the queen she has always been, the impeccable woman she always was."

33

The World Mourns for Celia

Celia could not have children, but she had nephews and nieces, godchildren, a loving and considerate husband, an adoptive son in Omer Pardillo-Cid, and dozens of friends and fans around the world who adored her. Celia was an exemplary friend, genuine and sincere, aware at all times of everyone's special needs.

Luis Falcón is one of the many "sons" that Celia never had. He listened to her for the first time when he was only seven, and right then he became her most passionate fan. By the time he was nine, he was president of the Celia Cruz Fan Club of Miami and had started calling her "aunt," but later he treated her as if she were his mother without any objection or jealousy from his real mother, who also became a good friend of Celia's. Falcón, who became an impresario based in Los Angeles, comments that he considers himself privileged, "First by God, who gave me the opportunity of sharing with my idol, because she was my idol; I say that there is no artist in the world at this moment who can give me the same emotional reaction as when I watched her perform. My heart would beat faster, like a child's. Yes, I feel privileged, and yes, I felt she was very special with me." Falcón was among the first to arrive in New York as soon as he heard of her passing, and he accompanied Pedro during the painful funeral.

On one occasion Celia had this to say about friendship: "I am a very joyful person who tries to be a good friend. I love what I do. Maybe that's why I'm so happy, and I want my laughter and my happiness to be contagious for everybody. In fact, when someone asks me how I want to be remembered, I always say the same thing: I want everybody to think of me as someone who was full of joy," and no matter what unimaginable level of popularity she reached, she never distanced herself from her fans because the higher she climbed, they followed. Celia had a very high concept of friendship, which for her meant attention, affection, and constant communication. She always found time in her heavy schedule of professional engagements to send greetings and congratulations to friends, male and female, and to the parents of her many godchildren (in Latin America there is a family-like bond between parents and godparents), no matter how far away they were.

In Cuba, of course, she left many friends who may or may not have forgiven her radical anti-Castro position, but who felt her death nonetheless as that of a member of their great musical family. The death of the most popular Cuban singer of all time, Celia Cruz, went practically unnoticed in her own country, where only family and close friends mourned her, in contrast to all the events in her honor all around the world.

The *Guarachera de Cuba* was not lacking in detractors

either. One of them, whose reflections epitomize a contrary, political opposition to Celia's glorification, was columnist Armando Benedetti. For a Colombian newspaper he commented that Celia's funeral had been "opulent, arrogant, excessive, endless. There was no sugar there, only money, funeral publicity for her as yet unreleased album, and the collections and anthologies that would surely come, and of course, the obscene politics of the Miami *"gusanería"* ["nest of worms," a derogatory term for the Cuban exile community], depriving death and Celia of the discretion and the decorum that the moment required." All of this is understandable, looking at it all with Latin American eyes accustomed to poverty, and being politically opposed to Celia's position, though the Miami community will surely feel offended by his choice of words, of sad remembrance. Besides, this has nothing to do with the thousands of fans who wanted to bid her farewell. He goes even further, suggesting that in the funeral cortège in Miami and New York, "the body of the deceased, the shroud, the coffin, the celebrant, the carriers of the book, the Holy water, the hyssop, the cross bearer and the candles, the sermonical, and the Holy water sprayer are not in harmony, but just the opposite, with the happy simplicity of the music that gave her life and that, nonetheless, could not save her from a vulgar mummification." But it did follow her wish to be bedecked with all her regalia.

Barely mentioned in the Cuban official media, the news of Celia's death spread like wildfire through what is wittily called *"radio bemba"* (the grapevine, or "people's lip radio"), and even though her music had been banned for more than forty years during her exile, a consternation was felt in the *solares*, or tenement houses, in Havana, where the unforgettable Guarachera was born, and had lived and sung. One of her old-time friends, singer Olga Guillot, said, "Celia's death is a great sorrow for me because we had been friends for a lifetime, we were always close. The world is in mourning, music is in mourning, and all the Cubans in exile, the two-and-a-half-million Cubans living in exile, all of us are in mourning for Celia." The famous *bolerista* recalled that they both had started their careers on Cuban radio while very young, making very little money, and that their situation had improved little by little, until Celia Cruz became "the greatest of all Cuban artists. She had earned this."

Another performer who got to know Celia well, through having shared the stage with her and enjoyed her close friendship is Mexican musician Marco Antonio Muñiz, who said he had the pleasure of having earned "her friendship, her fondness and affection while we were both performing in Mexico City as members of the Teatro Blanquita company."

Malena Burke, daughter of famous singer Elena Burke, Celia's friend and companion in various ventures while both were members of Las Mulatas de Fuego, was very emphatic when she said, "My mother and Celia adored each other. Celia made the thoughtful gesture at the last benefit for the League Against Cancer, when she found out about Mother's death, of making a donation in my mother's name. Without a doubt, there will be no other Celia. No one could replace her, because her image will stay as a permanent legacy."

In Mexico, the Cuban film actress and singer Ninón Sevilla, one of Celia's best friends, lamented that her death had come before Celia had been able to fulfill her most cherished dream, to return to her country. "I feel immense sadness. Whenever she was in Mexico, we always talked a lot. When we went to Veracruz or visited some other city in that country, she always said to me that she wanted to go back to Cuba before dying. It was her greatest dream, it's very sad that she could not have it fulfilled." Celia always recognized the merits of the gallant Miguelito Valdés (Mr. Babalú) as an interpreter of Afro-Cuban music. He was one of her great friends and a brother.

Celia always remembered how Miguelito Valdés died of a heart attack on Thursday, November 9, 1978, right on the stage of the Hotel Tequendama in Bogotá, singing with Tomás Santí's orchestra. (He managed to say, "I'm sorry, I'm sorry" before collapsing.) She feared that the same thing could happen to her in the Colombian capital. For that reason, she occasionally preferred to skip a Colombian tour if it included Bogotá, which is at 8,600 feet above sea level and could be detrimental to one's health. She had the same fear when she sang in Mexico City. She solved this by asking for an arrival with ample time for her to get accustomed to the altitude to be included in her contract, but in complete secrecy so that the press would not know. Only two days before her performance, was her presence in the city to be announced.

Colombia is among the countries that have most loved Celia. From 1955 on, she visited Colombia more than seventy-five times. The last time was on July 24, 2000. She also remembered Miguelito Valdés when talking about her eventual retirement from the stage. "Retirement is death, and I don't say this for artists, because many of them change their careers, but I think that inactivity is the cancer of the soul. I have always thought that I would retire the day God dims my faculties. Like Miguelito Valdés, I will perhaps say good-bye to life right on the stage."

Of course, her colleagues Tito Puente and Johnny Pacheco, as well the bandleader Isidro Infante, occupied a special place in her heart. She always considered Puente as her soul brother, and after his death, she included one of his songs in her next album in honor of the legendary *timbalero*. Her friendship with Johnny Pacheco lasted more than three decades. Pacheco and Masucci had been instrumental in her joining the Fania All Stars, and between 1974 and 1985 they recorded together six albums that undoubtedly also cemented Celia's world fame. Johnny's wife, María Elena Pacheco, known as Cuqui, was Celia's confidant during this time, just as Tita Borggiano, Rolando Laserie's widow, had been during her initial period. Both Laserie and his wife had been *"padrinos de boda"* (roughly equivalent to best man and matron of honor) in Celia's wedding, and Rolando had been a friend and colleague in numerous presentations.

The Queen of Salsa was the star of the concert *Celia Cruz y Amigos: Una Noche de Salsa*, at the Bushnell Park in Hartford, Connecticut, on August 11, 1999. It was a television special with the mambo and jazz legend Tito Puente (el Rey del Timbal), together with the RMM Orchestra under Isidro Infante. The album recorded live at this concert has been one of the major bestsellers for the record company owned by her friend and manager, Ralph Mercado. It includes thirteen numbers representative of Celia's big hits during the more than fifty years of her artistic career, such as *"Mi vida es cantar,"* *"La dicha mía,"* *"Babalú Medley,"* *"Azúcar negra,"* *"Cúcula"* (accompanied here by flutist Johnny Pacheco and La India, the so-called Princess of Salsa), *"El Guaba,"* *"Químbara,"* *"Usted abusó"* (in a duet with her inseparable *"Cabecita de Algodón"* or Cottontop, Pedro Knight), *"La vida es un carnaval"* by Argentine composer Víctor Daniel, and then *"Guantanamera"* with the whole cast.

When Celia was asked who was her favorite singer, she excused herself, very diplomatically, "because for ethical reasons I don't usually choose one over another, they are all my colleagues and my friends, and if I mention one, someone else will get upset. But a singer should be original and should not imitate. That is what I admire the most: originality." Among her friends, of course, were some of the most visible within the Cuban diaspora in Miami, who often made use of her popularity to express themselves against the Cuban regime, as guests on the television programs hosted by Cristina Saralegui or Gloria Estefan and her husband Emilio.

One of her faithful friends in Mexico was Daniela Romo, who also hosted a television program. When Celia visited Mexico's capital, she always appeared on her show. The Mexican singer said that "it was a privilege in my life that Celia honored me with her friendship, because she was the voice of her people. Her voice was heard all over the world." In addition, the Mexican performer recalled, "Celia Cruz always had a smile for everybody. A marvelous person, she had a tremendous capacity for enjoyment, she easily found a funny side to everything, her vitality was endless."

All the members of the Fania All Stars remember her with affection, as well as the various artists who collaborated with her in recordings or sang duets with her, like Luciano Pavarotti and Plácido Domingo, and from Spain, Rosario and Lolita Flores, daughters of her admired friend Lola Flores (who used to visit Celia's show in Madrid with her friends every night); and from the Dominican Republic, Vicente Fernández, Johnny Ventura, Kinito Méndez, Milly Quezada, José Alberto (el Canario), and Ángela Carrasco. Celia enjoyed a special friendship with the sensual dancer

Yolanda Montes (the famous Tongolele), whom she had met on one of her first visits to Mexico in 1948. "We never talked shop," Tongolele recalls, "we always got together at my place to play dominoes." When Joaquín González, Tongolele's husband, had his first heart attack, the Knights traveled to Mexico to be with them, and later when Joaquín died, Celia and Pedro, were again there to console her. Celia also had a long and fruitful friendship with Matilde Díaz, the star vocalist in composer Lucho Bermúdez's orchestra. He was her husband then, and she was one of the most sought-after singers. Celia had met her in 1952 in Havana, on one of Matilde's tours, when they were recording several numbers with the orchestra of Bebo Valdés. Celia had admired Matilde's beautiful voice when she first heard her on short-wave radio stations. Matilde wanted to have a child, but all her efforts had been useless. Then Celia, who was so devoted to the miraculous *Virgen de la Caridad del Cobre*, told her to pray to her. By a curious coincidence, one September 8, which is the day of the Patron Saint of Cuba, Gloria María was born to Matilde and Lucho. Of course, Celia was her godmother. Matilde fulfilled another of her dreams by recording with Celia "*Las pilanderas*," a *charanga-paseo* by Maestro José Barros, which in their voices acquires a new dimension. This Colombian singer became famous for her renditions of "*San Fernando*," "*Pepe*," "*Prende la vela*," "*La múcura*," "*Caprichito*," "*El secreto de mi voz*," "*El año viejo*," "*Salsipuedes*," "*Carmen de Bolívar*," and "*Kalamary*."

Celia had a pleasant memory of Marlon Brando when the famous actor invited Celia and Pedro for dinner at his Hollywood home. Brando had been in Cuba trying to learn to play the bongo, and he became a fan of Afro-Cuban music. During their visit, he promised to entertain them after dinner. They were also going to watch a boxing match on television later that night. However, with so many delicious dishes, swilled down with champagne, Celia fell asleep during the match and did not get to hear him playing the bongo, something she always regretted with her usual wit: "Poor thing, I left him all dressed up, and without getting to the prom!"

The Puerto Rican *salsero* Jose (Cheo) Feliciano, who for many years had been a member of the Fania All Stars and shared the stage with her, insisted that the greatest merit of the *Guarachera Universal* was to have triumphed in a musical world that had been up to then almost entirely male. "Celia's greatest accomplishment was that she entered and kept herself on top in a male world, because the *soneo*, or improvisation, in what we called *salsa* at the time she started, was exclusively a male thing," the distinguished *sonero* said. According to Feliciano, women used to sing *boleros* and ballads, but "Celia understood and assimilated the male way of singing and made it feminine, giving women that Caribbean flavor. That is why no one can fill her shoes."

Feliciano, who always considered himself one of her closest colleagues and friends, commented that the Queen of Salsa was a human being gifted with many virtues, and he attributed her success to the authenticity with which she conducted her career. "For me it's not easy to separate the artist from the human being. She was born to smile, and came with the mission to become a star, and near the end of her passing through this life, she succeeded. She was born to give the world a gift, to unite people, because in her beautiful way of singing and expressing herself, she united people," Feliciano declared about the Guarachera. "She was an elf, a gift of God to the world, I feel privileged to have shared more than thirty years close to her. Since she arrived in New York, she was always close to us; she was a friend of my wife, Cocó, all these years, and we toured together all over the world."

Feliciano recalled that one of the things that he found most striking was the pride Celia felt for being black. "The most beautiful anecdote I have of her is the one in which she allowed me to see how proud she was of being black, and it happened while we were in Africa. When the plane landed, Celia was the first to get off, and as soon as she stepped on African land, she knelt, kissed the earth, took a fistful, and tucked it inside her purse. She landed there as what she was, a queen in the midst of her people." The famous musician also remembers that "with any disagreement or misunderstanding that came up among the members of the Fania All Stars, *La Guarachera* always broke in to mediate, saying, 'But, what does it matter, if we are just a big family?' And everything was smoothed out. Since she was the only woman in the group, she was always very discreet when touring. There was always some funny note or positive attitude that she would share. If at any moment one of the boys did not feel well, or something was not right, she would tell him, 'Relax: when you get up on the boards, you are going to open your mouth and succeed, and you will see how your upset will disappear.' Celia was our aspirin for everything that went wrong."

34

Omer Pardillo-Cid

Celia and her husband used to pay visits to their
good friend María Hermida in New York
and, traditionally, they got together for dinner on Christmas Eve. María Hermida was also friends
with Magaly Cid, who had an adolescent son. He was
such a fan of Celia's music that he had a collection of her
records, as well as photos, and clippings of articles and interviews, of his much-admired singer. When Celia's friend
found out about the devotion that Omer Pardillo-Cid,
her friend's son, had for Celia, she invited them for the
following Christmas celebration so he would get to meet
Celia. Of course the boy, who was thirteen at the time, was
fascinated and nervous about meeting his idol, but he controlled himself when she said to him that it was unusual for
him to be interested in her music when most kids his age
preferred rock or another youthful rhythm. After this first

meeting, there were many other opportunities for Omer to see and speak to Celia.

When she joined her friend Ralph Mercado's RMM Records, Celia witnessed, as friend and mentor, the artistic development of Marc Anthony and La India. In order to fulfill the requirements for a course in communications at his high school, Omer Pardillo applied for an internship with RMM. He says he never used his friendship with Celia in order to get accepted, but fate had a surprise for him. The managers of the company needed to organize the folders containing information about Celia, and the job fell on Pardillo, who did it with such enthusiasm and dedication that he was offered a part-time job.

Later, in charge of some publicity tasks, he began to travel with Celia to engagements in the New York vicinity. With this basic experience, he became her exclusive publicist for three years. At this point Celia began doing music videos, which were the sensation of the moment, and all performers had to do some of their titles in video. Naturally, the bigger the success of a record, the greater was the pressure for a video. The specialized television channels are insatiable. And that was how Celia started making music videos. In general, they had a simple script in which the staging had to do with the lyrics. That was the case with "*Sazón*," which tells about an aspect of Celia and Pedro's domestic life. He is the silent co-protagonist while Celia cooks, watches television, or embraces her Cottontop, until she transforms herself into a star, with her *rumbera* costume, always joking and joyous. Celia also made videos for songs like "*Mi vida es cantar*," "*Que le den candela*," "*Guantanamera*," and her final—perhaps the best—"*La negra tiene tumbao*," with the participation of rappers and Latin actress Déborah.

The video has phosphorescent colors and a tone that wavers between erotic and funny.

In 1996, Pardillo was promoted to road manager at RMM Records, a position that consists in accompanying the performer during tours and solving any problem they might encounter. As the professional relationship grew, so did the affection between them, along with Celia's dependence on Pardillo's reliability and devotion to his work. They felt so close that Celia began calling him "my white son."

After the release of *Mi vida es cantar* in 1998, Celia decided to leave RMM Records. The speculation was that the performer was not satisfied with the oral financial arrangement she had with the company. As her fame grew, with the resulting increase in record sales, she thought she deserved preferential treatment and, naturally, more profits. Besides, according to some of her close friends, Celia was not comfortable with the fact that Mercado also represented Cubans on the island, such as Isaac Delgado.

Mi vida es cantar is a *salsa* album spiced with flamenco tones in *"Canto a Lola Flores"* and with the Colombian classic *"Salsipuedes"* by Lucho Bermúdez, a song her good friend, the late Matilde Díaz, had made famous. For this album Celia received the Latino Grammy for best album of tropical music, besides a special tribute for her career which spanned fifty years.

Once free from the association with Ralph Mercado, Celia and Pedro decided to keep Pardillo as her manager. With their experience and confidence, they decided to start their own company, Azúcar Productions, with Pardillo as president.

After this the young man, who started by collecting Celia's records and press releases, became their assistant, most intimate confidant, and business manager. So when an interviewer asked Celia who was her best friend, without hesitation she replied that Omer Pardillo and his mother had been very good to them.

During the final stages of her professional life, Pardillo was credited with encouraging her to experiment with diverse rhythms and to venture into unexplored paths in her musical career. He was also the mediator who worked hard to get her a lucrative contract with Sony Records, the company for which Celia recorded historic albums for the quality of her interpretations: *Siempre viviré* (2000), *La negra tiene tumbao* (2002), and *Regalo del alma* (2003), which reached the number one spot in radio, in distribution, and in sales around the world.

35

Un regalo del alma:
A Gift from Her Soul to Her Fans

A *fter her death,* Sony Records decided to push
ahead, to July 29, 2003, the release of Celia's last CD *Un regalo del alma*, which was
originally scheduled for the beginning of August. It is the posthumous album, recorded by *La Guarachera Universal* when
death was imminent. "*Ríe y llora,*" the first single by composer
Fernando Osorio and arranger Sergio George—who had composed her most recent hits—is a song calling for the full enjoyment of life: *Lo que es bueno hoy / quizás no lo sea mañana: /
he ahí el valor del momento, / he ahí el presente perfecto. Ríe
y llora / que a cada cual le llega su hora. / Ríe y llora / vive la
vida y gózala toda /* (What is good today / might not be good
tomorrow: / that is the value of the present moment, / that is
the perfect present. Laugh and cry, / for we are all on borrowed
time. / Laugh and cry, / live your life and enjoy it fully).

This is perhaps the album that took Celia the longest to finish. She had done many cuts before in one take. But by then she was under chemotherapy and radiation treatments, and already seventy-seven years old. It was her third album for Sony Records, and she was able to produce her idiosyncratic joy and her warm voice in each one of the ten songs included, plus a bonus: *"Siempre viviré"* (I Will Live Forever). This is a song characterized by its innovative style, without losing sight of the *salsa* genre with which the *Guarachera de Cuba* had been identified.

As a testament to the difficult times Celia was going through to record this album during the first months of 2003 (she had undergone an operation for a brain tumor in December 2002), she wrote a dedication coinciding with its title: "This album is a gift from my soul. I have decided that it has a deep meaning because, as you know, I have gone through some difficult moments. Your prayers and messages have been proof of your love, and they are the incentives that accompany me day by day. That is the reason why I have been able to record this album, and please allow me to dedicate it to those who now have helped me with their support." Among the people for whom she felt true affection and gratitude for sustaining her at this moment were her husband, Pedro Knight ("my eternal love: without him, I would never have existed"), her manager, Omer Pardillo-Cid ("I thank God He brought you into my life, you know how much I love you"), and "my true friends" Johnny Pacheco (*"mi dioso divino"*) and María Elena Pacheco. With her natural humility and generosity, she expresses a special gratitude: "to two angels at the Columbia Presbyterian Hospital who always took good care of me, Mercedes Perry and Felicia León, and to all the security personnel of the hospital."

Then Celia added as a conclusion: "This album is dedicated to you, who give me strength and hope. To my exiled Cuban people, scattered all around the world, and to the Cubans on the Island, who against all odds make my voice heard in all of Cuba." And as a premonition of her uncertain future, her dedication ends with some words for her admirers, who had loved her so much in each one of her vital periods: "May God allow us to meet again."

Celia recorded an astonishing number of albums, and *Regalo del alma* was a special production, not only because it was her last, but because it included songs that were really jewels in her crown, despite the difficulties she went through to record it. In this album Celia had a duet with El General, "Ella tiene fuego," and another one with Lolita, Lola Flores's daughter, "*Ay, pena, penita,*" a *guaguancó* with flamenco overtones. Other numbers include "*José Caridad,*" "*Me huele a rumba,*" "*La niña de la trenza negra,*" "*No estés amargao,*" "*Pa' la cola,*" and "*María la loca.*" With this album Celia topped a career that astonishingly spanned more than fifty years, as a singer who always enjoyed the favor of audiences for the quality of her voice, her renditions, and for her joyous themes.

Her sacrifice and dedication were rewarded posthumously with a Grammy, in the category of Best Salsa or Merengue Album, on February 8, 2004.

36

Celia Becomes a Legend

Celia started her career very modestly in Havana by entering contests, and her first awards were token sums of money that came at the moment when her family needed them the most. In time, she not only became the best-known and highest-paid Cuban singer in history, but also garnered success after success and gained recognition from all sorts of institutions, to the point of becoming the guest of honor in centers of political, economic, social, and cultural power of the Western hemisphere. In 1976, when her hit album *Recordando el ayer, con Celia, Johnny, Justo y Papo* came out and met with popular acclaim, the mayors of cities with large portions of Cuban residents, like Miami, Florida and Union City, New Jersey, as well as Dallas, Texas and cosmopolitan New York City (through its mayor Edward Koch) were eager to hand her the keys to these cities so that the Queen would feel at home and come to visit often. These were the first acts of recognition that the genial *Guarachera* received in the United States and which actually were the prologue to an avalanche of awards that she received as the quality of her voice and the love her audience had for her became more and more evident. Moreover, if it was true that her successful recordings were numerous, the applause and joyful response she got from her public performances all over the world were even more satisfying. Besides receiving keys to many cities, she was invited to events organized in her honor, and her fans were always ready to attend her concerts, wherever they were held.

Between 1977 and 1979, *Billboard* magazine and the *Daily News* awarded Celia Cruz the title of Best Female Vocalist. In June 1982, she was handed the keys to the city of Lima (Perú), and on October 23 there was an event in her honor, *Tributo a Celia Cruz*, at Madison Square Garden in New York City. The 1985 award ceremony of the Asociación de Cronistas de Espectáculos (Association of Entertainment Critics), known as ACE in the Spanish-speaking world, was in Celia's honor, and she sang a capella a few stanzas from her famous "*Yerberito*" (as she calls "*El yerbero moderno*") with other award-winners as her chorus, in this case, Plácido Domingo and Rocío Jurado. On September 17, 1987, she received her own star in the Hollywood Walk of Fame. Only two other Cubans had shared this honor in the U.S. film capital, the musician and television personality Desi Arnaz, and the Mambo King, Dámaso Pérez Prado.

Celia declared later that this was a recognition she had yearned for, adding that "all awards I have received have been imprinted in my memory. But I must say that the one I had to wait the longest for was the Hollywood Star. From

President Reagan to hundreds of illegals sent letters asking for this. That is why I have always said that this Star does not belong to me, it belongs to my fans." The idea came up on Pepe Reyes's radio program in Los Angeles, when the Chicano disc jockey asked the question: "Why is it that Celia Cruz, who is so famous and has performed so many times in California, has no Hollywood Star?" The question reverberated in Winni Sánchez, a determined Cuban journalist who immediately turned to the task of fund-raising for a campaign that received help from many people who wrote letters or donated money. Among them was designer Luis Vega, who did a poster that read *"Celia se lo merece"* (Celia deserves it), which was plastered all over the main cities around the country.

After this the idea snowballed, Celia Cruz finally got the Star which was a source of pride and satisfaction for her. When journalist Estela Pérez, from *Hoy* in New York, asked Celia which year had been most significant in her life, she answered immediately, "Privately significant and sad for me was 1962, when my mother died in Cuba and I was performing at the Teatro Puerto Rico [in New York], and therefore I had to go onstage to sing, and then return to my dressing room to cry. The other time was when I was granted the Star on Hollywood Boulevard, exactly numbered 6240. So many beautiful things!"

On March 3, 1987, Celia Cruz was listed in the *Guinness Book of World Records* for gathering the largest number of attendees at a single concert: 240,000 admirers of her music gathered in Santa Cruz de Tenerife (Canary Islands, Spain) during carnival season to see the Queen of Salsa perform. In turn, the Festival de la Calle Ocho in Miami, one of the largest celebrations of Latin music in the United States, elected her to be its presiding Queen, and offered a moving ceremony in her honor on September 28, 1989, with the inauguration of her Star. Some time afterward, decreed by the Office of the Mayor, a stretch of the famous Calle Ocho in Little Havana (Miami) was renamed Celia Cruz Way in 1991. In recognition of her accomplishments, Celia was declared Doctor Honoris Causa by Yale University, and that same year she performed with Tito Puente in the Tokyo Jazz Festival for ten days, during which she was acclaimed by an excited multitude.

The nineties started very favorably for Celia, especially generous in rewards for her artistic career. In 1990, after being nominated twelve times, she won her first Grammy in the Latin Music category, for her album *Ritmo en el corazón*, recorded with Ray Barretto. The President of Colombia, in honor of her musical contributions and her immense popularity in that South American country, presented her with the Medalla Presidencial de las Artes (Presidential Medal of the Arts). And in recognition of one of its most famous guests, Madison Square Garden in New York granted Celia a prominent space in the "Garden Greats' Wall."

In 1992, besides participating in the opening celebrations for the film *The Mambo Kings*, she traveled to California to unveil her wax image in the famous Hollywood Wax Museum, while New York Governor Mario Cuomo waited to present her the Hispanic Women Achievers Award. Then she received her second Doctor Honoris Causa in music, from Florida International University, with the delighted approval of the large Cuban community of South Florida.

Celia was also awarded the Lifetime Achievement Award, granted by Premios Encuentro, in Washington, D.C., and in 1993 she was admitted to the Movieland Hall of Fame in Buena Park, California.

On the professional level, she started a new stage of her performances with RMM Records, the company founded by her old friend Ralph Mercado in New York, with whom she cut an album, *Azúcar negra*. This production included the single "*Sazón*," composed by Emilio and Gloria Estefan and dedicated to Pedro Knight, her eternal companion, with Gloria and Jon Secada in the chorus. That same year Celia flew to Bogotá to be with her dear friend Matilde Díaz, who was going to be honored for her fifty years of artistic life, and with whom she sang a duet of "*Burundanga*."

Recognitions continued nonstop, and 1994 was the year she was at the Guantánamo Naval Base to sing for thousands of *balseros* who had escaped from Cuba. This visit to the base is the only time that Celia stepped on Cuban land since the beginning of her long exile, and her nostalgia was such that through a fence that separated her from Cuban territory, she took and kept a fistful of Cuban soil. "At that moment, I felt a heaviness, my heart shrank, and my eyes welled with tears that for a moment clouded the sky, which I saw much bluer, and the grass, which seemed to me to be greener."

1994 was a memorable year for Celia. She received the award Éxito de Vida (Lifetime Achievement) from the University of Panamá, which also established an artistic scholarship in her name. She then received one of the highest honors in the United States from President Bill Clinton as guest of honor in the White House: a Congressional Medal of the Arts, for her artistic contribution to the National Endowment for the Arts. The Billboard Music Award was granted to Celia for "*Mi vida es cantar*" (My Life is to Sing), and the Hall of Fame Award was bestowed on her in Miami, Florida. Later in the same year, she received an

ACCA award also in Miami Beach, and was elected Queen of the Musical Festival of Viña del Mar in Chile. The series of recognitions continued in 1995 when she was chosen Grand Marshall of the South Beach Festival in Florida, and in April she received a Star in the Paseo Amador Bendayan in Caracas, Venezuela, where Venevision TV Network produced a special in honor of one of its favorite performers, Celia Cruz. On a professional level, it was a fruitful year, with the production of the album *Que le den candela*, which included arrangements by Cuban musician Willy Chirino, and Celia's personal version of the classic black lullaby "Drume negrita" by Eliseo Grenet.

In May 1995 the film *The Pérez Family* had its premiere in Miami. Later the city of New Orleans honored Celia during its popular Jazz Festival. Los Angeles granted her the Olé la Vida award, and in Miami she received yet another Billboard award, this time for her entire artistic career. The Dominican Republic granted her the coveted Cassandra Prize, and in Washington, D.C. she received the Vida prize for her professional contributions. On September 29, 1995, Los Angeles gave her a Proclamation, and in October, Tito Puente, La India, Trilogy, and C&C Music Factory honored her during the celebration of the Hispanic Heritage Month at the Harlem Hospital. Celia was Grand International Marshall of the Hispanic Parade in the State of New Jersey, and the city of Hollywood (California) honored her with the DESI Award.

The following year, 1996, the list of awards did not stop: the Dominican Republic recognized her as the International Artist of the Year, and for the second time gave Celia the Cassandra Prize, granted by the Dominican Association of Art Columnists, and she was simultaneously invited to the Presidential Palace for yet another tribute. In

March, Celia received the ACE prize in the category of the Year's Most Extraordinary Figure, together with tenor Plácido Domingo and Mexican singer Luis Miguel. The prestigious Smithsonian Institute of Washington, D.C. granted her the Lifetime Achievement Award, and some of Celia's personal items were added to its collection. In the meantime, San Francisco declared October 25 to be "Celia Cruz Day." In 1997 she was celebrated in Mexico City with a Star in the Paseo de las Estrellas in the Plaza Galería. In spite of all these accolades, Celia remained nonpretentious, self-effacing, and full of a contagious joy that touched all of those lucky enough to be in contact with her.

In 1998 a Grammy nomination surprised her, in the category of best rap interpretation by a duo or group, for her version of *"Guantanamera"* with Haitian rappers Wyclef Jean and Jeni Fugita. She was recognized on a national level with the Hispanic Heritage Lifetime Achievement Award. This organization highlighted Celia's participation in fund-raising benefits for the fight against AIDS and againt cancer, as well as her collaboration in benefits for orphans in Honduras and for the handicapped in Costa Rica.

With the new millennium, the release of a new album was announced: *Siempre viviré* (I Will Live Forever), her first project for Sony Records, produced by Emilio Estefan Jr. and Óscar Gómez. It included her version of *"Uno,"* the first tango she sang since *"Nostalgia,"* at the beginning of her career, for which she won a prize in Havana. In honor of her old friend Tito Puente, his classic *"Oye como va"* was also included. In Chile, Celia received the Gaviota de Plata (Silver Seagull), granted her by the Viña del Mar Festival that year.

A recording that very quickly reached the top of the

charts was *Celia Cruz & Amigos: Una noche de salsa*, a compilation of thirteen representative hit numbers through an artistic career spanning more than fifty years. This album came out under the seal of RMM Records, some time after the musical "marriage" Mercado-Cruz dissolved. This album was recorded live during a concert on May 12, 1999, on the Bushnell Park stage in Hartford, Connecticut, and was televised by forty-nine Public TV stations in the United States. Also in 1999, she received her third Doctor Honoris Causa degree, from the University of Miami.

Another Latino Grammy nomination greeted her at the beginning of 2001, when she was also inducted into the Paseo de la Fama at the Jackie Gleason Theater for the Performing Arts in Miami Beach. On September 25, 2001, Celia released with Sony Records *La negra tiene tumbao,* which was a tremendous success and earned her a second Grammy for best salsa album in the United States. Her fame billowed and her music was heard throughout Europe as well as in stores in San Juan, Puerto Rico, or discoteques in Cali, Colombia.

Luciano Pavarotti then invited her to sing a duet with him, "*Guananamera,*" at the benefit concert he organized every year in Italy. This happened just a few days after Celia participated in the concert *Divas Live: The One and Only Aretha Franklin*, organized by the VH1 Network in honor of the Queen of Soul, and televised nationally and internationally.

In the fateful year of 2002, the seventy-six-year-old Celia Cruz, went on a world tour, brightening the stages where she performed with her happy, contagious rhythms. Panamá honored her with the Condecoración Nacional de la Orden Vasco Núñez de Balboa, for her incomparable artistic career, her relevant merits, and her collaboration in humanitarian and worthwhile causes. This recognition was awarded by President of the Republic Mireya Moscoso, during Celia's presentation at the Centro de Convenciones Atlapa, with a massive turnout of fans. This was the first occasion on which the President and her Cabinet had attended an entire artistic presentation. On January 6, during a concert in Yucatán, the keys to the city of Mérida were handed to her, and that day was "Celia Cruz Day."

A few days later, in Orlando, Florida, she received similar honors, delivered during her participation in the XIII Zora Neale Hurston Festival of the Arts and Humaniies. "I started this year with a lot of commitments and several awards. This gives me more energy and makes me eager to go on taking my music to my people," Celia commented during the ceremony. The indefatigable Latin star continued taking her voice, her rhythm, her joy, and also her *tumbao* to all the corners of the world, breaking all sorts of social and cultural barriers. To celebrate their fortieth wedding anniversay in 2002, Celia and Pedro went on a vacation trip through Europe, visiting Paris, one of her favorite cities, and then Rome, where in a splendid ceremony she received the keys to the city. They left afterward for Venice, where they finally enjoyed their long overdue honeymoon.

After recording countless albums and being granted more than a hundred awards throughout her fruitful career, on February 5, 2003, Celia received, together with Colombian singer Juanes, the greatest number of nominations for the Lo Nuestro prizes in Latin music, sponsored by the Univisión Network, earning four of these trophies that she took home. Around the same date, she received the Fundación Imagen award, created by the Hollywood film industry, and on March 13 made her first public appearance after her operation, in a multitudinous celebration in her honor at the Jackie Gleason Theater in Miami Beach, where musicians and vocalists performed some of her popular hits. They included Gloria Estefan, Marc Anthony, Arturo Sandoval, La India, Olga Tañón, José Feliciano, Milly Quezada, Alfredo de la Fe, Gilberto Santa Rosa, Patti LaBelle, Albita Rodríguez, Willy Chirino, Paulina Rubio, and Ana Gabriel among them.

After Celia's death on July 16, 2003, Congresswoman Ileana Ros-Lehtinen and her colleague Bob Menéndez, two Cuban Americans belonging to opposite political parties, presented a resolution in the House of Representatives of the United States to grant posthumously the Congressional Gold Medal to their compatriot Diva Celia Cruz, who had more than enough merits to receive such a prestigious recognition. By order of the Council of Union City, New Jersey, the state where Celia and Pedro lived for many years, a stretch between Kennedy Boulevard and Bergenline, heart of the Cuban community, was renamed "Celia Cruz Avenue."

New York Mayor Michael Bloomberg wanted also to take part in posthumous honors, and he announced the designation of a music high school in the Bronx as DeWitt Clinton/Lehman College/Celia Cruz in her memory. The curriculum of the Lehman College/Celia Cruz High School would include musical instruction and interpretation, and function as part of the DeWitt Clinton High School. The academic institution was designed in collaboration with Lehman College (C.U.N.Y.), with classes to be held at that institution.

The undeniable fact is that Celia Cruz was the main ambassador for Latin music in all the countries of the world, and that her marvelous voice and charismatic personality had the power to break all language barriers, and had men, women, and children singing, who all answered in chorus when Celia, at the end of the overwhelming *"Bemba colorá,"* would ask, *"¿Y cómo me llamo yo?"* (What is my name?). All would respond in unison, "Celia Cruz." And no doubt there is a word in Spanish that will be remembered, even in remote places: *"Azúcar!"*

37

Good-bye, Celia

In July 2002, the couple returned from a European trip celebrating their fortieth wedding anniversary. During a routine exam, Celia's physician detected a cancer of the breast, the same illness that ended her mother's life. The news was devastating, because although Celia had some minor complaints, she seemed to be in good health. Pedro consoled her, embraced her, and kissed her with the same affection and support he had always shown her, encouraging her to think that everything would be all right after a simple operation. They were determined to fight for her life with all the scientific resources available. In August, at the Hackensack Hospital in New Jersey, Celia underwent surgery to remove her left breast, and in September she returned to the hospital for a second operation. The whole situation was handled with the utmost discretion, and not even her closest fans got the news. Celia did not want her fans to pity her because of her illness.

On November 27, 2002, after two months of recuperation, Celia traveled to Mexico City, her second country of residence, where her performing-artist friends had prepared a well-deserved event at the Auditorio Nacional, in honor of her fifty-year career.

Iván Restrepo, a close friend of the Knights, who accompanied them on this occasion, recalled that before leaving for the ceremony, the couple had a heated argument in their hotel room, for reasons that he chose to keep secret. This upset the vocalist's disposition, and caused an unusual depression in Pedro, who kept frowning all evening. Toward the end of the show, which had the participation of her old friend Daniela Romo and the Conjunto Garibaldi, Celia began to lose control of coherent speech, babbling and rambling on.

The headaches that she began experiencing after her first operation were becoming worse, and she also suffered from fainting spells and shivering. Back in New York, she underwent intense testing, which confirmed the fatal diagnosis: a brain tumor. With her emotional character, her first reaction was to get rid of it immediately, but the situation was more complex than that. Celia had planned to start recording an album that had no title as yet—it was decided later to entitle it *Regalo del alma* (Gift from My Soul)—on December 15 with producer Sergio George, and she had some concerts scheduled in Latin America, but all of her commitments were canceled. "At the moment," commented Pardillo, "Celia is in the hands of the best doctor in the world, God. He is with her."

The couple then retreated to their home in Fort Lee to get ready for the next step on December 6, when she was admitted to Columbia Presbyterian Hospital in New York for a complex surgical procedure that would last six hours. Due to the medications she was taking, Celia slept often, but she was able to recognize everybody when she was awake. By her side were Pedro, her beloved Cottontop, her sister Gladys Bécquer, who lives in New York, and her manager and representative, Omer Pardillo. After she left the intensive care unit, she was transferred to a private room where nurses were with her twenty-four hours a day.

Numerous entertainment figures close to Celia came to visit her at the hospital, but access to her room was restricted. However, floral arrangements would not stop coming. The first ones to arrive were those from Emilio and Gloria Estefan, and from Julio Iglesias. She had no television in her room so she could rest better, and there was Andrea Bocelli and classical music in the background. During her period of recuperation, she followed a special diet, served at the hospital under medical supervision, but she had lost her appetite and ate very little. A complete recovery was expected, but she had to stay in the hospital in total rest. During those days, one doctor said that he had never had a patient as cooperative as Celia.

The news about her surgery surprised everyone in entertainment circles, her friends, and most of all, her fans around the world. From that moment on, her fans began calling New York radio stations to enquire about her health, and many of them even visited the hospital. On December 9, when the news about the seriousness of her condition was made public, she composed a letter to the press saying that though her life had been "a carnival and an open book," at this point she begged them to respect her privacy and that of her loved ones.

Despite the optimism that always had characterized her, she could not help feeling depressed when the results of the pathological tests came in. They confirmed that the excised tumor was malignant. Later, three additional inoperable tumors were detected in her brain. In those first days after the surgery, Pedro and Pardillo kept repeating that Celia was comfortable during the natural recuperation process, but that the nature of the illness was so private that they preferred to avoid speculating.

As soon as Celia felt better, they traveled to Hawaii for a rest, with four nurses constantly attending her. It had been Celia's wish to return to these Pacific islands, which she had visited before with her old friend Tongolele. She had taken Celia to all the shows of Hawaiian music until Celia, tired of Polynesian rhythms, wished to hear some *salsa*. Now, because of her convalescent state, it was an opportunity to enjoy nature in peaceful surroundings. Though she had some difficulty walking, with Pedro's help she went out to take a breath of fresh sea breeze and walk a bit along the shore.

For two weeks they were able to forget the hustle and bustle of the world, the demands of urban life, the telephone calls, the world news, and ceaseless rumors. Both of them always hoped she would overcome this illness, and they were annoyed when a journalist reported that her condition was serious, perhaps thinking, superstitiously, that by hiding her sickness, it would go away.

Upon her return to New York, Celia finished the necessary paperwork to establish a nonprofit organization devoted to benefitting the musical education of young Hispanics, and to raising funds for the fight against cancer. On February 14, 2003, the Fundación Celia Cruz was officially created for those important causes. For many years

Celia had put her talent and popularity at the service of many good causes, especially for the annual marathon of the League Against Cancer in Miami, where Celia helped raise millions of dollars that paid for the treatment of patients with limited economic resources. "What is the matter, why aren't these phones ringing?" she used to shout in the midst of the campaign, and when she asked people to contribute, the volunteers on the phones were then insufficient for the number of calls.

Celia then devoted herself to finishing the project that she had pending with Sony Records. Between February and March Celia recorded the album that would be her last: *Regalo del alma*. Since she had some speech difficulties due to her illness, and was even more weakened by the chemotherapy and radiation treatments, she had to record each song line by line with the help of the technical personnel. During the process of recording, she said she felt fine, happy and vital, and only complained that her legs ached (due to an undisclosed phlebitis). There was always a chair ready for her so she could rest when tired.

The Telemundo Network organized an event in Celia's honor on March 13, with distinguished guests in the Jackie Gleason Theater in Miami Beach. She was splendid in a blond curly wig that reached to her shoulders, a choker with strands of diamonds, a pleated two-piece suit long enough to cover her shoes, and a gray, long-sleeved blouson, with heavy makeup attempting to mask the ravages of her illness. She was listening and smiling, and applauded enthusiastically for all the participants. Celia had explained beforehand that she felt fine, that the event had been planned a year before, when her condition was not known. She said she was going to sing only one song, because she wanted to be relaxed. She also recalled that when there was a celebration in honor of her friend Lola Flores, she had wanted to sing a duet with each participant, and she ended up exhausted. Celia wanted to take her seat at the orchestra level and enjoy the show. At the end she climbed up to the stage and sang with the cast "*Siempre viviré.*" She suffered a brief moment of confusion, but got hold of herself quickly and said, "I want to thank God first, because when I got *la malanga esa* (that whatchamacallit), it did not do away with me, I am still here."

Celia then retreated to her home in Fort Lee. After a short while, with the help of her cousin Nenita and daughter Silvia Soriano, a nurse, Celia moved into a recently acquired penthouse with views of the Hudson River and the Manhattan skyline. She would live there only three months. She limited herself to hospital visits for observation and the chemotherapy sessions, but seeing that it all seemed useless, she decided to suspend the treatment. Her last public presentation was on April 2, 2003, for the annual gala in benefit of the Teatro Repertorio Español, in the elegant Plaza Hotel in New York. She was accompanied by the orchestra of José Alberto (el Canario). She looked gaunt and insecure, and only sang three songs in a dull voice that was but an echo of her former energetic and fluid clarion sonority, and whose lyrics, in spite of being very well known songs, she had to read from a paper on a music stand. From that point on her state of mind declined, she stopped fighting as if she had lost all hope, and her condition deteriorated rapidly.

When her brother Bárbaro died in Havana on May 6, 2003, none of her relatives had the courage to inform her. She was almost comatose, barely recognizing the people around her, though occasionally a glimpse of the old vital spark shined again. Monday July 14 was her forty-first wedding anniversary. Pedro knelt beside her and whispered, "Happy anniversary, my love." A tear ran down Celia's cheek, but she said nothing, returning to the stupor induced by her medications, and she finally took refuge in an unconscious state. On Wednesday morning, it appeared that the battle had been lost. Two hours before she died, Father Carlos Mullins was called to administer last rites. Already 81 years old, Pedro paced from one room to the other in the apartment in a vain attempt to calm himself. He looked tearful and desperate, without knowing where to turn, like a soul in purgatory looking for some respite, or like someone shipwrecked in the middle of an ocean, without hope of being rescued. His love, his life, his "*negra querida*" was leaving him. On Wednesday, July 16, surrounded by her loved ones: Pedro Knight; Cuqui Pacheco; her manager and adopted son, Omer Pardillo-Cid; her niece, Linda Bécquer-Dakota; her sister Gladys; her friends Luis and Leticia Falcón; and two nurses, Celia Cruz, the legendary singer of Afro-Cuban rhythms, *la Guarachera de Cuba* and Queen of Salsa with a happy "*tumbao*," died at 4:55 in the afternoon—victim of a brain tumor.

No one could accept that the most revered Diva in Caribbean music was gone. Pardillo, still in disbelief, said, "Celia was so vital, so solid, that I could not believe she was dead. I asked the doctors to check her over and over. I could never believe she was going to die. I am thirty years old, but with what I experienced with Celia and Pedro, I feel as if I were sixty. She was a goddess."

Pedro, in turn, was reluctant to believe that his companion in a thousand adventures through more than five decades since that remote date in 1950 when he helped her with the music sheets of the songs she was going to sing as a test for the Sonora Matancera, his dear Celia, was gone.

"I made a deep commitment to her," he told the journalists who interviewed him a few days later. "She never wanted to speak about her illness, and I have respected that. That is why I beg of you not to talk about the subject so I can keep my commitment to Celia." Pedro reminded them that he never thought that Celia was going to die so soon. "She was very strong, I called her 'the cast-iron woman' because she recovered quickly from any disease. I thought she was going to live longer. But He Who is on High decides, more than any of us," he concluded with resignation. Her very impressive funerals in Miami and in New York have been dubbed "The last tour of the Queen of Salsa, Celia Cruz." But her marvelous voice is still with us through her record-ings and her luminous call to joy, *Azúcar!* will be with us forever.

abacuá system of worship and secret brotherhoods of African slaves; *Carabalí*; *ñáñigo*

afro Cuban rhythm popular since the 1930s, used in *boleros* and lullabies

bachata an often raunchy song, accompanied by guitar and bongo drum

batá drums sacred drums used in Lucumí-Yoruba rituals

bolero slow dance and song with romantic lyrics

bolerista *bolero* singer

bomba vital Puerto Rican folk music with African influences

bongó usually two attached drums held between the knees, used in improvisations; bongo drums

bongosero *bongó* player

bugalú (boogaloo) New York fusion of Latin rhythms and soul or rhythm and blues

Carabalí term for a slave coming from Calabar, Nigeria

charanga a type of band originally created to perform *danzones,* later with flute, violins, *timbales*

chachachá (also cha-cha-chá) Cuban rhythm created in 1953 by Enrique Jorrín, of the Orquesta Aragón

clave a syncopated base pattern of Cuban dance music

claves small percussion instrument; two cylindrical pieces of wood struck against each other and giving the *clave* rhythm

clavero one who plays the *claves*

comparsa group of costumed musicians, singers, and dancers who perform during carnival season

conga a Cuban drum originating in the Congo, in three sizes, the largest being the *tumbadora.* Also a Cuban ballroom dance of the 1930s that became international

conjunto a combo, derived from the septet, based on trumpets and percussion with piano

corneta china high-pitched small wind instrument

cuatro a small guitar with ten strings, played in Puerto Rican country music

Cubop Latin jazz of the 1940s (mix of Cuban music and bebop)

cumbia traditional Colombian dance rhythm

danzón Cuban dance rhythm, popular in the 1920s and 1930s and still heard

danzón nuevo ritmo a more modern Cuban *danzón* with a fast portion with syncopated rhythm

danzonete a descendant of the *danzón,* with influences of the son, popular in 1929

descarga Cuban version of the jam session, with musicians improvising solos

guaguancó urban, erotic form of rumba, a vehicle sometimes for Latin jazz

guajira Spanish-Cuban nostalgic music from the countryside, played on the *tres*

guaracha old Havana musical genre, with humorous lyrics and a fast dance rhythm

guarachero-a one who sings and dances *guarachas*

güiro or **guayo** a serrated gourd or scraper played with a stick

ideophone musical instrument of tuned metal strips in a resonator box, derived from the African hand piano

Latin jazz jazz played with Afro-Latin rhythms and percussion

Lucumí term used in Cuba meaning Yoruba (of Nigerian origin)

mambí Cuban rebel who fought the Spanish in the War of Independence

mambo syncopated portion of the Cuban *danzón nuevo ritmo* or *salsa*; musical genre associated with Dámaso Pérez Prado in the early 1950s

maracas pair of gourds with handles, filled with seeds. Shaken to mark a constant rhythm

maraquero-a musician who plays the *maracas*

marímbula metal strips in a wooden box, used to play the *son*, early twentieth century

merengue musical genre of the Dominican Republic

montuno a section for improvisation in Cuban music and in *salsa*

orquesta típica an orchestra created to play *danzón*, adding brass instruments and a *güiro*

pachanga Cuban musical genre originated in 1959 by Eduardo Davidson; also rural festivity

paila name for *timbales* in Cuba

plena a traditional Puerto Rican rhythm with lyrics that tell about some news

pregón a street vendor cry from Havana in the form of a *son*

porro music from the Eastern part of Colombia

ranchera nationalistic Mexican or Chicano music

rumba a variant of the *son*, very popular in Cuba in the

1920s; which became an international ballroom dance in the 1930s. Also a solo percussion passage

salsa hot Latin dance, based on Cuban rhythms with new instrumentation, originating in New York, popular in the 1960s and 1970s *Salsa* (sauce) was a cry to encourage musicians

santera-o initiated priest of *Santería*

santería synchretic cult for the Lucumí-Yoruba religion, with some fusion of Catholicism

son one of the major Afro-Cuban musical genres originating in the Eastern provinces

soneo improvisation done by the singer

sonero originally someone who sings or plays the *son*. Also a singer who improvises *salsa* style

son montuno slow variation of the *son* from the Cuban countryside

tambora a couple of drums used for the Dominican merengue

timba (tumbadora) in Cuba, conga drum

timbales also called *pailas* in Cuba. replaced the tympani in the *charangas*. Two snare drums, cowbells and wood block, mounted on a metallic stand. Singular form, *timbal*, also used.

timbalero musician who plays the *timbales*

típica old-style *danzón* band with brass instruments

tres Cuban string instrument similar to a guitar, having three double strings

tresero or **tresista** musician who plays the *tres*

trova type of music popular in Eastern Cuba, where composer-singer also plays the guitar

tumbadora a barrel-shaped drum made out of casks held together by hoops; large *conga* drum

tumbao a rhythmic pattern that repeats for *conga* drum, sometimes for bass

vallenato Colombian folk music

watusi genre influenced by soul music, popularized by Ray Barretto in the 1960s

Discography

Celia Cruz with the Sonora Matancera

TITLE	DATE	COMPOSER	RHYTHM
A todos mis amigos	1958	Pablo Cairo	Guaracha
Abre la puerta, querida	1958	Guillermo Arenas	Guaracha
África	1958	Justi Barreto	Ritmo oriza
Agua pa' mí	1958	Estanislao Serviá	Guaguancó
Aguinaldo antillano	1958	Claudio Ferrer	Guaracha
Ahí na' ma'	1958	Senén Suárez	Guaracha
Al son de pillón	1965	Néstor Cruz	Afro
Al vaivén de palmera	1965	Salvador Veneito	Guaracha
Así quiero morir	1965	Oneida Andrade	Mambo Chachachá
Báchame	1960	Alberto Zayas	Guaguancó
Baho Kende	1960	Alberto Zayas	Guaguancó
Baila Vicente	1960	Roberto Nodarse	Son montuno
Baila Yemayá	1960	Lino Frías	Mambo
Bajo la luna	1960	Armando Oréfiche	Son montuno
Bongó	1960	Florentino Cedeño	Guaracha rumba
Burundanga	1960	Óscar Muñoz	Bembé
Comadre	1960	Celia Cruz	Guaracha conga
Camino para volver	1982	Tite Curet Alonso	Guajira
Cao cao maní picao	1982	José Carbó Menéndez	Guaracha pregón
Capricho navideño	1960	Roberto Puente	Son montuno
Caramelos	1960	Roberto Puente	Son montuno
Celia y la Matancera	1982	José León	Son montuno
Cha cha güere	1982	L. Reyes- S.Ramos	Guaracha
Changó	1965	Rogelio Martínez	Afro

Changó ta vení	1965	Justi Barreto	Guaracha
Cógele el gusto	1965	Santiago Ortega	Son montuno
Con un palo y una lata	1965	?	Guaracha
Contestación del			
marinero	1965	Cabrera-Rico	Merengue
Contentosa	1955	Sergio Siaba	Guaracha
Contestación a Aunque			
me cueste la vida			
(con Alberto Beltrán)	1955	Luis Kalaff	Bolero
Cuba bella	1965	Justi Barreto	Bolero
Cuídate bien	1965	Isaac Fernández	Guaracha
De Cuba a México	1965	Santiago Ortega	Guaguancó
De noche	1965	Piloto y Vera	Bolero
Desvelo de amor	1962	Rafael Hernández	Bolero
Dile que por mí no tema	1962	Tony Smith	Chachachá
Dime la verdad	1962	Vinicio Camilo	Bolero Rítmico
	1965	Vinicio Camilo	Bolero Rítmico
El aguijón	1961	D. en D	Guaracha
El barracón	1961	Senén Suárez	Afro
El becerrito	1982	Simón Díaz	Guaracha
El chachachá			
de la Navidad	1958	Gutiérrez-Collazo-Estivil	Chachachá
El congo	1958	Calixto Callava	Son montuno
El disgusto de la rumba	1958	Aldo Carrazana	Guaracha rumba
El guajiro contento	1951	Ramón Sanabria	Guajira mambo
El heladero	1960	Mercy Condon	Son montuno
El lleva y trae	1960	Isaac Fernández	Guaracha
El mambo del amor	1960	July Mendoza	Mambo
El merengue	1955	Alcibiades Agüero	Merengue
El pai y la mai (con			
Bienvenido)	1955	Daniel Santos	Seis chorreao
El que siembra su maíz	1962	Miguel Matamoros	Son
El viaje en la panga	1961	C. Leicea- C. Cruz	Conga
El yerbero moderno	1955	Néstor Millí	Guaracha pregón
Elegguá quiere tambó	1955	Luis Martínez Griñán	Afro
En el bajío (con Laíto)	1954	J.C. Fumero-Castro	Guajira montuno
En Venezuela	1954	Justi Barreto	Guaracha
Eterna Navidad	1960	Tony Pereira	Guapacha
Facundo	1960	Eliseo Grenet	Tango conga
Feliz encuentro	1982	Francisco Alvarado	Guaracha
Feliz Navidad	1960	Humberto Jauma	Bolero
Fiesta de Navidad	1960	Mario de Jesús	Guapachá

Goza, negra	1960	Bienvenido Fabián	Guaracha
Gozando	1955	Juan Bruno Tarraza	Chachachá
Guede Zaina	1952	D. en D.	Congo haitiano
Hasta fuérate con mi tambó	1961	José Claro Fumero	Guaracha
Herencia africana	1982	Javier Vázquez	Guaracha
Imoye	1965	Néstor Cruz	Guaracha
Ipso Calipso	1965	Carlos Argentino	Calipso
Jingle Bells	1958	J. S. Pierpont- C. Argentino	Guaracha
Juancito Trucupey	1958	Luis Kalaff	Guaracha
Juntitos tú y yo	1958	Felo Vergara (Bergaza??)	Guaracha
Juventud del presente	1961	Silvestre Méndez	Guaracha
La batahola	1961	Óscar Muñoz Boufartique	Guaracha
La clave de oro	1961	Eliseo Grenet	Conga callejera
La cumbanchera	1961	Enrique Silva	Guaracha
La danza del coyote	1951	Luis Martínez Griñán	Danza conga
La guagua	1951	Juan Bruno Tarraza	Guaracha
La isla del encanto	1951	Justi Barreto	Chachachá
La manía de mamaíta	1962	Julián Fiallo	Sonsonete
La merenguita	1955	Eridania Mancebo	Merenguito
La milonga de España	1965	Granada-Sobrevila	Milonga
La negra inteligente	1961	Elpidio Vázquez	Guaracha
La negrita sandunguera	1961	Bienvenido Fabián	Merengue
La sopa en botella	1961	Senén Suárez	Guaracha
Lacho	1961	Facundo Rivero	Canción afro
Lalle Lalle	1961	J.C. Fumero	Guaguancó
Lamento de amor	1982	Lourdes López	Son montuno
Las frutas y mi son cubano	1982	Senén Suárez	Guaracha
Llegó la zafra	1951	Enrique Bonne	Guaracha
Los ritmos cambian	1951	Justi Barreto	Chachachá
Luna sobre Matanzas	1956	Frank Domínguez	Bolero afro
Madre rumba (con Celio)	1956	Humberto Jauma	Guaracha
Mágica luna	1960	Welch-Merie	Guaracha
Malagradecido	1961	José Carbó	Guaguancó
Mango mangüé	1955	Francisco Fellové	Pregón
Marcianita	1960	Villota-Imperatore	Guaracha

265

Mata siguaraya	1960 Lino Frías	Afro
Matiagua	1960 Jesús y Rogelio Martínez	Guaracha
Melao de caña	1960 Mercedes Pedroso	Guajira mambo
Merengue arrimao	1965 C.M. Díaz	Merengue
Me voy a Pinar del Río	1965 Néstor Cruz	Son montuno
México, qué grande eres	1961 Calixto Callava	Son montuno
Mi amor, buenas noches (con Carlos Argentino)	1961 Roberto Puente	Bolero
Mi bomba sonó	1962 Silvestre Méndez	Bomba
Mi chaparra	1962 Salvador Veneito	Guaracha
Mi cocodrilo verde	1960 José D. Quiñones	Bolero
Mi coquito	1960 Salvador Veneito	Guaracha
Mi son den boso	1960 Lodwing Samson	Tumba curazoleña
Mi sonsito	1960 Isabel Valdés	Son
Mi tumba se rompió	1960 Roberto Puente	Guaracha
Mis anhelos	1961 Roberto Puente	Bolero
Mulense	1961 Florentino Cedeño	Guaguancó
Muñecas del chachachá	1961 Óscar Muñoz Bouffartique	Chachachá
Nadie me lo quita	1961 Mario de Jesús	Merengue
No encuentro palabras	1956 Ernesto Castro	Chachachá
No hay nada mejor	1956 Andrade- J.C. Fumero	Chachachá
No me mires más	1956 Aurelio Machín	Bolero mambo
No sé lo que me pasa	1956 Jesús Guerra	Son montuno
No te rompas el cráneo	1956 Humberto Jauma	Guapacha
Noche criolla	1962 Agustín Lara	Criolla
Nochebuena	1960 Lucho Bermúdez	Bachata
Nostalgia habanera	1962 Bobby Collazo	Canción criolla
Nuevo ritmo omelemkó	1962 Eduardo Angulo	Omelemkó
Oyá, diosa y fe	1962 Julio Blanco Leonard	Afro
Oye mi rumba	1965 Javier Vázquez	Rumba
Óyela, gózala	1965 Lino Frías	Guaracha
Óyeme Agayu	1965 Alberto Zayas	Lamento negro
Pa' gozar la rumba	1965 Eduardo Angulo	Guaracha
Pa' la paloma	1965 Antonio Machín	Guaracha
Palmeras tropicales	1965 Irma Murillo	Bolero mambo
Palo mayimbe	1965 Javier Vázquez	Bembé
Para tu altar	1965 July Mendoza	Pregón
Pepe Antonio	1965 Jacinto Ledo	Guaguancó
Plegaria a Laroye	1965 Francisco Varela	Afro

Poco a poco	1965 José Claro Fumero	Guaracha
Por qué será	1965 Roberto Puente	Guapacha
Pregones de San Cristóbal	1960 Senén Suárez	Pregón
Qué bella es Cuba	1960 Piloto Vera	Bolero chachachá
Que critiquen	1960 J.C.Fumero-Grande	Guaracha
Qué voy hacer	1960 Úrsula Suárez	Guaracha
Quinto Mayor	1982 Miguel Román	Guaracha

Rareza del siglo	1982 Bebo Valdés	Beguine
Reina rumba	1956 Senén Suárez	Guaracha
Resurge el omelemkó	1956 Javier Vázquez	Omelemkó
Retozón	1965 Calixto Callava	Son montuno
(El) rey de los cielos	1960 Oneida Andrade	Rezo lamento
Rico Changüí	1961 Calixto Callava	Changüí
Rinkinkalla	1965 Juan Bruno Tarraza	Afro
Ritmo de mi Cuba	1965 Silvio Contreras	Guaracha
Ritmo, tambo y flores	1951 Joseíto Vargas	Guaracha
Rock and Roll	1956 Frank Domínguez	Rock and Roll
Rumba para parejas	1951 Calixto Leicea	Guaracha rumba
Rumba quiero gozar	1951 Calixto Leicea	Guaracha rumba

Sabroso guaguancó	1951 Santiago Ortega	Guaguancó
Saludo a Elegguá	1961 July Mendoza	Afro
Sandunguéate	1961 Senén Suárez	Guaracha
Saoco	1954 Rosendo Ruiz Jr.	Guaracha
Sigo esperando	1954 Roberto Puente	Omelemkó
Silencio	1954 Elsa Angulo	Omelemkó
Suavecito	1962 Ignacio Piñeiro	Son
Suena el cuero	1960 Juanito Blez	Guaracha rumba
Sueños de luna	1960 Eridania Mancebo	Lamento

Taco Taco	1961 Néstor P. Cruz	Guaracha
Taína	1960 Mario Tenorio	Guaracha rumba
Tamborilero	1960 Evelio Landa	Son montuno
Tataliba	1951 Florencia Santana	Guaracha
Tierra prometida	1982 Henry Castro	Guaracha
Traigo para ti	1965 Calixto Leicea	Ritmo guasón
Tu voz	1952 Ramón Cabrera	Bolero mambo
Tumba	1952 Julio Gutiérrez	Guaracha
Tumba la caña, jibarito	1952 Rudy Calzado	Guaracha rumba
Tuya y más que tuya	1956 Bienvenido Fabián	Bolero mambo

Vallan Vallende	1956 Senén Suárez	Guaracha
Vamos a guarachar	1956 Salvador Veneito	Guaracha

Vamos todos de pachanga	1960 Lino Frías	Pachanga
Ven, Bernabé	1960 Ortega-Lara	Son montuno
Ven o te voy a buscar	1960 Rey Díaz Calvet	Bolero mambo
Virgen de la Macarena	1962 Bernardo Bautista	Guaracha
Ya llegó el carnaval	1952 Eduardo Angulo	Conga
Ya te lo dije	1960 Ramón Cabrera	Guaracha
Yemayá	1962 Lino Frías	Rezo bembé
Yembe Laroco	1962 Blanco Suazo	Guaracha
Yo te invito a mi país	1961 Jorge Zamora	Guaracha
Zahara	1961 Eligio Valera Mora	Bolero

Older Recordings by *Celia Cruz* with the Sonora Matancera live from Radio Progreso

TITLE	DATE	COMPOSER	RHYTHM
A guarachar conmigo	1953	?	Guaracha
Agua pa' mí	1953	Estanislao Serviá	Guaguancó
Ahora es cuando	1955	Juan Bruno Tarraza	Son montuno
Bajo la luna	1955	Armando Oréfiche	Son montuno
Cacumbia	1955	Alejandro Vázquez	Guaracha
Canto a La Caridad	1955	Eliodoro Colás	Bolero
Canto a Yemayá	1955	Enrique Herrera	Montuno
Comadre	1955	Celia Cruz	Guaracha conga
Con mi guaracha	1955	?	Guaracha
Cualquiera la baila	1955	?	Guaracha
El hombre marinero	1955	Ricardo Rico	Merengue
El merengue	1955	?	Merengue
El negro Tomás	1955	Eridania Mancebo	Afro
El Pacífico	1955	?	Guaracha
El son de los viejitos (mi "sonsito")	1955	Isabel Valdés	Son
Jerigonza	1955	?	Guaracha
Gozando	1955	Juan Bruno Tarraza	Chachachá
La cruz (palo bonito)	1953	Ricardo Rico	Merengue
La cumbachera de Belén	1953	Enriqueta Silva	Guaracha
La chambelona	1953	?	Conga
La ruma es mejor	1953	?	Guaracha
Luna sobre Matanzas	1953	Frank Domínguez	Bolero afro
Mambo de salón	1953	?	Mambo
Mango mangüé	1953	Francisco Fellové	Guaracha pregón
María la cocinera	1953	?	Guaracha
Me voy a Pinar del Río	1956	Néstor Pérez Cruz	Son montuno
Mi amor, buenas noches (con Carlos Argentino)	1956	Roberto Puente	Bolero
Mi chachachá	1956	?	Chachachá
No encuentro palabras	1956	Ernesto Castro	Chachachá
Oriente de mi corazón	1956	?	Guaracha
Oya, diosa y fe	1956	Julio Blanco Leonard	Afro
Oye, vida mía	1956	?	Bolero mambo
¿Por qué importa mi vida?	1956	?	Son montuno
Refrán	1956	?	Guaracha
Rock and Roll	1956	Frank Domínguez	Rock and Roll
Rompe bonche	1956	?	Guaracha
Rumba de cajón	1956	?	Guaracha
Rumba que quiero gozar	1956	Calixto Leicea	Guaracha

Rumba rumbona	1956	?	Guaracha
Saoco	1954	Rosendo Ruiz	Guaracha
Serpentinas en colores	1954	René León	Guaracha
Tápate, mi hermano	1954	?	Guaracha
Tu voz	1954	Ramón Cabrera	Bolero mambo
Tuya y más que tuya	1954	Bienvenido Fabián	Bolero mambo
Un paso pa'lante y un paso pa'trás	1954	Eridania Mancebo	Guaracha
Vivo para ti	1954	?	Bolero mambo
Yemayá	1954	Lino Frías	Bembé

Recordings by *Celia Cruz* with the Sonora Matancera live from radio station CMQ

TITLE	COMPOSER	RHYTHM
Abre la puerta, querida	Guilermo Arenas	Guaracha
Baila así		Son
Camagüeyano y habanero	J.M. Guerra	Conga
Contestación a El dinero no es la vida		Guaguancó
Ecuá		
El de la rumba soy yo (con Bienvenido Granda)		Guaracha
El tiempo de la colonia	Mario Recio	Afro
Guajiro, llegó tu día	Guajira	
Lacho	Facundo Rivero	Afro
María la cocinera	¿?	
Más linda es la rumba	Guaracha	
Mejor es la rumba		
Yo te invito a mi país	Jorge Zamora	Guaracha
Oye mi bongó		Guaracha
Prende la vela	Lucho Bermúdez	Guaracha
Tú no sirves pa'nada	Guaracha	
Yembe Laroco	Blanco Suazo	Guaracha

Most important albums by La *Guarachera de Cuba* (including reissues and compilations of classics)

1958
La Incomparable Celia (Seeco Tropical)

1959
Mi diario musical (Polygram)

1965
Sabor y ritmo de pueblos (Polygram)
Canciones premiadas (Polygram)

1966
Cuba y Puerto Rico Son (Tico)
Son con Guaguancó (Nascente)

1967
Bravo, Celia Cruz (Tico)
A ti, México (Tico)
La excitante (Tico)
Serenata guajira (Tico)

1969
Quimbo Quimbumbia (Tico)

1970
Etc. Etc. Etc. (Tico)

1975
Tremendo caché (Vaya)

1977
Only They Could Have Made This Album (Vaya)

1978
Brillante (Vaya)
Eternos (Vaya)
A todos mis amigos (Tico)

1979
La Ceiba (Vaya)

1980
Celia-Johnny-Pete (Sonido)

1981
Celia & Willie (Vaya)

1982
Feliz encuentro (BBO)

1985
Homenaje a Benny Moré, Vol. 3 (Vaya)

1986
De nuevo (Vaya)
La Candela (Fania)

1987
The Winners (Vaya)

1988
Ritmo en el corazón (Off-Beat)

1990
La Guarachera del Mundo (Sony)
Con Sonora Mantancera, Vol. 1 (T.H. Rodven)
Con Sonora Mantancera, Vol. 3 (T.H. Rodven)
Con Sonora Mantancera, Vol. 2 (T.H. Rodven)
Con Sonora Mantancera, Vol. 4 (T.H. Rodven)

1991
Canciones de Celia Cruz con La Sonora (Huub)
La Incomparable (Seeco Tropical)

1992
La verdadera historia (Rodven)
Tributo a Ismael Rivera (Vaya)
Celia-Johnny-Pete (Sonido)
La Candela (Fania)
Cuba y Puerto Rico Son (Tico)
Only They Could Have Made This Album (Vaya)
Quimbo Quimbumbia (Tico)

1993
Azúcar negra (CBS)
Los Originales (Sony)
Azúcar (Fania)
Etc. Etc. Etc. (Tico)
A todos mis amigos (Tico)
Boleros (Polydor)
Madre Rumba (Saludos Amigos)

1994

Homenaje a los Santos (Polydor)
Las Guaracheras de la Guaracha (Polygram)
Celia & Willie (Vaya)
Feliz encuentro (BBO)
Irrepetible (RMM)
Vamos a guarachar (Saludos Amigos)
Mambo del amor (Saludos Amigos)
Merengue (Saludos Amigos)
Homenaje a Benny Moré, Vol. 3 (Vaya)
Eternos (Vaya)
Tremendo caché (Vaya)

1995

Algo especial para recordar (Tico)
Irresistible (Sony)
Festejando Navidad (Polygram)
Época de Oro (PolyGram)
Nuevos éxitos (Tico)
Double Dynamite (Charly)

1996

Mi diario musical (Polygram)
Sabor y Ritmo de pueblos (Polygram)
Celia Cruz (Delta, 1996)

1997

100% Azúcar - The Best Of Celia Cruz (Rhino)
Bolero: Dos grandes ídolos (Orfeón)
La Reina de Cuba (International)
Con La Sonora Matancera (International)
El merengue (International)
También boleros (International)
Duets (RMM)
Cuba: Sus mejores intérpretes (Orfeón, 1997)

1998

Fiestón tropical (Orfeón)
Cuba: Guaracha y son (Orfeón)
Afro-cubana (Exworks)
Mi vida es cantar (RMM)
La Guarachera de Cuba: 1950-1953:
Celia Cruz and Sonora Mantancera (Tumbao, 1998)

1999
Sonora Matancera (International)
Con sabor a Cuba (Orfeón)
Tributo a los orishas (International)

2000
Celia Cruz and Friends (RMM)
Angelitos negros (Saludos Amigos)
Siempre viviré (Sony)

2001
La negra tiene tumbao (Sony)
Gozando, siempre gozando (Orfeón)
Tu voz (BCI)

2002
Canto a La Caridad (Orfeón)
Edición limitada (Universal Music Latino)
Hits Mix (Sony)
La negra tiene tumbao (Sony)

2003
Siempre Celia Cruz-Boleros eternos (EMI)
Regalo del alma (Sony)

Among the reissued numbers of note with the Sonora Matancera are the following productions: *Changó ta' vení,* with Celia Cruz (reissued in 2000), *65 Aniversario* (1995), *Azúcar y candela* (1999), *Clásicos de la música cubana* (1999), *Colección de Oro* (1990), *Con sabor a Cuba* (1999), *Cuba: Nostalgia tropical* (1998), *Este Cha Cha Chá* (1997), *Live On the Radio : 1952–1958* (1996), *Los tres grandes de La Sonora Matancera* (1994).

Bibliography

BOOKS

Betancur Álvarez, Fabio. *Sin clave y bongó no hay son*, Editorial Universidad de Antioquía, 2a Edición, 1999.

Carpentier, Alejo. *La música en Cuba*, Editorial Letras Cubanas, 1988.

Delannoy, Luc. *¡Caliente! Una historia del jazz latino*, Fondo de Cultura Económica, 2001.

Depestre Catony, Leonardo. *Homenaje a la música popular cubana*, Editorial Oriente, 1989.

Díaz-Ayala, Cristóbal. *Discografía de la música cubana 1925-1960*, CD-Rom.

Farr, Jory. *Rites of Rhythms: The Music of Cuba*, HarperCollins Publishers, 2003.

Fernández, Raúl. *Latin Jazz: The Perfect Combination/La Combinación Perfecta*, Chronicle Books, 2002.

Gómez, François-Xavier. *Orquesta Aragón: The Story 1939-1999*, Lusáfrica, 1999.

Linares, María Teresa. *La música popular en Cuba*, Instituto del Libro, La Habana, 1970.

Loza, Steven. *Recordando a Tito Puente*, Random House Español, 2000.

Martínez Rodríguez, Raúl. *Benny Moré*, Editorial Letras Cubanas, 1993.

Mirós, Gilda. *Celia Cruz, Sonora Matancera y sus estrellas*, Edición de autor, 2003.

Morales, Ed. *The Latin Beat: The Rhythms and Roots of Latin Music from Bossa Nova to Salsa and Beyond*, Da Capo Press, 2003.

Moreno-Velázquez, Juan A. *Desmitificación de una diva: La verdad sobre La Lupe,* Traducción de Carlos José Restrepo, Editorial Norma, 2003.

Muguercia, Alberto y Ezequiel Rodríguez. *Rita Montaner*, Editorial Letras Cubanas, 1984.

Orovio, Helio. *Diccionario de la música cubana*, Editorial Letras Cubanas, 1992.

Pérez-Brown, María. Mamá: *Hijas latinas celebran a sus madres*, HarperCollins Publishers, 2003.

Puente, Tito and Jim Payne. *Tito Puente's Drumming with the Mambo King*, Hudson Music, 2000.

Ramírez Bedoya, Héctor. *Historia de la Sonora Matancera y sus estrellas*, Edición del autor, 1996.

Roberts, John Storm. *The Latin Tinge: The Impact of Latin American Music on the United States*, Oxford University Press, 1979.

Serna S. Carlos E. y Markoté Barros Ariza. *La Sonora Matancera: Más de 60 años de historia musical*, Ediciones Fuentes, 1990.

Valverde, Umberto. *Celia Cruz: Reina Rumba*, Arango Editores Ltda, 2a Edición, 1995.

_____. *Memoria de la Sonora Matancera*, Caimán Records, Inc., 1997.

NEWSPAPERS AND MAGAZINES
Cambio, Bogotá, July 2003
Caribe con Son y Ton, Barranquilla, September 2003
Clave, A Journal of Latin American Arts & Culture,
  Washington, D.C.
Cristina, La Revista, Miami, Año 13, No. 9, 2003
El diario/La Prensa, New York, July 2003
El Heraldo, Barranquilla, July 2003
El Nuevo Herald, Miami, 2003
El Tiempo, Bogotá, Colombia, 2003
Esmeralda, Tu revista, New York, September 2003
Hoy, New York, July 2003
Huellas, Revista de la Universidad del Norte, Barranquilla,
  Colombia,
Números 67 y 68, 2003.
La Gaceta de Cuba, Havana, January-February 1993
La Libertad, Barranquilla, 2003
People en Español, USA, October 2003
Revista Aló, Bogotá, July 2003
Semana, Bogotá, July 2003
The New York Times, New York, July-August 2003
TV y Novelas, USA, August 2003
Vanidades, USA, September 2003
Vista, USA, August 2003

AUTHORS OF ARTICLES, ESSAYS, REVIEWS, NOTES CONSULTED
Aparicio, France R. The Blackness of Sugar: Celia Cruz and the Performance of (Trans)Nationalism, Cultural Studies, Theorizing Politics, Politicizing Theory, Volume 13 Number 2, April, 1999.
Aquino, Fernando. *el diario/La Prensa*, New York
Arias Satizábal, Medardo. *Diario Hoy*, New York
Arteaga, José. El negocio de la salsa, internet
Avendaño, Manuel E. *el diario/La Prensa*, New York
Batista, Carlos. *AFP*, Havana
Bayona, Mauricio. *El Tiempo*, Bogotá
Benedetti Jimeno, Armando. *El Heraldo*, Barranquilla
Borrero, Rosario. *El Heraldo*, Barranquilla
Caicedo, Guarino. *El Tiempo/Hoy*, Bogotá
Castro, Eunice. *Vanidades*, Miami
Child, John. Profiles, internet
Corzo, Eduardo. (Chicago), *Revista Esmeralda*, New York
Donado, Jacqueline. *el diario/La Prensa*, New York
Enesco, Miguel. AFP, Miami
Fernández, Raúl. Celia Cruz, Artista de América Latina, Deslinde, July-September 1997
Fernández-Jiménez, Georgina. *Vanidades*, Miami
Fernández-Soberón, Miriam. *el diario/La Prensa*, New York
Ferreira, Rui. *El Nuevo Herald*, Miami
Fleites, Alex. (Havana), *Revista Esmeralda*, New York
Fundora, Ernesto. *El Nuevo Herald*, Miami
González, Dámaso. *el diario/La Prensa*, New York
González, Igor. *Diario Hoy*, New York
Guarín, Marta. *El Heraldo*, Barranquilla
Hernández-Beltrán, Ruth E. EFE, New York
Jaimes, Manuel. *Diario Hoy*, New York
Jiménez-Ramírez, Mercedes. *Diario Hoy*, New York
Lewis, Evan. *el diario/La Prensa*, New York
Loboguerrero, Cristina. *el diario/La Prensa*, New York
Louis, Néstor. "Celia Cruz with Nestor Luis" (Interview) www.nestorluis.com)
Luis Llanes, José. *Diario Hoy*, New York

Marín, Mar. EFE, Havana
Martínez de Pisón, Javier. Independent journalist, New York-
    Miami
Martínez, Edwin, *Diario Hoy*, New York
Medina Rendón, Jorge. *El Tiempo*, Bogotá
Montalvo, Izadeli. *el diario/La Prensa*, New York
Moreno-Velázquez, Juan A. *el diario/La Prensa*, New York
Muriel, Tommy. Fania All-Stars: Tres décadas de sabor y no
    quieren parar, Internet
Noriega, Zoraida. *El Heraldo*, Barranquilla
Pardo Llada, José. journalist, Cali, Colombia
Paredes, Julio. *el diario/La Prensa*, New York
Pérez, Edwin. *El Nuevo Herald*, Miami
Pérez, Estela. *Diario Hoy*, New York
Pérez, Miguel. *el diario/La Prensa*, New York
Reynaldo,Andrés. *El Nuevo Herald*, Miami
Rivas, Josué R. www.ElPuenteLatino.com
Rodríguez, Ichaso Mari. *Vanidades*, Miami
Sanchis, Eva. *el diario/La Prensa*, New York
Solano Alonso, Jairo. Ismael Rivera: El Sonero Mayor, Internet
Sotola, Carolina. *Diario Hoy*, New York
Taillacq, Evelio. *El Nuevo Herald*, Miami
Urgilés, Nube. *el diario/La Prensa*, New York
Utset, Joaquím. *El Nuevo Herald*, Miami
Vanconcellos, Ricardo. *el diario/La Prensa*, New York
Vizcaíno, Argelia María. La cruz de Celia, Internet

VIDEOS

Celia Cruz: La única, programa Son Latino, Televisa, México
Celia Cruz: The Queen of Salsa, produced by Dick Brima
Historia de la música afrocubana
Homenaje a Celia Cruz, Special program of Telemundo, Miami
    Beach
Reina Rumba Celia Cruz, conversation with Umberto Valverde,
    filmed in Barranquilla, Colombia
Rhythms that Speak-Salsa
Yo soy Celia Cruz, a documentary by Hugo Barroso, Miami